THE SIMPSON TRIAL IN BLACK AND WHITE

By

Tom Elias and Dennis Schatzman

General Publishing Group, Inc.
Los Angeles

For information:
General Publishing Group, Inc.
2701 Ocean Park Boulevard
Santa Monica, CA 90405

Library of Congress Cataloging-in-Publication Data

Elias, Tom
        The Simpson trial in black and white / by Tom Elias and
Dennis Schatzman.
            p.   cm.
        Includes index.
        ISBN 1-881649-92-X
        1. Simpson, O. J., 1947---Trials, litigation, etc. 2. Trials
(Murder)--California--Los Angeles. 3. Crime and the press--
United States. 4. Mass media and race relations--United
States. 5. Newspaper court reporting--California--Los Angeles.
I. Schatzman, Dennis   II. Title.
KF224.S485E43   1996
070.4'4934573'025230979494--dc20   96-3740
                                                                    CIP

ISBN 1-881649-92-X

Printed in the USA
10 9 8 7 6 5 4 3 2 1

General Publishing Group
Los Angeles

TABLE OF CONTENTS

ACKNOWLEDGMENTS

TOM ELIAS

This book could never have happened without the faith and confidence of my wife Marilyn, herself a superbly skilled and gifted reporter. Her emotional support and practical suggestions during the difficult months of the trial and the many weeks of writing were invaluable. Her editing ideas as I wrote my chapters served to hone both my thoughts and my words. Some suggestions from my son Jordan were also vital. He helped bring focus to my chapters by encouraging me to write about my own feelings and beliefs, which were never before a conscious part of anything I'd written.

I might never have attempted this book without the clever thinking of my good friend Deborah Kraut. During a dinner at which I talked about the problems of covering the Simpson trial, she first voiced the idea of a book presenting contrasting black and white views of the case. I let the idea percolate for weeks after her initial suggestion before asking my friend, colleague and seatmate Dennis Schatzman to join me in this effort.

I also owe a debt of gratitude to our publisher Quay Hays and to the editor on the project, Murray Fisher, for their unqualified faith that two reporters who had never before written a book could turn out work of high quality in a relatively short time. Their patience and forbearance became key factors when certain chapters were delayed beyond our initial deadline. And it was Murray who kept Dennis and me on track in the debate that makes up our last chapter.

One other person should get immense credit for my part of this book, even though he had no direct involvement with the project. That is my journalism teacher at Highland Park High School in Highland Park, Illinois, John Munski, who taught me the skills of reporting, editing and interviewing that I was to use through a long career. His never-failing good humor and solid expertise gave me the ability to handle any story I've ever been thrown into, from the Charles Manson murder case to presidential politics and investigative projects.

Our colleagues at the trial also provided an assist. Frequent hallway discussions with men and women like authors Joseph Bosco and Dominick Dunne, Shirley Perlman of *Newsday*, David Dow and Bill Whitaker of CBS News and Mike Tharp of *U.S. News* helped focus and crystallize my thinking about the many complicated issues we dealt with every day.

DENNIS SCHATZMAN

This treatise could not have been published had it not been for the help and influence of the men and women listed below, both living and dead. This is a two-parter. Part I, the men and women who helped shape my journalism philosophy:

Sylvester Henry Scovel, Upton Sinclair, Lincoln Steffens, George Skuyler, Percivil L. Prattis, Ethel Payne, Frank Bolden, Teenie Harris, H.L. Mencken, Theodore White, Kyle Palmer, Elizabeth Oliver Abney, Sam Lacy, Sherley Uhl, Eddie Jeffries, Antero Pietella, Edwin Guthman, Eugene Roberts, Edwin Diamond, Lu Palmer, Chuck Stone, William Raspberry, Linn Washington, Robyn Denise Yourse and Bill Boyarsky.

Now to Part II, the personal side. Sir Walter Raleigh once said, "If it appears that I have seen more than others in my life, it is because I stood upon the shoulders of giants."

It begins with Robert Bailey, my Sunday School teacher at Pittsburgh's Bethel African American Episcopal Church. He taught us not only the Bible, but black history.

Morris Stewart, Sr., my late Boy Scout leader, made men of boys. Our troop was the first black troop to win Pittsburgh's citywide window display award.

Mildred Berry, my Lemington Elementary School English teacher, taught me how to read and write with purpose. She also gave me P.L. Prattis's address.

Mary Alice Babusci was my homeroom teacher at Peabody High School. It was she who told me not to buy that crap the guidance counselor was putting down that the only place for a black student with a 3.4 g.p.a. and 1206 on his college boards was a state teacher's college. Ditto Philip Fienert, the school's activities director who opened my eyes up to worlds I had never seen before.

Ludwick V. Hayden, William C. Weaver, Edwin Harr and Wayne Sadowsky were four teachers who made me think, think, think, and after that, think some more. Sadowsky I think about every day. For it was this chemistry teacher who told our class, "It's not how smart you are that counts, its whether or not you know how to get the information you need."

James Edward Banner, my track coach at the University of Pittsburgh, always told us that if we are to be defeated, it wouldn't be because we weren't prepared. He also said that as long as he lived, if he heard that we were messing, he would kill us. I believe him.

Dr. Joseph P. McCormick, II, a Howard University political scientist and fellow member of Kappa Alpha Psi Fraternity, always let me rummage through his library whenever I traveled to Washington, D.C.

Quay Hays, our publisher, trusted us and it is because of him that we are at this point today. Their crack editor, Murray Fisher is, as we say in the black church, "still water."

The men and women of the Los Angeles *Sentinel* have always been with me. Ditto the gang at WVON-AM Chicago. Every week on "World Perspectives," Cliff Kelly made me look like an expert.

My daughter Cicely Rae Schatzman, age 13, taught me about DNA. She had recently won second place in her school's science fair on the subject, "How Long Does it Take for a Substrate to Dry?" I took copious notes.

My best friend, my lover, my soulmate and my administrative assistant, Sandra Mancha, provided the emotional backbone that was needed to complete this task. I owe everything to her.

Finally, none of this would have been possible without the oversight of my Lord, Jesus Christ, the Almighty. In praising Him, I wholeheartedly agree with Sandra, "To God be the Glory."

INTRODUCTION
SHARED EXPERIENCES

They shared the same seat through more than eight months of the O.J. Simpson double murder trial. Week after week, Thomas D. Elias, then of Scripps Howard News Service, and Dennis Schatzman, covering the proceedings for the black-owned *Los Angeles Sentinel* and the National Newspaper Publishers Association, saw the defendant's bull neck and distinctive profile and the changing hairstyles of lead prosecutor Marcia Clark from precisely the same angle. Both analyzed every move the large troupe of lawyers made. Both watched the jurors closely from the third-row seat they occupied directly in front of the witness stand. But even though they heard the same testimony and observed the same people and events from precisely the same spot, Tom Elias and Dennis Schatzman saw two very different trials.

Elias became convinced in the early days of the case that O.J. Simpson murdered his ex-wife Nicole and her friend Ronald Goldman. Schatzman remained equally sure throughout that police had trumped up a case against Simpson and could never prove him guilty. From the first week of the trial, the two men engaged in spirited debates over the evidence and how it should be interpreted. Schatzman believed police frequently plant evidence, especially when African American defendants are involved. Elias felt the notion of a widespread police conspiracy against Simpson was absurd because it would have required the almost instant involvement of at least half a dozen cops, all of whom would be risking their careers and pensions. Elias believed the blood evidence was compelling; Schatzman thought the blood easily could have been planted in locations as varied as Simpson's Ford Bronco and the rear gate of Nicole Simpson's condominium.

As impassioned as these debates often became, they were never mean-spirited, always marked by mutual respect and even humor. Elias and Schatzman, thrown together by Judge Lance Ito's supposedly random press seating chart, developed a friendship and became the odd couple of the trial.

Like most of the six dozen-plus reporters regularly covering the Simpson matter, Elias and Schatzman weren't certain until Jan. 20, 1995, three days before the trial began, that they would even have a seat in the courtroom. On that morning, Jerrianne

Hayslett finally posted the long-awaited seating chart for the trial. There would be only 24 press seats, but hundreds of organizations wanted them. A place in the courtroom would be a plum; exclusion could be a career-threatening disaster. Without a seat in the courtroom, reporters would be in a sort of journalistic purgatory— almost in heaven, but with a stout oak door and a troop of deputy sheriffs blocking the way in.

Elias and Schatzman arrived separately, with no inkling that they were about to be paired. They also didn't yet have any clue about Ito's ironic sense of humor in seating members of the press. Hayslett, the court's chief public information officer, posted Ito's list on the west wall of the 12th floor elevator lobby, amid a forest of television camera tripods, lights and cables erected by electronic news organizations large and small. For Elias and Schatzman, the list brought good news.

Elias had been especially anxious because his news service expected him to attend virtually every court session—but failed to respond on his behalf when the Associated Press first invited editors to write Ito and request seats at the trial. Elias was on vacation in France at that time, the end of August 1994, and because his editors failed to act, he was left off the preliminary press seating list issued in mid-September.

Hayslett assured him that if Scripps Howard editors finally did write to Ito and if he regularly attended pre-trial proceedings, arrangements might still be made to accommodate him. But until he saw the final seating chart, he wasn't sure whether he would be inside or out in the cold.

Schatzman hadn't worried much about getting a seat. He knew his publisher, Kenneth Thomas, had communicated with a long-time friend, Municipal Judge Veronica MacBeth, seeking assurances that the black press would not be excluded. Schatzman knew the letter had been passed along to Ito. The Thomas letter was prompted by Schatzman's concerns that larger news organizations would bump specialized media like the *Sentinel*. He had seen regular pre-trial attendees like the *National Enquirer*, Agence France Presse and the Japanese Sports News Service cast aside. But Schatzman attended pre-trial proceedings so regularly, often arriving early to take a courtroom seat on a first-come, first-served basis, that he easily proved to the judge he and the *Sentinel* had a sustained interest. So both Schatzman and Elias got a seat. But not one seat each. It was one seat to share. Now they had to organize it, deciding who would sit in for which days and hours.

The *Los Angeles Sentinel*, the Scripps Howard newspapers and the *Pasadena Star-News*—three outfits with almost nothing in common—were to occupy seat C-12, four seats west of the aisle in the third row of the courtroom spectator section. From that spot, Elias and Schatzman could see the defendant's profile—but only if they leaned forward a bit, looked slightly left and around the broad shoulders of CBS-TV correspondent Bill Whitaker. They looked directly into the eyes of witnesses and had a head-on view of Judge Ito, unless an exceptionally tall person occupied the victims' family seat directly in front of them. They saw the backs of Marcia Clark's then-curly locks and Christopher Darden's shiny, clean-shaven head. To see the jury, they had only to glance to their right, around the tall and sturdy frame of best-selling author Joe McGinnes.

Seat C-12 was beside authors Joseph Bosco and Jeffrey Toobin, who shared a space, but had little else in common. To the right in C-13 sat the unlikely (and unwilling) triumvirate of American newspaperdom's most bitter rivals: The *New York Daily News*, the *New York Post* and New York *Newsday*. Incredulous at first about being thrown together, reporters Ann Bollinger of the *Post*, Michelle Caruso of the *Daily News* and the irrepressible Shirley Perlman of *Newsday* worked out their sharing peaceably from start to finish.

Judge Ito assured the press through his ever-agreeable mouthpiece Hayslett that these assignments were made on a completely random basis. But with *Newsweek*, *U.S. News*, *Time*, *Sports Illustrated* and *People* magazine sharing another seat (C-5), not too many in the usually suspicious press corps were buying that one. Other mixed pairings included the *New York Times* sharing a seat with the Spanish-language Los Angeles newspaper *La Opinion*, and the ferociously competitive Channels 5 and 9 in Los Angeles, who were also forced to share.

All these strange bedfellows had to decide how to divide their court time. Elias took it on himself to call a meeting of his trio first thing the next Monday morning, the day opening arguments were to begin and the day the strictly-enforced seating chart took effect. As usual, he exited the express elevator on the 12th floor at about 7:30 a.m., punched the combination 2-1-3 into the lock on the print pressroom door, then went to the snack bar one floor up.

When he returned, Elias looked around for Schatzman and *Star-News* reporter Kathy Braidhill. They weren't there yet. So he paced the floor impatiently, wandering in and out of the neighboring broadcast news center. Braidhill appeared next, eager to use the seat in the afternoons, but wanting little part of the morning sessions. She sometimes taught early-morning aerobics classes for side income.

The usually gregarious Schatzman popped off the elevator at about 8:10, but he was in an obviously bad mood. Looking pained and exhausted, he plopped onto one of the folding chairs in the hallway area Court-TV had staked out with a few strips of duct tape. Elias came over and said, "Hi, we need to work this out."

"Get the fuck away from me," Schatzman snapped with no warning. Elias blanched and walked away. He headed for a nearby bank of pay phones to check his office telephone messages and make his routine daily call to his boss in Washington, D.C., while whatever had set Schatzman off dissipated. Elias knew Schatzman represented the black press at the trial and he knew feelings of racial slights could be aroused inadvertently. But all his contact with Schatzman during the long pre-trial process had been matter-of-fact, so he didn't expect trouble when he went back to try again at starting a meeting.

"Hey, man, I apologize, that had nothing to do with you," Schatzman said. "Let's get on with it." Later, Elias and his colleagues learned that Schatzman was out of sorts because his stomach cancer was acting up. The same ailment was to get him tossed out of court about a month later, when pain medication made him drowsy and he dozed off for a moment in the courtroom, in full view of Judge Ito's hidden joystick-operated audience-scanning camera.

But once their meeting started, it ran smoothly. Arrangements made in that moment were to last through the entire nine months of trial. And within days, Schatzman and Elias began talking regularly about everything from football and politics to their kids. Elias beamed while talking about his son, a Yale University sprinter, and Schatzman harkened back to his days as an All-American middle-distance man at the University of Pittsburgh. Eventually, they got around to serious and spirited discussions of the trial.

They found they disagreed on almost everything about it, from the time line to the credibility of many of the witnesses. These discussions continued for months. Each man would sit in C-12 for hours at a stretch, trying to concentrate on the testimony and arguments. But at times their minds wandered and Elias wondered how Schatzman could possibly be watching everything from precisely the same angle and still see it so differently. Schatzman, in turn, wondered how Elias could be so naive about the way the system worked.

Their sometimes heated talks led first to a series of stories in which Elias became the first national reporter to explore the reasons for the black/white divide in public opinion about the trial, and later led to Schatzman's emergence as a regular television presence explaining the African-American point of view on the trial.

Their debate, like the public's, continues.

CHAPTER 1
THE VERDICT

TOM ELIAS

Justice Stinks

Two hours after the verdicts came down, the mostly-black crowd was still thick on the north side of Temple Street opposite the Criminal Courts Building. They stood three or four deep all along the block between Spring Street and Broadway, rejoicing and occasionally cheering wildly, as if they'd been watching a football game and their team had just scored a touchdown.

In a way, it had. "Live with it," one black man shouted directly in my ear as I walked to my car after attending the defense team's gloatingly surreal victory press conference, staged in Judge Lance Ito's courtroom and attended by more than a dozen Simpson relatives who seated themselves in the jury box. Still exhilarated, the man shouted, "O.J. is free and so are we!"

I heard much more than his actual words when that black man aggressively accosted me. The deeper message from him and the rest of the crowd chilled me to the bone. "It's OK for blacks to murder whites," he and the other street-corner celebrants seemed to shout. "It's our turn now. You've been doing this to us for centuries, with white juries clearing white men accused of killing and lynching blacks. Now we've stuck it to you, at least this once. A mostly black jury at last has done to you what the Rodney King jury did to us."

Months earlier, I had thoroughly documented the racial divisions spawned by this seemingly endless trial, and some of the reasons for them. But I realized in that moment I still lacked a true feeling for the depth of America's split over Simpson. I began to comprehend more completely that evening, when a colleague told me about her own verdict-day experience.

She'd witnessed the reading of the jury's decision in a small battered women's shelter in the suburban Los Angeles San Fernando Valley. Its exact location is a tightly kept secret, so that the women there need have no worries about being found by the brutal and angry men they have fled. The racial mix in the shelter was not quite representative of its area in the sun-bleached valley. There was only one black among the eight women taking refuge. The shelter ordinarily has no TV, but on this morning, the women all gathered around a set specially brought in for the verdicts at 10 a.m. They watched intently as Ito asked the jurors whether they had reached verdicts. When court clerk Deirdre Robertson read the rulings, their response was mixed. White and Latina women wept or walked disgustedly off to their rooms, fists clenched in frustration. But the lone black woman wasn't the least bit upset. She merely nodded, then explained that the verdict wouldn't encourage men to batter their women in the belief that they'll never have to pay for it, because, after all, "Even with all his money, Simpson still spent 15 months in jail." No one even attempted during his trial to dispute Simpson's decade-long history of wife-beating. But that didn't stop other black women in other domestic abuse shelters around the nation from taking to network television with expressions of delight at seeing him acquitted. This, despite the fact that almost without exception, the batterers they had fled were black. Racial identity simply proved far stronger than the violence that had been done to them.

The living rooms of those shelters were emblematic of all America. Every post-verdict opinion survey showed whites unified against the acquittal as they rarely are about anything. Blacks, on the other hand, seemed almost unanimous in their approval of the speed with which the jury reached its decision and the nature of its irreversible ruling.

Fred Goldman, aggrieved father of one murder victim, laid the racial split at the feet of chief defense attorney Johnnie Cochran. "Single-handedly, with his 'Dream Team,' he's managed to shove a wedge between the races that's larger than we ever could have imagined," he told his solemn fellow congregants at Yom Kippur services the day after the verdicts were delivered. Goldman plainly believed the nine blacks on the jury took to heart Cochran's final argument urging them to send a message that racists like Detective Mark Fuhrman would not be tolerated in this case.

Goldman's attributing the racial split to defense tactics rather than spontaneous emotion resonated truly with what I had been told while writing one of the first newspaper analyses of the racial tensions raised by the trial. To many in the black community of South Central Los Angeles, Simpson was a highly improbable martyr around whom to rally. "He has never done much for this community," Celes King told me in one interview. The bail bondsman and onetime president of the Los Angeles NAACP chapter chuckled as he added that "about the only thing he does down here is get his hair cut." The rest of Simpson's time during his life before the murders, King said a bit ruefully, was usually spent in the company of white friends and amid the opulent surroundings of Brentwood and the nearby Riviera Country Club, whose spectacular golf course regularly hosts professional tournaments like the PGA. Still, King was sympathetic to Simpson all through the trial, even offering to post bond for him if and when a judge granted bail. Yet he consistently shook his head in disbelief that the privileged Simpson could have become a symbol of the battle against oppression for black America.

Meanwhile, Goldman was far from alone in his outrage. Television executives had never seen anything like the outpouring of the next ten days. When Simpson considered televising a pay-per-view interview to replenish his coffers, angry cable TV subscribers mounted an unprecedented national protest campaign. "We have never gotten so many calls on anything," reported William Rosendahl, an executive of Century Cable Television, the largest cable system in Los Angeles. "I think we'd be idiots to put on an O.J. show, we'd lose so many subscribers."

Even more infuriated whites telephoned NBC television's western headquarters in Burbank, California, when that network agreed to air a live hour-long interview with Simpson eight days after his acquittal. The protest ended only when Simpson canceled the interview, ironically complaining that NBC's Tom Brokaw had been "sharpening his knives" in preparation. Predictably, leading the protest was the National Organization for Women. But the extent of feeling it bared was not predictable. "We did not have to generate anything. We did not phone-bank it," Tammy Bruce, leader of NOW's Los Angeles chapter, reported afterward. "We did not do anything that grass roots organizations normally have to do. (The public outrage) was just there."

Even in the 1990s era when the "angry white male" became a truism in American politics, such unified feeling was without precedent. "I think that right now, we have an emotional riot in L.A.," said Patty Giggans, executive director of the Los Angeles Commission on Assaults Against Women, after Simpson backed off the interview.

The protests and the racial split made me think of my final morning of trial coverage: verdict day. In the 12th floor hallway where coveted courtroom passes were distributed daily to reporters, I encountered Andrea Ford, a black woman and a veteran reporter who covered most of the trial for the *Los Angeles Times*. Speculation was rampant—and evenly split—at that moment about the meaning of the jury's swift return. "A guilty verdict," I remarked to Andrea and a few others within earshot, "would be a real statement against racism. It would prove to the world that all African Americans are not just a bunch of automatons who respond automatically whenever someone yells 'racism.'" Andrea swallowed hard and said nothing, but her face became an eloquent sneer. We didn't speak often before, but we've spoken not a word since.

I believed that morning the jury would come in the way I hoped they would, returning the guilty verdict Simpson so richly deserved. Months of blood evidence—much of it uncontroverted—along with the presence of Simpson's hair at the crime scene, plus rare and unusual carpet fibers from his car, were enough to convince me. Evidence about shoeprints and the fact that he owned and had been filmed wearing one of the relatively few pairs of Aris gloves precisely like those found at the scene clinched it for me. Then you could add Simpson's prior record of beating his wife before, during and after their marriage.

Afterward, the celebrations staged at black churches in Los Angeles and elsewhere reinforced the cold-blooded message I received on leaving the courthouse. My colleague Dennis Schatzman now says my hearing this message from the rejoicing African Americans was a racist act. I say baloney. He excuses the reaction of black celebrants by comparing Simpson's case to the 1991 shooting of fifteen-year-old honor student Latasha Harlins in a small grocery store in South Central Los Angeles. Schatzman says there was no significant white reaction after Korean-American shopkeeper Soon Ja Du received only a slap on the wrist for killing the teenage girl when she appeared to be shoplifting a candy bar. He's wrong. There was outrage then from many white groups. And many of the same pundits Schatzman now calls racist for decrying the Simpson verdict also lambasted Judge Joyce Karlin, who let Mrs. Du off with a $500 fine and probation.

If Schatzman wants to compare the Simpson case outcome to Harlins, fine. That case was an insult to blacks, and I said so in my column at the time. The Harlins result told African Americans it was OK for an Asian shopkeeper to shoot any black—even a sweet child—who acts suspiciously for a moment. That was wrong. So were the Simpson verdicts and the celebration that surrounded them. In fact, the Simpson outcome should be an insult not just to whites but to every American, because it said you can get away with murder if you're popular enough with the jury.

Schatzman calls this a "sick analysis" that "demeans a whole race." The fact that I received a racist-seeming message from the black celebrants demeans only those who sent that message. It wasn't the whole black race, but only the celebrants whooping it up, who seemed to be putting the white race on notice. The only reason anyone in the crowd of Simpson sycophants outside the courthouse said anything to me on verdict day was because I'm white.

Other whites obviously sensed a similar racial animus. African Americans got the same kind of message in 1992, when a lily-white suburban jury acquitted all the white policemen who beat motorist Rodney King to a pulp a year earlier. That jury in effect told blacks that many whites didn't care what policemen do to blacks. African Americans responded immediately with the Los Angeles riots, the deadliest urban disturbance in U.S. history. The message of the celebrants after the Simpson verdict was an extension of the tit-for-tat instinct behind those riots: Some blacks were now saying they don't care what other African Americans do to whites or Koreans or other ethnics. Revenge is sweet, they implied. If a Du could escape with virtually no punishment, if a white jury could give white cops carte blanche to beat a black man like King, then it's also OK for a mostly black jury to retaliate in kind in the Simpson case.

Nowhere was this message more clearly communicated than on college campuses. Students at the elite and virtually all-black Howard University in Washington, D.C., cheered wildly as the verdicts were read; white and Asian-American students at UCLA watched silently, in obvious disbelief and dismay.

The white students at UCLA likely would not have argued with what John Mack, president of the Los Angeles Urban League, said after the end of the Simpson trial: "Mark Fuhrman confirmed what most African Americans have felt right along and known right along. In South Central Los Angeles, too many Mark Fuhrmans have harassed and brutalized people. Los Angeles will never be the city any of us want it to be until this problem is truly addressed. People have to stop burying their heads in the sand. I really believe the jury is still out on L.A."

But the Simpson jury wasn't sitting in judgment on Mark Fuhrman. Sure, Fuhrman said he found a bloody glove at Simpson's home. Sure, he found a drop of blood on the door of Simpson's car. But even without any of the evidence Fuhrman found, there was plenty to convict Simpson. This was what I thought and still believe—and it remains the conviction of mainstream white America.

But that's not how mainstream black America thought about this case. Those African Americans who paid close attention to the six months of evidence presented by prosecutors—a group which apparently didn't include most of the jurors, who often had trouble staying awake, let alone fully comprehending what they were shown and told—seemed to line up with the thoughts of a street musician who set up shop in Rastafarian dress on a shopping mall near the courthouse on verdict day. "I don't have much doubt that he killed those people," the dreadlocked artist said. "But he's not guilty. This country owes us blacks a lot for all that's gone down over the last 400 years. We wanted O.J. free because of all that." So for some, it was as if Nicole Brown Simpson and Ronald Lyle Goldman died to expiate the racist sins of all America for centuries past. That's hardly what I thought American justice was supposed to be about.

The jurors themselves denied any such racial motivation. "This case wasn't racial at all," the onetime Juror No. 10, Gina Rosborough, said one week afterward. "I was just giving a verdict." But if race wasn't an issue, despite Cochran's many attempts to make it central, then the jurors had to conclude that all of the prosecution's evidence was at least suspect, that none of it had any substance or merit.

Marcia Clark, Christopher Darden and the 23 other prosecutors who worked virtually full-time on Simpson's case wrapped up their effort with one large poster-board listing some of the evidence that had never been controverted at any point in the trial.

Their list included the drops of Simpson's blood to the left of the bloody footprints leading away from the dead bodies, Simpson's blood on the glove found at the crime scene and blood found on the floor of Simpson's foyer hours before police drew a small vial of blood from his arm. They also left no doubt that Simpson repeatedly beat his wife over a period of years. Darden called this the "long fuse" gradually burning down to the moment of explosion on June 12, 1994.

It all added up to a "weak case," said the former Juror No. 7, computer technician Brenda Moran. For her to believe that, she and other jurors had to put more weight on the fact that they didn't trust key detectives in the case than on the hard evidence those detectives could not have planted and were never shown to have touched. Testimony and a letter from former real estate broker Kathleen Bell about her mid-1980s encounters with Fuhrman were a key factor for Moran, she said. "When I read the letter, he had made a statement that a white woman and a black man together—if he stops them for any reason and there's no problem, he'd find a problem," she said two days after the verdict was rendered. "So in my mind he's not credible. I couldn't believe anything he would say." In short, the Moran reasoning goes, if Fuhrman was guilty, Simpson was not.

She also said she and her colleagues paid no attention to Simpson's long history of wife-beating. "This was a murder trial, not domestic abuse. If you want to get tried for domestic abuse, go in another courtroom and get tried for that," Moran smirked.

That, of course, ignored years of research showing that fully one-third of women murdered by husbands or lovers have been beaten by them before. It ignored Nicole Simpson's own prediction—never allowed into evidence—that Simpson would kill her and get away with it. For the jury to ignore that history and the uncontroverted evidence, its attention and consciousness must have been diverted elsewhere. And Moran's statements about the Bell-Fuhrman letter make it clear race was that diversion, regardless of the defensive statements jurors made afterward.

The statements of many black clergymen in the immediate aftermath of the verdicts were further evidence that, like the jurors, even highly educated and articulate African Americans saw the case racially, and were therefore not surprised when the prevailing white view was so different from their own. At the Parks Chapel AME Church in the ethnically-mixed Los Angeles suburb of San Fernando, the Reverend Jordan Davis predicted a "subtle riot" in which tensions would increase between whites and blacks. He urged his mostly-black congregants to "stick together" and pray for "those 12 jurors who had the courage to do the right thing."

At the First African Methodist Episcopal Church in South Central Los Angeles, the Reverend Cecil Murray warned church members not to gloat. "There are people walking around a little high-handed after the verdict. It's understandable. After 300 years, you get something that looks like a break. But we still have a lot of breaks to go." There was that thought again: that the Simpson verdicts were somehow justified by the sweep of black history.

These comments only served to reinforce the impression that every poll showed was left on most whites by the verdict-day celebrants. Emanating from some of the African American community's most prominent and responsible spokesmen, they essentially rubbed salt in the wounds of whites convinced that Simpson, despite his charm and his wide smile, is a murderer.

The tone was very different during Yom Kippur services at Temple Beth Chaverim in the Los Angeles suburb of Westlake Village, where Fred Goldman went for succor the day after his son's probable murderer was set free. Rabbi Gary Johnson cast no racial aspersions that morning. Instead, he resorted to Yiddish humor, as Jews often do when confronted with tragedy. Before introducing a brief talk by Goldman, Johnson told one of the many Chasidic folk tales about the eccentric people of the fictitious Polish town of Chelm, who often held skewed views of their world.

In the story, the Jews of Chelm went to the town's chief rabbi seeking justice. He told them they should go to Warsaw and buy some. They went, and quickly found two men eager to sell it to them. These men sold them a large barrel, supposedly full of justice, which they carted back to Chelm. The townsfolk opened it in a public ceremony in their main square—and suddenly the area became suffused with the odor of dead fish. None of the adults dared speak up about this travesty. But the children piped right up. "Justice stinks!" they complained loudly.

But America is not Chelm. And it was not only children who cried out when the O.J. Simpson jury returned its not guilty verdicts after less than three hours of deliberation. The furious included front-row courtroom spectators and journalists, feminists and United States senators. But Goldman and his family, perhaps the most aggrieved parties throughout Simpson's trial, cried out loudest.

Goldman lost a son whose only "crime" was his attempt to return a pair of eyeglasses to their rightful owner. The father watched for months from courtroom seats in either the first or second row as the carefully-chosen jury laughed at each joke told by defense attorney Johnnie Cochran, but took few notes when prosecution witnesses testified. He listened with incredulity when Anise Aschenbach, one of only two Caucasians on the jury, told a television interviewer that "I think he probably did it...chances are good he did it, and that's a shame," but added that she went along with the jury majority because "I thought of all the months, all the money, this case not being resolved..." and because she felt prosecutors didn't adequately prove their case.

Goldman's grief, like that of his daughter Kim, exploded into a shriek of pure pain when Robertson twice pronounced the words "not guilty." It was a nightmare, he said, second only to the moment he learned that his treasured son was murdered. No one else in the courtroom reacted so strongly, although disappointment was easy to read on the clenched jaws of Nicole Brown

Simpson's mother and sisters. But the Brown family seemed to have suffered from mixed feelings through much of Simpson's trial. In varying degrees, they depended on Simpson economically for years before the murders, helping him to manage the rental car and fast food businesses he owned. Simpson had also come through with college expenses for Nicole's sisters. All through the trial, eldest sister Denise was the only Brown willing to say she previously had any clue their former son-in-law and brother-in-law occasionally beat and humiliated his wife—their daughter, their sister.

Nor would the Browns explain why they had never urged her to escape his orbit. Even when Nicole's diary was published, with its revelations about how the couple lied to cover up the beatings Simpson administered to her, they said nothing. This was consistent with what psychologist and author Susan Forward reported about the two private sessions she had with Nicole Simpson in 1992, two years before her death. "She said she was beaten to a pulp on regular occasions," Forward told me in an interview. "And she said her family consistently urged her to stay with O.J. and work things out." In the hallway outside Judge Ito's ninth-floor courtroom, the surviving Brown sisters sometimes bantered with Simpson's sisters and adult children as the trial progressed. They often wore revealing micro-mini skirts—so blatantly sexy that Mike Tharp of *U.S. News* looked them over disbelievingly one day, rolled his eyes, turned to me and said just one word: "Bimbo-rama." Their frequent palling around with the family of the man accused of slitting their sister's throat led Simpson sister Carmelita Durio to explain on one such morning, "You know, we have been family for years."

But Goldman had no connection with Simpson other than through the murder of his son. His anguish and grief were unadulterated. So, too, were the shock and dismay of many in the small crowd allowed into the courtroom for the reading of the verdicts. Author Dominick Dunne, seated in the front row beside the Browns—and himself the frustrated father of a murder victim—turned white in shock. It was the same in the 12th-floor print press room, three floors above the courtroom, where the verdicts were recorded on two television monitors. Stunned silence reigned for a few moments, before the mass of reporters recovered their equilibrium and quickly began filing urgent stories.

The cheers of the mostly black crowd outside the courthouse and other African Americans around the nation contrasted sharply with that courtroom atmosphere. They couldn't have been better targeted if their underlying intention had been to arouse white fears. Just as the deepest fear of slaveholders has always been an armed uprising by their chattel, so white America secretly fears an uprising by a long-oppressed black underclass. The Simpson verdicts were a kind of revolt by a jury dominated by African Americans, encouraged by lawyer Cochran's appeal to disregard the evidence in favor of racial considerations. And because the jury's tactics involved no riots or looting, they aroused even deeper fears than did the urban uprisings which have swept through Los Angeles, Washington, Detroit and other major cities in the last half of the 20th Century. Precisely because African Americans had now shown themselves capable of using the same system whites had long employed to oppress blacks, white fear rose to new levels, producing thousands of letters-to-the-editor in newspapers across the nation and the outpouring of feeling against any television outlet that might give Simpson a forum.

Schatzman says white reaction to the verdict amounted to sour grapes: "How dare you people beat us on our own court?" was the subtext he saw in white complaints. Again, he is correct up to a point. But he doesn't go far enough. The white fear is that putting blacks in control of court decisions might cause them to acquit purely on the basis of race. That's what Cochran called for in his closing argument and it's what white jurors have often done, all the way back to the *Hannah Warwick* case Schatzman likes to cite. Dennis also says the Simpson trial may have been the most important since *Brown vs. Board of Education*. If so, it's because we've long known that guilty whites can manipulate the legal system if they've got enough cash or popularity, and now we know that blacks can, too. There should have been no surprise when this made whites uncomfortable.

All those feelings were clearly evident on a personal level as much as a week after the verdicts, when a small group of black celebrants drove to Simpson's Brentwood neighborhood in hopes of catching a glimpse of their hero. They stood along the south side of Sunset Boulevard near its intersection with Rockingham Avenue. Across the heavily traveled street, white residents of the area out for a morning run stopped and stared. The two sides said nothing, but their glares were as hot as laser beams.

There were no white riots, however, to compare with the black uprising that followed the first Rodney King beating trial. Instead, analysts all over America noted a change in the way whites felt about African Americans. Wrote Roger Boesche, a political science professor at Occidental College in a Los Angeles suburb, "Even liberals, in the face of cheers by African Americans who saw the not-guilty verdict as a victory over racism, will say: 'I supported affirmative action; I applauded programs for the poor, and I thought Rodney King's attackers were guilty. But I am still jeered as a racist. To hell with it. I'm going to close my doors and pull down the shades. It's time to retreat to private life and ignore public affairs." This, Boesche said, is how white people riot.

If he is correct, and that feeling truly prevails even among white liberals, then it may be "look out below" for black America. For without white liberal support, there would never have been a Head Start and there might be far fewer public health clinics. Affirmative action would not be merely an embattled practice; it would never have happened. Asked Boesche, "If most whites, including then-President Bush (whose Justice Department staged the second King beating trial, the one that produced prison terms for the most brutal cops), could see the injustice of the first Rodney King verdict, then why can't African Americans see the obvious injustice of this verdict?"

History is the answer to his question and the reason for the divide exposed—but not created—by the Simpson verdicts. The haves believe they can afford to sift through evidence dispassionately and arrive at reasoned conclusions. The have-nots know police have often rigged the justice system against them, so they can easily believe it's happening again, especially when a Fuhrman makes it clear that some policemen are willing to perjure themselves.

The outcome left some whites to wonder how they can react

positively when they're convinced they've just been shown that a defendant like Simpson can get away with murder merely because of the legacy of racial injustice. Fred Goldman may provide their most useful role model. Rather than venting anger, as he sometimes did during the trial, or continuing to rail at the verdicts, as he initially did after they came down, Goldman by the next day was capable of taking a larger perspective.

"We as a nation have been turned upside down," he told his fellow congregants on the Yom Kippur holy day. "We've gone from being concerned about the victims and their families to being more concerned about defendants and criminals." And he vowed to spend much of the rest of his life working to improve the lot of victims in the justice system. "Perhaps," he said, "if we all speak up, this kind of thing will never happen again."

DENNIS SCHATZMAN

Sex, Lies and No Videotape

There's nothing in the sport of boxing more demoralizing than the old "one-two" combination. Ask Billy Conn, former light-heavyweight champion and a native of Pittsburgh, Pennsylvania, my hometown. In a 1938 non-title fight with Heavyweight Champion Joe Louis, Conn was said to be ahead "on points" going into the 13th round. White folks, ears glued to their Motorolas, were drunk with ecstasy, my father, the late Clyde M. Schatzman, recounted to me 30 years later.

Max Schmeling aside, white America took the position that Louis' 1937 pummeling of the German, known as the "knockout that struck a blow for Democracy," was *then*; this was *now*. Almost to a U.S. Aryan, they were rooting for Conn. Then out of the corner of Conn's right eye came the left hook. His left eye probably didn't see the companion right cross coming in from the opposite direction.

Conn, America's latest "Great White Hope," went crashing down to the canvas. Predictably, black Pittsburghers went apeshit, much to the chagrin of many "mill hunks" living in and around Conn's native Lawrenceville and Bloomfield sections of the Steel City. Many blacks daring to venture out of the predominantly black Hill District, which was bordered by both areas, found themselves waking up in the emergency room of Passavant Hospital.

All this, of course, reminded me of the events of October 3, 1995 and the weeks that followed. The first left hook came at approximately 10:08 a.m. Pacific Time. Deidre Robinson, Judge Lance Ito's able and efficient clerk, read the verdicts—not guilty on both counts. Even the usually articulate Johnnie Cochran, O.J. Simpson's lead defense attorney, could only manage a joyful "ugh." Kim Goldman, Ronald Lyle Goldman's younger sister, and my choice for the "Profiles in Courage" award, broke out into loud sobs. Dominick Dunne, *Vanity Fair*'s journalist-in-residence, was seen sitting there next to the Brown family incredulous, with his mouth wide open. The right cross came twelve days later with the staging of the Million Man March in Washington, where 1.18 million mostly black men (the actual count conducted by Naval Intelligence via laser-heat head count) snubbed their noses at white America.

Retaliation would come swiftly and in very nasty, insulting ways. Generally, the entire African American race was put up for ridicule by many legal pundits and journalists—all white, mind you—on network television and in print. Even my colleague on this book made arrogant and, in my opinion, borderline racist comments that made me seriously think about canceling this project.

We should have seen the hint from the jury earlier than we did. Once the jurors were given their instructions, it took them all of five minutes to select a forewoman, a 51-year-old black woman. This group of eight black women, one black man, two white women and one Latino was certainly wasting no time taking care of business.

All month—in fact—all year, the virtually all-white contingent of legal "experts" that graced the radio and television airwaves had been predicting a hard-fought conviction at best or a hung jury at worst. About two hours into deliberations, the jury called for the only evidence they would need to review: the testimony of Allan Park, the limousine driver who drove up to the Simpson estate at 10:25 p.m. on the night in question to take the former hall-of-famer to the airport.

Park had testified that he "hadn't noticed" whether Simpson's Ford Bronco was on the street next to the mansion at the time of the murders. By inference, I suspect, the jury also surmised that the limo driver never heard a Bronco pull up, nor did he see a Bronco with its lights being turned off as it was parked. In the still of the night in fashionable yet paranoid Brentwood, either action would have instantly been noticed by a bright young man like Park.

Two hours after the transcript of Park's testimony was read back to the jury, Judge Ito heard three beeps, the signal that they had reached a verdict. A stunned Carl Douglas, the only defense attorney within miles of the courthouse, sat with his client and tried to read the notoriously poker-faced jury. He couldn't.

But dozens of pundits thought they could. "When no one in the jury looks at the defendant," Peter Arenella, a UCLA law professor, told a national audience, "that usually means a guilty verdict." Laurie Levenson and Stan Goldman of Loyola University School of Law in Los Angeles, Robert Pugsley of L.A.'s Southwestern University Law School and a cast of thousands joined Arenella in making that assessment. Only a few like Greta Van Susteren of Georgetown University School of Law and Ira Reiner, the latest Los Angeles County district attorney to be ousted from office for perceived incompetence, would venture out on a skinny branch and predict acquittal. Said Reiner: "In such a high-profile case, I cannot believe that a jury would come back so soon with a conviction." Ito, also stunned, but knowing that most of the defense attorneys were out of town or otherwise preoccupied, sealed the verdicts until the next morning.

In predominantly black and brown South Central Los Angeles, and all places similarly populated, it was a night of fitful rest. Linda Johnson Phillips, a self-styled professional "court watcher," said she tossed and turned all night. She had proclaimed all along that Simpson was innocent. Along with her sister Rose, Phillips had sat in on every major Southern California trial involving blacks in the last several years. She had been "blessed" to get a seat in the Simpson courtroom 43 times. The 36-year-old wife and mother would be at 210 West Temple to win one of only seven designated public seats for one last time.

Either due to the good Lord or to one last lucky roll of the dice, Phillips' number was the second one randomly picked by the deputy sheriff. "But you know something," Phillips told me later, "I was a little skeptical because the number called before mine was 187. And, as you know, 187 means 'murder' in the California Criminal Code."

At the hour of reckoning, I was one of two guests in the Los Angeles studio of the New York-based cable TV show, *News Talk Television*, a syndicated national talk-format program. My girlfriend, Sandra Mancha, watching the verdict on a monitor in a back room, was sitting with her hands in the praying position.

In the program's New York studio, three lawyers—two black females and one white female—along with an Asian jury consultant, all cast their bets for conviction. My colleague, Ed Lawson, a Rastafarian-coiffed businessman who had sued the Los Angeles Police Department for harassment in a case that was upheld by the U.S. Supreme Court, felt the verdict would be acquittal. I still wasn't sure.

When the verdicts came down, Ed and I could see the courtroom reaction from our vantage point—and we could certainly hear Sandra from way in the back room: "Oh Lord Jesus! Yes, yes, yes, Lord!" Ed and I were cool. Both of us were veterans of the television game. We took the emotional high road. But deep down inside, we were doing background vocals for Sandra: "Oh, Lord Jesus! Yes, yes, yes, Lord!" In the back of the courtroom, Linda Johnson Phillips, dressed in her trademark all-black ensemble, was doing all she could to keep from breaking into a loud cheer. She was shaking with jubilation.

Later that day, several afternoon and evening television news programs would contrast reactions of students at various law schools across the country. At Loyola Law School, the reaction was very subdued, with a spattering of black students expressing mild glee. But at Howard University in Washington, D.C., the scene was reminiscent of the one that took place on May 17, 1954 when the U.S. Supreme Court handed down the landmark decision in *Brown vs. Board of Education*, striking down segregation in the nation's public schools—tumultuous celebration.

Later that day, and in the days that followed, the white-controlled legal press would launch a spin control that the Nazi propagandist Josef Goebbels would have envied. Southwestern Law School's Robert Pugsley took dead aim at defense lawyer Cochran, calling him a "demagogue" for using the "race card" by comparing Mark Fuhrman to Adolf Hitler in an effort to get the predominantly black jury to strike a blow against racism and police incompetence.

Pugsley conveniently forgot to mention that it was original defense attorney Robert Shapiro who purchased the cards on Fuhrman and brought them to the party. But white people didn't want to hear that. And as we all learned, Pugsley and his colleagues in the legal spin patrol were talking to whites—and only whites.

Stan Goldman, the Loyola Law School legal eagle, was so incensed with the jury's verdicts that it was all he could do to keep from calling them a bunch of incompetent fools. He even hinted that Simpson would get his comeuppance in civil court where, he predicted, the Brown and Goldman families would bleed O.J. dry. My colleague Tom Elias has written in this book that "the celebrations staged at black churches in Los Angeles and elsewhere sent a chilling message to me and millions of other white Americans: It's OK for blacks to murder whites, the celebrants seemed to shout at us. 'It's our turn now. You've been doing this to us for centuries with white juries clearing white men accused of killing and lynching blacks. Now we've done it to you, at least this once. A mostly black jury has at last done to you what the Rodney King jury did to us.'"

When I first read that unbelievably sickening prose, I went to my Latasha Harlins file just to make sure that I didn't miss anything. Harlins was the 15-year-old black honors student whom the world witnessed on videotape being murdered—shot in the back of the head—by Korean grocer Soon Ja Du. After a jury found Mrs. Du guilty of manslaughter, Superior Court Judge Joyce Karlin, a person who admitted from the bench to being afraid of blacks, gave the businesswoman probation and a $500 fine.

When asked why she gave such a wildly unbelievable non-sentence, Karlin said that she could not find a jail suitable for Ms. Du. No one in the black community had ever heard of such a thing. A judge not being able to find a jail suitable for a "nigger"? Search as I might, I couldn't find one article—not one—by Elias or anyone else that said Karlin's obviously racist ruling told the world it was all right to murder blacks. I guess we could jot that one down as one of those grammatical rules something like "the you is understood." Of course it's all right to murder blacks. Everyone knows that. There is ample precedent. Need we write about it?

Elias' sick analysis was just one of dozens of observations that white journalists would put uncensored on the national wire.

Much of it, like his, was meant to demean a whole race generally and the predominantly black jury specifically. Consider the Oct. 16, 1995 *U.S. News and World Report* editorial by its owner, Mortimer B. Zuckerman, who had the nerve to print that since most of white America felt Simpson was guilty, then something must definitely be wrong with blacks since they believed overwhelmingly that he was innocent due to lack of evidence.

"The Simpson verdict was a sensational example of the conviction among African Americans that crime in general is not so much a matter of wrongdoing as it is one of prejudice," Zuckerman said without offering any intellectual proof, "and an issue of racism rather than reason. It is easy to understand why blacks are suspicious of the system. It is perplexing and dismaying to find the level of feeling so intense even in 1995 that many African Americans can make a near martyr out of a man who has no history in the civil rights struggle and who is a proven wife beater. It must surely be that for many blacks, the trial was not about O.J. Simpson but about reparation."

This drivel coming from a man with the worst record of hiring and retaining blacks of any major publication in the nation? Who did he consult on this editorial? His maid or butler? If so, no doubt they told him in typical Stepin Fetchit fashion: "Yowsah boss. Youse right, mastah Zuckerman."

He closes by writing: "The platitudes that 'the jury has spoken' and 'our system of justice has worked its will' do not suffice. Now many whites have joined blacks and lost confidence in the ability of jurors of the opposite color to reach an honest verdict based purely on the evidence before them."

To many blacks, what Mort was really saying is this: This ain't no basketball game, no Broadway performance of *The Wiz*, this is the criminal justice system. *Our* system! How dare you niggers beat us on our own court? Fuck the evidence. If we say that planted blood drops are evidence, that's the end of the ballgame. If we say that one of Simpson's hairs was found at the Bundy Drive murder scene, a venue where Simpson played with his kids constantly for six months, and his hair is probably all over the fucking yard, then that's enough evidence to convict!

Mort said all that in his own magazine.

But the vast majority of vicious propaganda was heard over the airwaves. On the *Leeza* show, I was pitted against two paragons of journalistic virtue, an editor for the supermarket tabloid, *The Globe*, and a reporter from *A Current Affair*, a program whose only purpose is to provide comic relief between the evening's news programs and the situation comedies that follow.

On *Leeza*, these guys are trying to tell the predominantly white studio audience that I didn't know what I was talking about when I dissected the evidence for them to show that the "mountain of evidence" they thought they had was really just a trumped-up minor landfill. Never mind that I was a freaking judge for three years and that I had forgotten more about evidence than any one of them would ever know. But it was, again, just another example of the white boys trying to rest on their perceived superior laurels and gain sympathy from an audience who feels just as they do—that no matter how experienced the Negro is on the subject matter, he doesn't know as much as us.

Sometimes the venom took on comedic qualities. On the day after the verdict, I was to appear at 11 a.m. on KABC's popular *Michael Jackson Show* in Los Angeles. I arrived a little early to see Dominick Dunne work the guest mike. Jackson, a strident yet generally fair native Brit, saw me in the control room, and both he and Dunne invited me to join them.

Alas, it was not to be a good outing for Dunne. Prior to my entering the studio, he had pretty much had his way in lambasting the jury, Johnnie Cochran, Greta Van Susteren and anyone else he didn't agree with. When I forced him to talk about the evidence, things got really silly. I reminded both my host and my friend Dunne that since Simpson was bow-legged and pigeon-toed, why didn't the bloody shoeprints reflect that? To which Dunne responded: "Maybe he changed the way he walked because he killed them." That's what Dunne actually said on a live radio show being simulcast both on CNN and on *America's Talking*.

Which brings me to Tammy Bruce, president of the Los Angeles chapter of the National Organization for Women. Bruce, who also hosts her own talk show, has never been a friend of the black community even in the most quiet of times. After the verdict, she took to the streets and to the airwaves to tell all who would hear her that "a murderer was walking the streets." She forced Simpson to cancel his appearance on NBC with Tom Brokaw and Katie Couric. I went back to my Latasha Harlins file to see what fervor she had revved up for the murdered sister. Just as I thought. Nothing. Worse, she never returned calls from the Latasha Harlins Justice Committee. Double standards? But, of course.

The jurors, naturally, took a beating both in the media and in the white community. And it wasn't just the nine blacks. Some of the worst vitriol was saved for the two white women. "Those two," I overheard one white man tell his companion in a coffee shop on fashionable Beverly Drive, "are the modern day Hester Prynnes. Instead of them wearing the scarlet 'A,' they should be forced to wear a scarlet 'T' for 'traitor.'"

Traitor, they say? Just one more example of the fact that many whites really believe the criminal law system is their system and their system *only*. Which, I suspect, is why the worst characterizations were saved for Johnnie Cochran. No black lawyer has been more viciously lampooned than Cochran, the man who helped win acquittal for Simpson. Only two in recent history even come close, former judge, now Congressman, Alcee Hastings and the late Thurgood Marshall.

Hastings was serving a lifetime appointment on the Southern Florida federal bench when one of his Kappa Alpha Psi fraternity brothers, a Washington attorney named William Borders, was accused of attempting to bribe Hastings on behalf of two organized-crime figures coming before the judge. Both were tried separately; Borders was convicted, but he never rolled over. Hastings hired his girlfriend to represent him and told the world that he was going to "beat the daylights out of the government's case."

Once he made good on his promise, nine white boys (and one black) in the Florida judiciary appealed to the U.S. Senate to have Hastings impeached. The Senate, with the help of a handkerchief-headed Detroit congressman named John Conyers, once a friend of Hastings, impeached the jurist in a less-than-subtle act of sleight-of-hand double jeopardy. Hastings got even, though. Once he got his bar license back, he promptly ran for Congress and won. Now Conyers has to look him in the eye every day. I wonder if Conyers is wearing a scarlet "T."

In 1965, Thurgood Marshall was appointed the nation's first black solicitor general by President Lyndon Johnson. The appointment was met with stiff resistance from Southern boys in the Congress and from newspapers sympathetic to their cause. And all of the papers were not located in the South, either. When he won the first of his 33 (out of 34) cases before the Supreme Court, the *Chicago Tribune* used black dialect to poke fun at him. "Hell, I ain't had de jitters in de Supreme Court," the paper lampooned, "since de day I was admitted to practice nearly 30 years ago. But dat day, O boy! You coulda heard mah knees knockin' way out in de hall." (from *American Diary*, by Enoch Waters; Path Press, 1987).

Cochran was being lauded by black America as the second coming of Thurgood, winning arguably the most important case since Marshall persuaded a majority of Supreme Court justices to uphold *Brown v. Board of Education*. Whites, however, called Cochran a race-baiter, a demagogue and a dirty player. After Fred Goldman criticized him for comparing rogue cop Mark Fuhrman to Adolf Hitler, the black lawyer's office was flooded with death threats.

Enter the Nation of Islam security force and all hell broke loose. On Michael Jackson's radio show in Los Angeles, the host and Dominick Dunne both took great pains to criticize Cochran for hiring Farrakhan's boys. I reminded them on the air that the Nation of Islam's prices are much lower than Pinkerton's—and they don't carry weapons.

Reviewing the double-standards issue again as it relates to Cochran, no better example can be given than a comparison between him and the parent-murdering Menendez Brothers' defense attorney Leslie Abramson. While Cochran was being skewered for successfully defending Simpson, Abramson was praised as a brilliant defense attorney, which she is. But while Abramson was rewarded with an opportunity to host her own nationally televised legal talk show, Cochran's reward was to be invited to appear as a guest on Abramson's pilot show along with former LAPD Chief Daryl Gates, former L.A. District Attorney Robert Philibosian and yours truly. Cochran proceeded to join a long line of black leaders to be suckered by the media into denouncing Nation Of Islam Minister Louis Farrakhan and his Million Man March.

Speaking of the march, that event certainly didn't help matters any. As if the Simpson verdict wasn't enough, now white America had to endure seeing 1.18 million black men in the nation's capital, all but threatening to remove the blindfold from the woman holding the scales of justice in front of the Supreme Court.

Even *Saturday Night Live* got in on the stereotyping act. During the news portion of the show, the commentator asked "President Clinton" why he came all the way to Texas on the day of the march. To which "Clinton" said, "Because there's a million black guys in Washington."

But perhaps the most poignant explanation for the mass criticism of the verdict and its trial participants came from "Marie," a caller to the *Michael Jackson Show*. Choking back tears, Marie asked Jackson and Dunne "What are you saying to us? I watched and listened to the trial from gavel to gavel. I know exactly what went on. I just want to let you know that I am not crazy, okay? But are you saying to us that because we are black and supported the acquittal of O.J. Simpson, that we are wrong; and because you are white, and disagreed with the verdict, that you are right? Is that what you're saying to us?"

Yes, Marie. That's exactly what they were saying.

CHAPTER 2
THE CRIME

TOM ELIAS

I Hate This Story

I don't want to cover it! Keep me away from this case! Those thoughts, directed fervently but silently to my editors in Washington, D.C., were a first for me. In all my life, I had never wanted to duck a story. But this one was different.

From the moment O.J. Simpson became a prime suspect in the murders of his ex-wife Nicole and her friend Ronald Goldman, I wanted to get away from the story. It was a terrific story, I knew, with all the elements of great drama: sex, violence, money, power, glamour, celebrities, expensive sports cars and blood on the floor. I didn't immediately think of race, but that was to come, and soon. But instead of arousing my interest, these murders made me want to run as far away as possible. This sensation never went away, and it never stopped feeling odd. I had spent 25 years as a newspaper reporter and I instinctively run toward hot stories, not away from them.

Typical was the night in 1989 when my wife Marilyn and I flew from New York to Athens on a TWA Lockheed L-1011 which suddenly turned around over the mid-Atlantic and headed back to America, landing in Boston. The plane taxied to a runway far from any terminal and police with bomb-sniffing dogs immediately surrounded it. They herded the passengers as far as possible from the aircraft, but I wouldn't go with the others. Flashing a press card, I dashed back toward the plane despite Marilyn's frantic pleas to stay with the other passengers, out of harm's way. And I eventually filed a story on the false alarm.

I've always been attracted to stories with big-time potential. Murders never turned me off, no matter how gruesome. I never wanted to run away from the Charles Manson murder case during my years as a young reporter with the *Santa Monica Outlook*. The 1969 Ypsilanti murders didn't arouse nausea when I wrote about them as an Associated Press reporter in Michigan. Like many news junkies, I've been attracted to other people's tragedy like a moth to a light bulb. When the Loma Prieta earthquake struck the San Francisco area in 1989, I was in my car en route to the disaster area within minutes. I headed straight for the epicenter of the 1994 Northridge quake in Los Angeles. I've never quailed before rampaging brush fires, mobs of rioters or the bodyguards around politicians and movie stars.

But I wanted nothing to do with the O.J. Simpson case. It was a gut feeling, one I didn't deeply understand until months later. There were also physical sensations. When I learned that O.J. Simpson was the principal suspect in the two brutal slashing murders, I felt I'd been dealt a blow to the stomach. By the time police made it clear that they had no other candidates and considered the case solved, I had remembered Simpson's 1989 wife-beating conviction. As more and more evidence appeared to pile up against him during the week after the murders, I felt increasingly nauseated. I began to realize this would be a very important news story, one I would almost surely cover until its finish. And I just didn't want to do it. I wanted no part of the case.

But that wasn't how I felt when I first heard the news. Sorrow is all I felt at 7 a.m. on Monday, June 13, 1994, when radio news shows reported that police had found the mutilated bodies of Nicole Brown Simpson and her friend Ronald Goldman. Another tragedy for O.J. Simpson, I thought. How terribly sad. I immediately remembered how he'd lost a young daughter in a swimming pool accident and had been divorced from his first wife. Beyond that, it seemed like a routine murder story, nothing extraordinary in Los Angeles, where a night without at least one slaying is rare.

My initial feelings were scarcely different from those of most other people I saw. The regulars at my workout gym took brief note, expressing their own sorrow before returning to discussions of the stock market and the basketball playoffs. Then more news began to filter in. Simpson had flown back to L.A. from Chicago. Simpson had been handcuffed briefly by police. Simpson was considered a suspect.

As I heard those developments, something clicked. I remembered his conviction for beating his wife and I wondered if this was the same woman. I felt an ever-increasing sense of dismay. Soon the Simpson murders were the hottest topic of conversation everywhere I went. Almost everyone I saw that morning was white, and almost everyone I saw assumed that Simpson was the murderer.

But there was no talk of race. No one thought of O.J. Simpson, football hall-of-famer, pitchman for Hertz Rent-a-Car, occasional sports announcer and rather inept movie funnyman, as black. He was just plain O.J., almost without any racial identity. Yes, the victims were white, but that had no obvious bearing on anything. My feelings were reinforced when news reports recounted details of the 1989 spousal battering, when police early on New Year's morning found a bruised, muddy and whimpering Nicole in the yard of the Simpson mansion on North Rockingham Avenue in Brentwood, dressed only in a bra and sweatpants. Race had nothing to do with it. This was simply the story of a big, strong bully regularly beating and bruising his much smaller and weaker wife.

That impression grew stronger when Los Angeles City Attorney James Hahn released copies and transcripts of several phone calls from Nicole to 911 emergency operators. In one tape of a 1993 call, the operator asked a frantic, terrified Nicole to stay on the line until police could arrive, so that authorities could hear whatever was transpiring. "He's fucking going nuts!" Nicole shouted. "He broke down the back door to get in...I don't want to stay on the line. He's going to beat the shit out of me." No, she panted, her ex-husband had not been drinking or taking drugs. It was just his temper.

Suddenly I was back in the bucolic Chicago suburb of Deerfield, Illinois, running for my life around the big oak trees in our shady backyard. I had accidentally spilled some lemonade on my older brother Peter, and he was going to make me pay. Round and round the yard we went until he eventually caught up with me. I fell to the ground and he began pounding away. How I eventually escaped, I don't remember. But this was not an unusual incident. For years, Peter, three years older and far larger than I, would pummel me mercilessly. "I really did want to kill you," he remembered years later, as an adult. My problem was that

I never knew what might make him explode; when we might be off on yet another chase through the trees and grass and bushes, inevitably ending with me on the ground beneath his vengeful fists. Our parents rarely stopped these episodes. They couldn't control Peter's temper either. They called his flashes of anger "lion attacks" because his fury reminded them of the unleashed rage of a large and ferocious wild animal.

Between these attacks, the young Peter could be completely charming, kind and generous. But I never knew what might set him off, when an attack would come. I loved my brother, but I lived in constant terror of his fiery temper. He shared my home and could get at me any time he pleased, so there was never hope of permanent safety from these beatings. Even when I tried to lock him out of my room, he would force the door open.

In short, I knew exactly how Nicole felt on the night she died and for years before. She had loved him for years, but she couldn't be sure when he might turn violent. He had access to her homes and her children, and even when she tried to lock him out, he would beat the door down. In tapes and transcripts of all her panicked calls to the 911 service, she never made a racial reference—and neither did he. His attacks on Nicole had no more racial motive than what my brother did to me.

When a police report from 1989 showed that Nicole cried to police that officers had been called to her home eight previous times and had done nothing to stop O.J., I deeply understood her rage and frustration. My parents also broke up some of my brother's attacks, though far from all, but they never really did anything to him. There was no therapy and there was no improvement until I was large enough to defend myself and Peter outgrew his sudden flashes of temper.

In the immediate aftermath of the Simpson murders, it quickly became public knowledge that authorities never did anything significant to him either, even after he pleaded no contest to spousal battery charges. A few telephone therapy sessions, a few community service hours, that's all. For me, this story was like a forced revisit to the worst parts of my childhood. I had long ago forgiven my brother and my parents, and thought I'd forgotten all about those "lion attacks." But they came flooding back as radio news shows played and replayed the 911 tapes. I couldn't stop the memories from surfacing.

I was not allowed to put these parallels out of my mind as the murders quickly developed into a big story, and my job was to cover major news stories in the West whenever they broke. So it was no surprise when my phone rang. My editors weren't going to let me evade this story. No chance. They wanted me to visit the Simpsons' Brentwood neighborhood, filled with distinctive and expensive homes, and write a story on the prevailing mood the day after the murders. It was to be the first of 131 Simpson-related news and feature stories I would write over the next 15 months, detailing virtually every aspect of the trial.

On this bright June 13, the murders were all anyone could talk about in Brentwood. The mechanic who serviced Nicole's white Ferrari Testarossa with vanity license plates reading L84AD8 (late for a date) seemed shaken. "I miss her," he said. "She was such a nice lady, always bright and happy. I remember the last time she and O.J. came in together, she was all chirpy, but he looked kind of angry."

Such descriptions surfaced all around Brentwood, where habitués of the Toscana restaurant and the Starbucks coffee shop where Nicole often liked to relax spoke of incidents in which Simpson would suddenly appear and his ex-wife's exterior calm would shatter. Virtually none of the neighbors, waiters or workers were African American. Brentwood is almost lily white, a place where black people are made to feel unwelcome. Lester Sloan has been one of them. A veteran *Newsweek* photographer, he lived in a Brentwood apartment not far from Nicole's condominium. He remembered episodes in which police patrol cars followed him into the garage of his building, then questioned him sharply about his employment and whether he, in fact, lived there.

That never happened to Simpson. Police usually recognized him because of his football and acting fame, so he didn't get that kind of treatment. In fact, after the 1989 incident, police let him drive his $130,000 Bentley Turbo-Rocket off into the darkness, never even arresting him for the mauling he later admitted giving Nicole. They followed up much later, then didn't protest as a judge accepted his no contest plea and meted out a slap on the wrist.

Simpson wouldn't get off so lightly this time. He was taken to police headquarters downtown, where detectives took a blood sample and a statement. They ransacked his house, looking for connections with the killings and coming up with little. But as the week wore on, police leaked word that blood samples from the crime scene matched Simpson's type. They also confirmed that two bloody gloves had been found, one near the mutilated bodies, the other behind Simpson's house. Race never entered any discussions with police or Simpson's own lawyers, first Howard Weitzman and later Robert Shapiro.

A sense of incredulity persisted as police apparently didn't want to arrest Simpson. Why not? Why did they allow him to travel to suburban Orange County for Nicole's funeral when he was the leading suspect in her murder? Was he getting special treatment because he was black and police were afraid to move too fast in the wake of the Rodney King incident, or was he handled gently because he was a celebrity, or both?

Refusing all inquiries, police never clearly answered those questions, but guesses about why Simpson was handled with kid gloves came from all sides. "It cuts down on costs (and) it's less embarrassing to the suspect, who's not convicted yet," said black attorney Milton Grimes, well known locally for representing beaten motorist King, whose 1991 clubbing by police eventually led to the 1992 Los Angeles riots. "If you have a person who's an unknown...you have one set of circumstances; and if you have someone who's well known and the person has strong ties to the community, then you're going to have another set of circumstances." So, even Grimes, who was to become a leading exponent of the view that police acted in a racist manner, offered no such opinion at the time. Public defender Jeff Brown of San Francisco attributed Simpson's soft treatment to his celebrity status. Had he been just another black suspect in a South Central Los Angeles murder, "He would have been in the can so goddamn fast it made your head spin," Brown told a reporter.

But Shapiro met with robbery-homicide unit detectives Philip Vannatter and Tom Lange at mid-week after the murders, agreeing to make Simpson available for an interview, or surrender if they insisted. They didn't insist until 8:30 a.m. on the Friday after the murders, June 17, when they called Shapiro and he agreed that O.J. would turn himself in at 11 a.m. It was only when Simpson failed to appear at the appointed hour that the case took on new national proportions. A major celebrity was now on the lam. No one spoke about his race. Rumors floated in bunches, like balloons at a political convention, and they popped just as easily: He'd been abducted by his ex-wife's family. He was already dead, a suicide beside the grave of Nicole. My editors heard a plausible one: that Simpson was holed up in his ex-wife's condominium, the murder scene, about to shoot himself. Go over there and check it out, they instructed me.

When I arrived, a full block of Bundy Drive outside Nicole's condo was packed with about 400 bystanders. A line of television cameras pushed at the yellow crime-scene tape police had stretched around the building. Shoulder to shoulder, cameramen jousted for prime vantage points allowing them to film the walkway where the bodies were found. I burrowed through the crowd into the first row, only to be elbowed backward by two cameramen who were afraid I'd block their view of police carrying out Simpson's body. Elbowing right back, I finally got the spot I wanted. But the crowd dissipated as quickly as it had gathered when Detective Ron Phillips emerged to assure the mob that Simpson was nowhere near. The rumor that he was there had started after a man purporting to be Nicole's father asked the small group of curiosity seekers outside her condominium to call 911, and someone complied.

In fact, Simpson was more than 50 miles south, cruising toward the Mexican border in a white Ford Bronco—almost identical to his own—driven by his old friend and former teammate Al Cowlings. At 5:51 p.m. he was located by police tracing down a Cowlings cellular telephone call. The discovery of Simpson, heading south in a car containing his passport, more than $8,000 in cash and a fake beard, came almost an hour after old friend Robert Kardashian read Simpson's maudlin semi-suicide note to a national television audience. "I think of my life and I feel I have done most of the right things," Simpson said in his handwritten letter, full of misspellings. "So why do I end up like this? I can't go on. No matter what the outcome, people will look and point. I can't take that. I can't subject my children to that."

But he could and he did. Americans did much more than point at Simpson after Cowlings' Bronco was located. They watched engrossed for almost three hours as A.C. took his old buddy O.J. on a tour of Southern California. TV stations sent their traffic helicopters to join the chase, which proceeded at a stately 45 miles per hour, looking like a police-escorted motorcade as it swept under scores of bridges loaded with homemade "Go O.J.!" signs. Finally, Simpson emerged from the car in his own driveway, clutching a family photograph. Police allowed him to reenter his house and telephone his mother before taking him off to jail.

The crowd on Sunset Boulevard just south of the Simpson mansion on Rockingham that night provided some clues about the divisions to come when Simpson went on trial. "Juice! Juice! Juice!" they chanted as Simpson was driven past in the back seat of a gold-colored Ford sedan, surrounded by detectives. The arrest scene had overtones of a collegiate pep rally, I reported that night. One fan said he followed the chase all the way from Anaheim (about 60 miles) because "He's a hero no matter what happened." Another fan, a black man, said he went to the arrest scene because "He's an African American and I was afraid the cops would blow him away if someone wasn't watching."

That was the first time I heard race injected into the case. It demonstrated to me that no matter how many privileges the police allowed Simpson, some blacks would always see a racist tinge to his arrest. But I wasn't buying it. There was his run for the border. His blood at the scene. And his history of beating one of the victims. I thought then that police had arrested the right man, and nothing I saw in the months of courtroom scenes that followed has changed my mind.

DENNIS SCHATZMAN

"It's Not What it is. It's What it Looks Like it Is."

T he clock hadn't even struck 6 a.m. on the morning of June 13, 1994 when I realized that events of the night before would change not only my journalistic life, but forever alter the landscape of the "criminal law system" and how it relates to L.A.'s deteriorating race relations. On that morning, Kent Shocknek, the morning anchorman for Los Angeles' KNBC appeared on my television screen with the news that Nicole Brown Simpson, the estranged wife of O.J. Simpson, and a male friend of hers, had been found brutally murdered in the front yard of Nicole's trendy West Los Angeles condominium on Bundy Drive.

Simpson, the anchor said, was at that moment on an American Airlines flight coming back to Los Angeles from Chicago where he had arrived on a "red eye" just hours before. At about 6:15 a.m., Marshall Lowe, then my managing editor at the black-owned *Los Angeles Sentinel*, called. "This is your baby," Lowe barked into the receiver. We both knew what he was talking about. "You know the deal," he said. The deal. That phrase pretty much explains what the criminal justice life is really all about for a black man, particularly one who has been suspected or accused of doing something illegal or offensive to a white person.

I speak with some authority on that issue. As a kid growing up in Pittsburgh, Pennsylvania, I saw how black boys were treated differently than white boys by white policemen and others involved in the criminal law system. (Notice I didn't say "criminal justice system." You'll rarely see that phrase written anywhere by me.) I remember one day Michael Fiore and I got into a fight after school right in front of Weitz's television repair shop on Lincoln Avenue. Mr. Weitz knew both of us. It was the kind of neighborhood where everyone knew everyone. He asked us to stop fighting and, of course, we didn't. So he called the cops. They came promptly, brandishing handcuffs, and took only *me* to the police station. Fiore walked away with his friends, laughing at my misfortune.

All the way to the station, I'm screaming at the two white cops. "Why am I the only one going to jail?" The policeman riding in the passenger's side, turned around. Feigning a backhand, he told me to shut up. I kept screaming, of course. "You racists!" Finally, the officer had had enough and he slapped me. I went berserk. I just motherfucked them repeatedly until we pulled into the police station parking lot. The desk sergeant called my father, who had to take off work to come and get me.

As I was analyzing where this Simpson story was going, I couldn't get past that roadblock that said, "Black man, white victims? Black man goes to jail; does not pass 'go'" Even a wealthy black man named Orenthal James Simpson is bound by the rules of reality as I understood them: "The easiest person in America to convict, whether the defendant is actually guilty or not, is a black man."

My first excursion into the case of O. J. Simpson as prime suspect came with my telephone interview with then-Commander, now Deputy Police Chief David Gascon, the LAPD's chief spokesman at the time. Gascon, a quiet, unassuming and honorable man, at first deftly danced the dance that we journalists and seasoned spokesmen often engage in. The commander told me that Simpson's initial flight left Los Angeles International Airport at 11:45 p.m. Sunday night. His flight arrived at Chicago's O'Hare International Airport at 5:34 a.m. Central Time and he checked into a hotel near the airport at approximately 6 a.m. When he heard of his ex-wife's murder, I was told, Simpson caught a return flight at 9:41 a.m. and arrived in Los Angeles at 11:08 a.m. Monday morning.

From that point on Gascon's responses to my questions became evasive. "Was Mr. Simpson a suspect?" I asked.

"We have not said that publicly," said Gascon.

"Then why was Simpson handcuffed on his property the moment he arrived from the airport?" I asked.

"That was a mistake," Gascon claimed.

Mistake, my ass, I thought to myself. I had been around for a long time and I knew for a fact that to handcuff a black man is standard operating procedure for law enforcement agencies, especially in Southern California, no matter how rich or well-known the black man may be.

Earlier that year, former Olympic triple jumper and track coach Al Joyner was stopped in Hollywood and questioned by LAPD officers about his late model car. He was handcuffed and harassed before being let go. A few moments later, Joyner was stopped again and the procedure was repeated by two different white officers. After filing a lawsuit against the city, Joyner won a $250,000 settlement.

A few years earlier, former baseball hall-of-famer Joe Morgan was handcuffed and arrested at the Los Angeles International Airport because police believed that—you gotta be sitting down for this one—Morgan, a national television sports commentator, "fit the profile of a drug trafficker." He, too, settled with the local government for a quarter of a million big ones.

Ditto former UCLA and Los Angeles Lakers star forward turned real estate broker Jamaal Wilkes. This native Angeleno, whose countenance is almost as well known as Rodney King's, was stopped in his car by LAPD officers, handcuffed and thrown to the pavement. Reason: Officers claimed Wilkes had a busted taillight. His eventual settlement payday was also in the quarter-million range.

The way black men are treated by white cops, white judges and prosecutors of any hue does not come without ample historical precedent. Dating back to the 1600s, black men accused of wronging whites have been treated worse than whites who were accused of committing similar infractions. While mentally reviewing the initial plight of O.J. Simpson, I considered the 1640 Jamestown, Virginia case, *In Re: John Punch.*

Punch, a black indentured servant, ran off with two white Dutch servants. Where three indentured servants could have run to in the densely wooded Jamestown area, I don't know. But all three were caught by local constables and brought before the local justice of the peace. The two white servants were found guilty, sentenced to four additional years of indentured servitude and given an afternoon of public flogging in the town square. Punch, however, was given a courtesy lashing in the town square *before* being dragged before the JP, whereupon the good magistrate remanded Punch to remain an indentured servant "for the rest of his life." As an exclamation point, the JP ordered Punch to endure an additional public flogging.

In legal terminology, the Latin phrase *stare decisis* means "let stand what has already been decided." This is the basis for acknowledging legal precedent. In the history of legal precedent, the case of John Punch became the one that legalized the perpetual slavery of the black man and woman in the southern states of America.

I have learned that whites tend to ignore examples of disparate treatment, especially when they have already become focused on the "guilt" of a black man accused of violating the rights of a white person. This was what I suspected was the case here in Brentwood. As *Time* magazine's Nancy Gibbs would remind her readers in the June 27, 1994 edition, Simpson's wealth would assure that he would not be treated by the "criminal justice system" (her words) as it treats other black men suspected of wronging whites. That false belief prompted me to think of the 1667 Virginia case, *In Re: Hannah Warwick.*

Warwick, a white "maiden servant," was accused of stealing from her boss, a black innkeeper. The justice of the peace found Warwick guilty of multiple thefts, but ruled additionally that Warwick was absolved from serving jail time or paying any fine because, according to the ruling, "the person that she was bound to obey was a 'negar' (black man)." The psychological precedent set in this case was that despite one's wealth and status in the larger community, if one is black, he is still a "negar." Therefore, I knew what the deal was, as Marshall Lowe realized. Simpson, despite his celebrity status, was in for an uphill battle, just like virtually every other black man accused of a crime against a white victim.

Something else struck me as being peculiar that week. The murders were performed in a series of brutal knife slashings in the still of the night in a quiet, upscale white neighborhood. It seemed to me to be highly out of the ordinary that an athlete who was formerly in as violent a game as football would kill two people in that way. When I was a University of Pittsburgh student, I was housed on one of the athletic floors in the dormitory. I was attending the school on a track and field scholarship. One of the residents of the floor was none other than "Bromo" Seltzer, a starting linebacker on our 1-9 football team and a real sick puppy. Seltzer would get drunk, especially after a loss, and start throwing people down steps, out windows. If neither exit was available, he would just beat you wherever you were. There was a guy talking on the telephone one evening. All of a sudden you heard a sickening wail. Seltzer had punched the guy in the stomach, causing the young man to throw up blood and food particles all over the floor.

Another pillar of the U of P college community was one Rodney Fedorchek, celebrated 6'6" tight end and a reputed opposite-sex abuser. Fedorchek, now a dentist in suburban Alliquippa, would get drunk and engage in fights with his girlfriend. One night, she had apparently had enough and told him to take a long walk off a short pier. Dejected, Fedorchek came running down to my room crying his eyes out. He wanted me to help him get his girlfriend back. I mean, this guy is bawling like a sissy. I thought that shit was both funny and pathetic at the same time.

The point is this: Athletes from Bronco Nagurski to Jim Brown to Steve Garvey to O.J. Simpson have been loud, boisterous and extremely physical in their brutalization of their fellow human beings. They usually don't exhibit the same *modus operandi* as the notorious assassin in Ken Follett's book *Eye of the Needle* or Carlos in any of Robert Ludlum's books. They just kick people's asses or shoot them and the whole neighborhood usually hears it or sees it.

The murders of Nicole and Ron, by contrast, were done in the quiet of the night. We would later learn that no one heard or saw anything, except the dog. Strange, I thought, very strange. In that week's June 16 *Sentinel*, I also reported on an interview I had with Howard Bingham, the longtime personal photographer of former Heavyweight Champion Muhammad Ali. Bingham was also on O.J.'s American Airlines flight to Chicago. "I saw him on the plane," Bingham told me early Tuesday morning, June 14. "Once we landed, we talked for a while at the baggage claim area where he picked up his golf clubs and a bag." Bingham added that Simpson didn't appear to act out of the ordinary or as if something pressing "like murder" was on his mind. In another interview later that week, Bingham swore up and down that he never saw any cuts on Simpson's left hand, a contention that would loom ever more important in the months to come.

Simpson was always the prime suspect in the double murders. He had been so deemed as early as the wee hours of June 13 when four detectives, led by Mark Fuhrman, would enter Simpson's Rockingham Avenue estate and seize control of the property and all of its internal and external contents without the benefit of a search warrant. Someone asked me that week whether or not I thought the detectives would have pulled such an illegal stunt if the property had belonged to someone like Frank Sinatra. "Did they get away with that," my friend asked, "because Simpson was black?" The question brought me back to my days in judiciary school at Wilson College in Chambersburg, Pennsylvania, when Harrisburg attorney James Morgan, an instructor and legal counsel to the Special Court Judges Association, told our class one morning: "It's not what it is, it's what it *looks* like it is." Whether it was an act of double standards or not, it certainly *looked* like an act of double standards.

I didn't visit the Bundy Drive murder scene, the Rockingham estate or the Mezzaluna restaurant, or attend the funerals of the victims. I have never been nor will I ever be a pack journalist rolling along with the crowd. Besides, I work in what I call the "specialized media." The *Sentinel* is not unlike *Time* magazine or *Golf Digest* in that it publishes weekly, which allows for more substantial news analysis. We have not only the luxury to report what people say, but also the ability to dig deeper to find out why they said what they said, all in the same story.

Thus I spent the week, among other things, analyzing the role the media would play in covering this blockbuster story. I was also preparing to participate in a joint Harvard University/University of Southern California-sponsored conference entitled "Beyond the Los Angeles Riots: What More Can We Learn?" What I thought was the most provocative aspect of this story—second only to race and justice—was the celebrity or "prominence" factor.

Several years ago, I wrote in *Editor and Publisher* about "the black press and its role in modern society." Among the many topics I covered were the factors that determine "what makes news." One of the factors I described was "prominence" and how it upped the ante on what becomes a newsworthy item. Coincidentally, the example I used to describe prominence read thusly: "People get divorces every day without fanfare. But when O.J. Simpson gets a divorce, that makes news."

At the time of that writing, I was the 29-year-old city editor of the *New Pittsburgh Courier*, one of the nation's oldest and most respected black-owned newspapers. I don't think I knew the details of the divorce then. In the week of June 13, 1994, however, the news media accounts made it clear. *Time* reported that Simpson had divorced his first wife Marguerite shortly after their then-youngest child, Aaron, drowned in the family's backyard pool.

Prominence, I suspected, would play a large role in the coming events. In my opinion, his notoriety would work both for and against Simpson. O.J.'s considerable wealth, gained by his prominence, was already beginning to pay off. Attorney Robert Shapiro, who would replace Howard Weitzman (of automaker John DeLorean fame) as the defendant's lead attorney, began putting together the defense machine that would later prove too invincible to stop in the courtroom.

Shapiro's entry into the case reminded me of a 1925 Detroit case involving Dr. Ossian H. Sweet, a black neurosurgeon who moved into an all-white neighborhood. White neighbors began stoning Dr. Sweet's fashionable home on a regular basis. One day a mob gathered in his yard, many of them threatening to storm the house. When they did, Sweet and his brother opened fire and several of the rabble were taken to the hospital. The case became such a *cause celebre* at the time that Sweet's fraternity, Kappa Alpha Psi, and the NAACP secured the legal services of the legendary Clarence Darrow.

One of the questions Darrow asked of witnesses during the trial was, "Was there a mob gathered in front of Dr. Sweet's home?" All of them answered in the negative. "If that's the case," he asked, "What do you call more than 79 white people gathered in front of Sweet's house, a welcoming party?" Darrow would eventually get Sweet off, but the neurosurgeon's life would never be the same. He went mad and could never regain his medical practice. I suspected the same fate would befall Simpson.

Soon after the funerals of Nicole and Ron, I was invited to be a panelist in that Harvard-USC symposium analyzing the role of the news media as it related to minority response and participation in the April 29-May 2, 1992 Los Angeles Rebellion (notice I didn't say "riot"). The coordinator was no less a media giant than Marvin Kalb, the respected television and newspaper journalist.

Among the 100 or so journalists and other participants sitting in the audience was the legendary Edwin Guthman, the former national editor of the *Los Angeles Times*, editorial page editor of the Pulitzer Prize-winning *Philadelphia Inquirer* and former advisor to the late President John F. Kennedy. Just before it was my turn to speak, Jeff Wald, another panel participant and TV news director of Los Angeles' KCOP, closed up his cellular telephone and asked to make an announcement. "I'm sure the audience and my fellow panel colleagues would be interested to hear," Wald began, "that O.J. Simpson will be turning himself in to the police at 11:00 a.m."

Several working journalists both in the audience and on the panel broke for the only pay telephone in the building. But neither I nor any of my panel colleagues left our seats. Nor did we let the audience down that day. We were accurate in our analysis and our truthfulness about the role of the media during the rebellion. In a phrase, we did our job that day as we had on the day of the rebellion—a task made more dangerous when the police abandoned the flashpoints, something I suspected they would never have allowed to happen if the rebellion had occurred in a white neighborhood.

Just before the afternoon session officially commenced, word spread like wildfire that Simpson was "on the run" and that one of his good friends, attorney Robert Kardashian, was reading a "suicide letter" from the now fugitive. The hall quickly emptied of virtually all the working journalists, myself included. While driving back to the office, I heard on the radio that Simpson was spotted riding in the back of a Ford Bronco driven by his friend

Al Cowlings, and holding a gun to his temple. I agonized to myself: O.J., have you lost your goddamned mind? Have you any idea who you are fucking with? The LAPD, you stupid asshole! They will kill your black ass!

This is not a game where the referees will throw a yellow flag and stop play at the sight of one tiny infraction. In Southern California, the police are not only the referees, but they also often act as the judge and the jury in the streets. As an officer hissed at me once, "Your newspaper, my streets." So I knew what I was talking about. Unlike Simpson, I didn't live or work in Brentwood. In fact, even to this day I have never been to Brentwood. My understanding of the police is that if you're black or brown, you will more than likely get beaten to smithereens or killed by the local constabulary, especially if you run from them. You see, running from the police in Southern California requires the pursuing officers to submit more paperwork. Thus the price one pays for running from the cops, whether one is black, white, brown or yellow, is often a good old-fashioned ass-whipping, on which the LAPD in particular is a universally recognized authority.

I thought to myself: How many times have I written stories about how police in this particular venue resort to shooting or beating first and asking questions later? Three immediately came to mind. One was the 1993 shooting death of Daryl Harts, a fraternity brother of mine whom police claimed pulled a gun on them. Harts, however, was a recent graduate of the Rio Hondo Police Academy and wanted desperately to become a police officer. Therefore, his shooting at police is a story that didn't make sense to me. Further, the police never released a paraffin test on Harts to prove he actually did shoot a gun at the officers.

Another incident involved tow truck driver John Daniels, Jr., who was shot and killed by a Los Angeles police officer as he was driving out of a service station. For some reason Daniels refused to stop when an officer told him to. The officer promptly shot him through the driver's side window while the truck was still moving. The officer's report claimed that the shooting was necessary to prevent Daniels from hurting pedestrians. So he shoots him, leaving a huge tow truck to drift into heavy traffic without a live driver? That's protecting the public?

Lastly, there was a rotund Pasadena barber named Henry Bryant. LAPD officers who had stopped him thought he looked suspicious. For some reason, Bryant drove away, eventually jumping out of his car and leaping into someone's swimming pool. While Bryant floundered in the water, officers shot him with an electric taser, nearly electrocuting him. Then they hogtied him and threw him face down into the back of the squad car. He died almost instantly.

So I feared for O.J. Simpson, a man who most white Americans considered like "one of us" as opposed to "one of *them*." Like Harts, Daniels and Bryant, he was in danger of being a recipient of justice meted out on the street instead of in the courtroom.

"Please let him get to a courtroom," I cried to myself. At the time, I thought that would be a good idea. I had been a district court magistrate in my native Pittsburgh almost 15 years ago. I knew the basic rules of jurisprudence. He would get a fair trial, I thought. As later events would confirm, I was both right and wrong about that.

Not only was this "biggest story of my career" getting bigger and bigger by the minute, it was also bringing back other painful memories. As a college student, I pledged Kappa Alpha Psi Fraternity. On November 2, 1968, I and several other pledges (Marvin Greer, Dorel Watley, Dwayne Cooper, Mack Randall, Joseph Brown, W. Thomas Whitaker, James B. Catlin, Frederick Wells Hill, Johnny Clark, Rossie Sanford Jackson and Eric Garrison) took a chance and kidnapped one of the regional officers of the fraternity and dumped him off in a cemetery about six miles from the University of Pittsburgh campus.

About four hours later, we were all rousted from our beds and brought before the fraternity officer. "With tears of anger streaming from his eyes, and borrowing words from Franklin D. Roosevelt, Joseph P. McCormick (now a distinguished professor of political science at both Brown University and Howard University) said to us that "this is a day that shall live in infamy." For the next month or so, our pledge line was the recipient of several severe ass-kickings from Kappas from Penn State, Ohio State (among them

Mike White, now mayor of Cleveland, Ohio), Cheyney State and Tennessee State in Nashville, Tennessee. We survived it, but we will never forget it.

As I pulled into the *Sentinel's* parking lot, I was certain that June 17, 1994 would become for me a new day that would live in infamy. The events that followed over the next 16 months made reality of my worst fears.

CHAPTER 3
THE PRELIMINARY HEARING

TOM ELIAS

It's a Lying Shame

Shame and lies. Virtually every person in the courtroom for O.J. Simpson's preliminary hearing on two charges of murder knew those were the fundamental themes of the proceeding. For six days in July 1994, police steadfastly lied about the motivations for their actions in the early morning hours of the previous June 13, just after the slashed bodies of Nicole Brown Simpson and Ronald Goldman were found outside her luxury condominium. But defense lawyers were not to challenge that lie seriously until many months later, when police prevarication became one of the central weaknesses of the state's case against Simpson. There was only one reason why attorneys Robert Shapiro and Gerald Uelmen didn't make a serious effort to undermine that lie: shame.

The police lie came first. As the four homicide detectives who were called to the murder scene took the witness stand one by one in the courtroom of Municipal Judge Kathleen Kennedy-Powell, their story was identical. All said they went together to O.J. Simpson's estate on North Rockingham Avenue, about two miles from the murder scene, to inform him of his ex-wife's murder and to see that the couple's two young children were properly cared for. They all said they entered Simpson's property without a search warrant because they feared foul play had occurred inside.

Detective Mark Fuhrman made the claim first. "We didn't enter with any intention of finding anything," insisted the man who testified that he found on Simpson's estate a bloody glove, matching one discovered at the crime scene, presumably dropped by the killer. Then came detective Philip Vannatter, who said, "We were within five minutes of a very brutal murder scene. I knew it was connected with Mr. Simpson because his ex-wife was one of the victims." After repeatedly trying and failing to rouse someone inside, and after Fuhrman pointed out a spot of what appeared to be blood on the door of a Ford Bronco parked near one gate to the estate, Vannatter added that "I became concerned we might have another murder scene, or someone injured inside. So we decided to go over the wall. I was looking for people, not evidence."

It seemed as if hardly anyone in the courtroom audience believed this for a moment. The police claim immediately became a standing joke. Every reporter, every visiting lawyer knew that police routinely question ex-spouses whenever there is a murder. As Vannatter would later testify, the ex-husband is usually one of the first questioned. In Simpson's case, there was even less doubt. His history of wife-beating was common knowledge at the West Los Angeles division of the LAPD. So any detective who didn't consider him an immediate suspect would have been derelict in his duty. In short, detectives Fuhrman, Vannatter, Tom Lange and Ron Phillips went to Simpson's estate not principally to inform him of anything, but to question or arrest him.

Fuhrman testified that he was the guide on the short trip, because he knew precisely where the Simpson mansion stood. This led to the single most embarrassing moment of the entire preliminary hearing. It came when defense attorney Uelmen, retired dean of the Santa Clara University law school, violated one of the cardinal rules of cross-examination. That rule is simple: Never ask a question when you don't know the answer in advance. First, Uelmen asked Fuhrman why police went to Simpson's house. Answer: "We didn't want Mr. Simpson to be notified by the media." Uelmen than asked how Fuhrman knew the location of the Simpson home. The answer came back quickly. Fuhrman had been there before. Gulp. Uelmen immediately changed his line of questioning. But he had been taken by surprise, and Simpson's reputation had been further tarnished.

Mark Fuhrman, it developed, had been called to the Simpson home in 1985 while he was still a uniformed officer. His job was to break up a domestic dispute in which O.J. Simpson shattered the window of his then-wife's Mercedes-Benz with a baseball bat. Uelmen knew this the moment Fuhrman mentioned that he had previously been called to the estate. But the braintrust of Simpson lawyers, which had not yet evolved into the so-called "Dream Team," was at least as concerned about his public image as about getting him off without a trial.

When Uelmen and Shapiro tried to discredit the police story, their hands were tied by the Simpson camp's desire to preserve as much of his previously benign public image as they could. They attacked the detectives' statements, but only to a limited extent. Shapiro's strongest statement: "We are going to show the four officers in charge left the crime scene...not to go to Mr. Simpson's to notify Mr. Simpson, but because of the celebrity nature of Mr. Simpson...How many detectives were necessary to make a notification?...If Mr. Goldman were the sole victim, would the same sort of investigation have taken place?" Neither Shapiro nor Uelmen wanted Simpson's sordid history as a batterer fleshed out on national television. So even when Uelmen inadvertently stumbled into that arena—which could have led to exclusion of the evidence found at Rockingham—he quickly backed off. As a result, Fuhrman's and Vannatter's statements stood without elaboration until much later in the trial. Neither Uelmen nor Shapiro knew it at the time, but this was to be one of their very best moves.

Prosecutors also did not call on Fuhrman to explain. For if he had testified about the exact nature of his previous visit, no reasonable judge could conclude anything other than that police went to Simpson's home because he was their prime initial suspect. But prosecutors believed they could not afford to admit that Simpson was an instant suspect—and they never would admit it through the entire trial—because that admission would spotlight one of the first and worst of the many police errors in the investigation: They entered Simpson's estate without a search warrant. Their combing of the property went on for more than two hours before Vannatter finally swore out a warrant. If any judge had ruled that this delay lacked sufficient cause, all evidence seized during that time could have been suppressed.

"We had just left a very bloody murder scene," Vannatter recalled on the witness stand. He and the other detectives reported they got no answer in their attempts to buzz the Simpson house from a gate outside. "No one knew of any (Simpson) travel plans, there were no lights on in the house, there was blood on (Simpson's) Ford Bronco and we knew there was supposed to be a full-time maid," Vannatter said. "At that point, I became very concerned. So, he said, he authorized Fuhrman to scale the wall. None of this, Vannatter insisted, was done with the intent of arresting Simpson but only of informing him about the crime.

Defense lawyers didn't buy any of this. But they never dared mention the obvious: that Simpson's long history of domestic abuse led police to suspect him from the start. By focusing on Simpson's past record, including the 1985 baseball-bat incident, Shapiro and Uelmen could have thoroughly discredited the well-orchestrated police excuse for the detectives' precipitate actions. But preserving Simpson's wholesome public image was clearly more important to his side than debunking the stated police reasons for their intrusion.

That intrusion swiftly became the central controversy of the preliminary hearing. Tension grew all week as Judge Kennedy-Powell first heard arguments and then considered whether to allow use of evidence gathered before police acquired their warrant. To allow that evidence in, argued Uelmen, "would turn the Fourth Amendment on its head and say that the less (police) know, the more (they) can do." He said the walls and gates around Simpson's house demonstrated that Simpson wanted and expected the constitutionally guaranteed right to privacy.

But prosecutors claimed the police intrusion was "minimal." Detectives, argued lead prosecutor Marcia Clark, did not force an entry into any building and did not search the interior of Simpson's house until they did get a warrant. The arguments put immense pressure on Kennedy-Powell who, like all California judges, must face reelection every six years and knew her term had less than four years to run. Well aware of the fact that Los Angeles voters had ousted Judge Alfred Gitelson two years after he rendered an unpopular decision on school busing in the early 1970s, and that California voters had fired former California Chief Justice Rose Bird because they believed she was soft on crime, the judge considered her decision for two days before coming down on the side of the prosecution.

"I don't find anything improper about the police conduct, with the idea that they went to the Simpson home to find the father," she said, buying the detectives' story wholesale. "The place for two small children is with their family." As for Uelmen's eloquent Fourth Amendment argument, Kennedy-Powell was having none of it. The police, she said, did not go in "like storm troopers...I disagree with the defense argument that this means the end of the Fourth Amendment...In my mind the Fourth Amendment is alive and well...the court finds that (police) were, in fact, acting for a benevolent purpose in light of the brutal attack and that they reasonably believed a further delay could have resulted in the unnecessary loss of life."

This was one of what would become a string of Pyrrhic victories for the prosecutors, as they won legal battle after legal battle and scored one public relations coup after another. The first of these empty triumphs came with the very first preliminary hearing witness. Demonstrating a sophisticated sense of drama, prosecutors called the previously-unheralded and unknown Jose Camacho to the stand. Camacho, a salesman for the downtown Los Angeles knife store Ross Cutlery, testified that he sold Simpson a 15-inch German stiletto barely four weeks before the murders, when O.J. was filming a TV show nearby. The implication was clear: Prosecutors believed that knife was the murder weapon. But Camacho's testimony proved pointless when Simpson's lawyers turned over the knife to Kennedy-Powell in a manila envelope which would not be opened until many months later. Camacho sold his story to the *National Enquirer*, but was never called as a witness in the actual trial.

The prosecution victory in the fight for admission of evidence seized before police obtained a search warrant appeared at first to be an even more significant coup than Camacho's testimony about Simpson's buying a large knife. But this victory may have eventually lost them the war. The fact that Shapiro and Uelmen didn't pursue their motion to suppress the glove and other Rockingham evidence as vigorously as they could eventually redounded to Simpson's great benefit. At the time, other lawyers questioned the defense strategy. "Beating his wife in 1989 does not necessarily mean Simpson committed this murder," said constitutional scholar Roger Jon Diamond. "Shapiro would help himself with respect to this motion if he brought up that this was common knowledge in the LAPD's West Los Angeles division. If Shapiro can create a backdrop that the police had a suspicion of Simpson at the scene, it would greatly help this motion." But Shapiro and Uelmen did none of that, and outside lawyers immediately hailed the prosecution victory. "This is the most critical decision on the admissibility of the evidence," said Samuel A. Pillsbury, a criminal law professor at Loyola University of Los Angeles.

His conclusion was to prove correct, but for all the wrong reasons. For it was only because of the Kennedy-Powell decision that prosecutors were allowed to use the bloody glove Fuhrman claimed to have found on Simpson's property. Because they needed Fuhrman to testify about how the glove from Simpson's estate was found, and where, it became mandatory for them to call Fuhrman as a witness. Other detectives could have testified about the blood drop on the Bronco door, also found by Fuhrman. But the warrantless search ensured Fuhrman's presence at trial. He eventually became a central issue by himself, casting doubt not only on the glove he found but on everything else police did. Without Fuhrman, prosecutors would have had only one glove, the one discovered at the crime scene. Without the warrantless evidence, Fuhrman would have been a minor figure in the case, one whom prosecutors could have called as a witness if they wished, but not a necessity. If prosecutors hadn't been so eager to bring in the warrantless evidence, the defense might not even have known Fuhrman existed.

As Uelmen was to declare during a pretrial hearing on September 21, 1994, "We were unaware of any involvement of Fuhrman in gathering evidence until he testified (in the preliminary hearing). He made no reports. Here we were confronted with a detective at the preliminary hearing without any opportunity to investigate his background at all. We were unaware Detective Fuhrman was going to testify until he did." But once defense attorneys began investigating him, it wasn't long before they discovered the racist tendencies that would eventually turn the prosecution's highly-touted legal victory into a disaster.

But it was no worse a fiasco than the decision that led to the preliminary hearing in the first place. This choice was made by Los Angeles County District Attorney Gil Garcetti. Garcetti decided even before Simpson's arrest to pursue a grand jury indictment rather than expose the full range of prosecution evidence during a preliminary hearing. Because the grand jury meets only in the Criminal Courts Building in downtown Los Angeles, the case would move there from suburban Santa Monica, whose courthouse has hosted numerous trials and proceedings involving celebrities from Michael Jackson to Elizabeth Taylor and Christian Brando. Most criminal cases from the Brentwood district of Los Angeles are heard in Santa Monica, far closer at hand than the downtown courthouse.

Garcetti maintained ever afterward that he had no choice but to move the trial downtown, claiming that security at the Santa Monica courthouse would have been inadequate to handle the death threats and crowds he knew would accompany the Simpson proceeding. "Downtown was the only place we could have held this trial," he told me. The credibility of that statement, repeated often in subsequent months by the district attorney, was placed in doubt by the way the first trial of parent-killers Erik and Lyle Menendez was conducted in another branch courthouse in Van Nuys. That facility features less security than Santa Monica's, but the fully televised Menendez I went off without a hitch, even though the unsequestered jurors frequently mingled with reporters during smoking breaks on the courthouse steps. So long as no one mentioned the trial during those encounters, there was no problem—and no problem ever arose. Result: The second Menendez trial was set in the same branch courthouse.

Plenty of others also felt Simpson's case should have stayed in Santa Monica, close to the crime scenes and with a jury pool that would have been almost 79 percent white. "The case belonged in Santa Monica," said retired Judge Leonard Wolf, presiding judge in Santa Monica from 1986 to 1989. "And it could have been tried there...A number of major criminal cases have been tried in Santa Monica." Garcetti's gamble was plain when he moved the Simpson case downtown: Because grand jury proceedings are secret, neither the defense nor the public would know for months all the evidence an indictment might be based upon. Balanced against this was the fact that the jury pool in the downtown area contains a far higher percentage of African Americans and other ethnics than are available on the West side of Los Angeles.

For the defense, the move downtown had some obvious potential advantages, assuming that black jurors are more likely than whites to acquit black defendants. This assumption became popular during the trial of the black youths who beat trucker Reginald Denny during the opening moments of the 1992 Los Angeles riots. The young men were convicted only of minor offenses and given short sentences largely because of the ethnic composition of their jury, essentially reversing the outcome of the Rodney King beating trial which set off those riots. But Garcetti heatedly disputed that claim. "Black jurors convict black people all the time," he told me. "I have just as much faith in black jurors as in white."

One obvious question: If Simpson's prosecution was based on a racist conspiracy—a claim defense lawyers made central to their case and one echoed by my colleague Dennis Schatzman—why didn't Garcetti leave the case in Santa Monica, where the jury almost certainly would have included more than one or two whites? If Garcetti were planning an old-fashioned "rat-fucking" of Simpson, as Dennis suggests, why take the case downtown, where Simpson was certain to find a more sympathetic jury?

Nevertheless, the apparent ethnic advantage to the defense could have been offset by the secrecy of grand jury proceedings. But the grand jury didn't keep the case very long. On June 24, Shapiro succeeded in an unprecedented legal maneuver: He managed to interrupt a grand jury proceeding and get the panel thrown off a case it had begun to hear. He was able to do this because days earlier, Los Angeles City Attorney James Hahn released tapes and transcripts of several frantic telephone calls a desperate Nicole Simpson had made to 911 emergency operators as her husband threatened and attacked her. One of the 23 grand jurors acknowledged that he had heard those tapes while watching television at home before hearing the Simpson matter. "I doubt that any (grand jurors) did *not* see it," said the grand juror, who spoke to me on condition of anonymity. "If you watched TV at all, you couldn't help hearing them."

Schatzman would have us believe the only reason for releasing those tapes was to "bring down the tremendously high Q-scores Simpson enjoyed," to destroy his popularity. Not so. The newspapers, TV and radio stations that pushed for releasing the tapes were trying to satisfy a public hungry to know more about a celebrity who had suddenly shot into new prominence. This was no racist plot; it was just the press doing its job. And city attorney James Hahn was simply complying with media requests not only because they were legitimate, but also to avoid getting involved in an embarrassing lawsuit he was bound to lose.

The result was that Shapiro went before Cecil J. Mills, a former Democratic state senator then sitting as Los Angeles County's supervising criminal judge, arguing that the grand jurors could no longer be objective arbiters. Mills immediately stripped the grand jury of any role in the case. The move, Mills said, was necessary to "protect the due process rights of Mr. Simpson and the integrity of the grand jury process." Said Shapiro, "We look forward to finally presenting this evidence in a public courtroom...to hearing live testimony under oath from the witnesses."

The witnesses he meant were all to be prosecution witnesses, for Shapiro had now secured for Simpson the best of both worlds: Because of Garcetti's action, a jury with at least a significant number of African Americans was assured. And because Shapiro succeeded in removing the cloak of grand jury secrecy, the defense would get to see the nub of the prosecution case months before the start of an actual trial. This allowed plenty of lead time to devise ways of undermining key witnesses like Fuhrman and their evidence.

That's just what happened in the preliminary hearing. Vannatter testified. Fuhrman testified. Deputy Coroner Irwin Golden testified. Los Angeles police crime laboratory technicians testified. Houseguest Brian (Kato) Kaelin took the stand to talk about the thumps he felt and heard in the night. Several neighbors of Nicole's testified to a time-line dependent on the barking of Nicole's Akita dog, also named Kato. By the conclusion, it was obvious there had been at least some serious errors by authorities investigating the case.

The testimony of Mrs. Simpson's neighbors produced one of the memorable moments of the trial for reporters working in the print press room, then located in a windowless cubbyhole on the 11th floor of the courthouse. On a day dominated by testimony about barking dogs and bloody paw prints, the distinguished *New York Times* correspondent B. Drummond Ayres Jr. attempted to maintain some dignity amid the noise and crowded conditions of the makeshift press facility. His editors made this difficult, trying to help him compose his story. Finally Ayres exclaimed in a Southern drawl that everyone in the room could hear, "You mean you want me to put the *dog* in the *lead?*!" In fact, the dog did become the lead in his story—and almost everyone else's, too.

The scene in that press room and in the hall just outside, where courtroom passes were given out daily, also provided a few clues to the future. Television cables stretched everywhere in the 11th floor hallways, frequented daily by hundreds of newly-called jurors reporting to the jury holding room. Camera crews occupied virtually the entire main hall. It wasn't long before Judge Lance Ito demanded that the press be moved off that floor for fear that the good behavior that prevailed at the first Menendez trial wouldn't be repeated by the much larger press corps turning out for Simpson. That's why, when new and more permanent press quarters were meted out, they were one floor up and reporters were asked to stay off the 11th floor.

Clues about the difficulties that would later plague both prosecutors and defense lawyers began to emerge even before the preliminary hearing. As the county grand jury began hearing testimony against Simpson on June 17, 1994—the same day Simpson declined to turn himself in and eventually was arrested—deputy district attorneys called several witnesses who would later prove so unreliable or biased that they would never be called on to testify in open court.

One of those witnesses was Jill Shively, a resident of Santa Monica who claimed to have been driving near the murder scene on the night of the crimes. She told the grand jury that Simpson almost struck her car with his Ford Bronco as he sped from the rear alley behind Nicole's condominium onto a side street and then into the northbound lane of Bundy Drive. After the near collision, she said, Simpson "turned around and glared at me." Shively was branded an unreliable witness, however, when she misled prosecutors by telling them that before bringing her story to them, she had spoken to no one except her mother about what she saw. In fact, Shively had sold an interview to the television tabloid show *Hard Copy* for $5,000 before her June 21 grand jury appearance. Under questioning by Clark about that apparent contradiction, Shively said she meant no harm with the interview. "I am, I was nervous and hadn't slept all week and wasn't really thinking," she told the grand jury. "I wasn't trying to hide anything because I knew it was being aired the next day, and I assumed I would be involved in the trial, so I wasn't doing anything to break the trust."

Clark reacted harshly and possibly self-destructively, telling grand jurors to "completely disregard the statements given and the testimony given by Jill Shively in this case. I cannot allow her to be part of this case now that she has proven to be untruthful as to any aspect of her statement." So Shively—the prosecution's last, best hope for an eyewitness who could place Simpson at the crime scene—disappeared from the case. Later, of course, Clark would sign a $4 million contract to detail her version of the case. If Shively became unreliable when she accepted a $5,000 payment, what does that make Clark?

Another disappearing witness was Keith Zlomsowitch, the manager of the Mezzaluna restaurant where Nicole Simpson ate her last meal and where Ronald Goldman worked as a waiter. Zlomsowitch, who dated Nicole and had at least one sexual encounter with her while she was estranged from Simpson, described to the grand jury several incidents in which Simpson appeared suddenly in front of their tables while they were eating in various restaurants in Beverly Hills and on the West side of Los Angeles. He told the grand jury he felt "very intimidated," especially on one occasion when Simpson introduced himself and announced, "She's still my wife." He also testified that Simpson once confronted him and told him he had observed through a window as Zlomsowitch and Nicole engaged in a sex act on a living room couch in the house Nicole rented for a time on Gretna Green Way, about two blocks from the murder scene. But the Zlomsowitch testimony was never heard again, as Garcetti and Clark completely abandoned their early portrayal of Simpson as a threatening stalker.

The grand jury transcripts reveal that police also believed they found blood in the drain of Simpson's bathroom sink. Criminalist Dennis Fung claimed he discovered some there, but prosecutors never used that information either at trial or in the preliminary hearing. And the quick disposition of Shively was similar to what was to happen later to several defense witnesses. For a time, defense lawyers hoped to get major exculpatory evidence from Frank Chiuchiolo, a convicted burglar from rural Northern California who told investigators he saw two men in dark clothing near the back gate of the murder scene. Chiuchiolo said he was in the area to case homes for his next burglary. Had he testified, he might have been able at least to dispel the police notion that Simpson acted alone. But Chiuchiolo was quickly discarded when police in his hometown of Yreka dismissed him as a convicted thief, liar and longtime con man trying to capitalize on the Simpson case.

The experience of both sides with witnesses like Shively and Chiucholo showed that Simpson's case from the outset was not seen by most whites as even marginally racial. It drew groupies, not bigots. Its celebrity nature far overshadowed any racial overtones. No crowds of tourists ever swarmed the small grocery store where Latasha Harlins was shot in 1991. Only a few went to the intersection of Florence and Normandie Avenues, where the 1992 Los Angeles riots began with the televised beating of trucker Reginald Denny. But fans swarmed every scene important to the Simpson case. From its first days, the O.J. case had more in common with the suicide of Marilyn Monroe and the drug overdose of John Belushi than with any racially-motivated crime. This was why Grave Line Tours, the Hollywood-based firm which employs remodeled hearses as it ferries tourists to the sites where movie and television stars have died, quickly added the Simpson scenes to its macabre itinerary.

So police lies, the Constitution, legal tactics and Simpson's shame over his history as a wife-beater all became central factors in the preliminary hearing, but racial issues never entered the proceeding. Shapiro and his cohorts avoided bringing up that subject just as assiduously as they tried to keep the disgrace of Simpson's prior domestic abuse out of the public's consciousness. No one involved at this stage of the case thought Simpson's skin color had any relevance to the crimes of which he was accused. Shapiro even promised to try to keep race out of the eventual trial. Famous last words.

DENNIS SCHATZMAN

"You Mean There Really Wasn't a Bloody Ski Mask?"

Several years ago, I was driving down Los Angeles' Jefferson Boulevard. We became tired and needed a place to rest. So I stopped with a lady friend of mine in one of the area's "sleep-cheap" motels for a few hours of peace and quiet. The lady and I were sitting around the table reading magazines when we heard through the paper-thin walls next door a man laying some serious pipe on his paramour. Apparently when the feeling got good to him and he was beginning to feel like Zeus, the man shouted out to her: "Show me what you got, goddammit! Show me what you got!"

Which brings us to the subject of the O.J. Simpson preliminary hearings and the events that led up to them. In June 1994, the public first got a glimpse at the prosecution's tactics. Fortunately, many of those tactics, designed to put Simpson in a negative light before the trial, were exposed early. The ultimate result was that Presiding Superior Court Judge Cecil Mills dismissed the predominantly white grand jury, forcing the prosecution to "show me what you got," or in other words show the defense and the public what it had in the form of evidence against Simpson in a preliminary hearing.

Essentially, the slick tactics came in four phases: the release of the infamous "911 tapes," the convening of a grand jury, the leaking of damaging and often untruthful information against Simpson and the prosecution's numerous attempts to delay giving information, under discovery, to the defense.

Shortly after Simpson was arrested following the chase, LAPD officials released to the news media copies of the 911 tapes from October 1993. What the tapes revealed, among other things, was that Simpson was angry because he saw Nicole on her living room couch performing fellatio on Keith Zlomsowitch, a restaurateur whom Nicole had been seeing since 1992. The releasing of the tapes was done without any resistance from either LAPD Chief Willie Williams or Los Angeles City Attorney James Hahn. A request came in from news media attorneys, under the Freedom of Information Act, asking for release of the tapes. Without going to a judge to get official permission to hand over the tapes, "They just acted like a couple of street whores," I told one talk-show host, Warren Olney of KCRW's *Which Way L.A.* "They just gave it up."

What happened next was predictable. Television news shows all over the nation began airing the tapes. One newspaper, the South Los Angeles County *Daily Breeze*, a Copley newspaper, ran a phone number on its front page daily urging its readers to call in and listen to the tapes. I asked Jean Adelsman, the *Daily Breeze*'s managing editor, whether she gave any thought to whether or not the airing of the tapes violated Simpson's right to a fair trial. "No!" she said matter-of-factly. And she spoke for most of the nation's news media as well.

I thought the airing of the tapes was done for one reason and one reason only: to bring down the tremendously high "Q-scores" Simpson enjoyed. A "Q-score" is a measure of a celebrity's positive penetration with the audience. The higher the "Q-score," the more likely the celebrity gets work in movies, television shows and commercials. One example of how Simpson was regarded prior to the double murders is indicated in the British Broadcasting Company's August 1994 one-hour documentary on Simpson. Title: "The Mr. Nice Guy Murders."

Never mind that the tapes were nearly inaudible, the constant airings gave the impression that Simpson was almost a maniacal killer. Others disagreed. "Did you hear what he's saying on the tapes?" Carl Nelson, Peabody Award-winning journalist for Los Angeles' KJLH-FM, asked me. "He's talking about (Nicole) sucking some guy's 'johnson' on the living room couch while the kids are upstairs."

Moving on to the short-lived grand jury, Los Angeles County District Attorney Gil Garcetti opted to bring his evidence against Simpson before the 23 predominantly white permanent jurors beginning on June 17, 1994. The benefit to the prosecution is that these hearings are closed to the public and the media and witnesses cannot bring attorneys with them.

It's important to note here that while he was a USC undergrad, Garcetti and a fellow pre-law student named Donald Segretti, along with Dwight Chapin and others, used to perform dirty tricks against people running for student council office. The process was called "ratfucking." Both Segretti and Chapin would go on to ratfuck on a grander scale for a Whittier College graduate named Richard Nixon. So Garcetti, in my opinion, bore watching.

Among those who testified before the grand jury were Brian "Kato" Kaelin, Simpson's guest-house tenant; Dr. Irwin Golden, a deputy coroner; Jose Camacho, a salesman who sold Simpson a 15-inch stiletto just weeks before the murders; Allan Park, the limousine driver who took Simpson to the airport; Thano Peratis, the registered nurse who took blood samples from Simpson after the murders; detectives Tom Lange and Philip Vannatter, the detectives who searched Simpson's estate with and without a search warrant and Dennis Fung, the LAPD criminalist who collected blood samples at both the Bundy Drive murder scene and at Simpson's Rockingham Avenue estate.

All that, however, would come to naught. Judge Mills put a stop to the grand jury for two reasons. One, the release of the 911 tapes, in Mills' opinion, violated Simpson's right to due process of law. Further, someone either in the District Attorney's Office or within the LAPD leaked to the media that a "bloody ski mask" was found at the murder scene. As it turned out, there was no bloody ski mask, as indicated by this exchange before Municipal Court Judge Patti Jo McKay:

Shapiro: "Your honor, I have been given a list of evidence in the prosecution's possession, and I see no notation of a bloody ski mask. So then there is no ski mask?"

Clark danced around that question by saying that the papers given to Shapiro listed all the evidence in the district attorney's possession.

Judge McKay: "So you are saying there is no ski mask?"

Clark: "There is no ski mask."

Also, KCAL-TV's newsman David Goldstein reported on July 1, 1994 that a knife had been found in Chicago where Simpson had traveled on the night of the murders. Like the ski mask, the knife story would later be proven untrue. As it turned out, each was leaked to the media by unnamed sources either within the district attorney's office or the LAPD. Mills realized, in my opinion, that the incidents previously described fell in line with the case involving Dr. Sam Shepard, a Cleveland physician accused of murdering his second wife. His 1954 conviction was overturned because, according to the U.S. Supreme Court, Shepard didn't receive a fair trial because the prosecution leaked damaging information to the public, much of it evidence that never came to trial. The attorney who effectuated the conviction reversal was F. Lee Bailey, the Boston attorney who would loom ever important for the Simpson defense team in the months to come.

Since the grand jury convenes downtown, the preliminary hearing would have to be held downtown, according to Garcetti. This was a boon for the defense, and people in the African American community were ecstatic. Blacks have long been skeptical about whether or not a closed grand jury hearing would be conducted according to Hoyle. Besides, this was becoming the "Trial of the Century" and everyone wanted to see what was going on. Plus, the defense got to see at least a portion of what the prosecution had on the defendant.

The preliminary hearing opened on June 30, 1994 before Municipal Court Judge Kathleen Kennedy-Powell. The tension was so thick you could cut it with a knife, if you'll excuse the expression. The news media and the general public were seated first, about 8:50 a.m. Then came the Goldman family. Shapiro and attorneys Gerald Uelmen, Robert Kardashian and Shapiro's associate Sara Caplan, by far the sexiest attorney to grace the courtroom at any time during the trial, walked out of the holding cell area at 9:03 a.m. The Brown family entered the courtroom at 9:05 a.m.

Now everyone was waiting for O.J. Simpson. "It's so quiet you could hear a pin drop," I wrote in my notes. The lawyers remained standing, waiting for their famous client. Finally Simpson entered from the holding cell area, wearing a black suit, white shirt and a red polka dot tie. Members of both the Goldman and Brown families were holding hands during this time.

The first order of business concerned how many of Simpson's

hairs can be obtained by the prosecution for analysis. Shapiro claimed that the prosecution needed between one and seven hairs. Clark countered that the prosecution needed at least 100 hairs "or you can't make an effective comparison." Shapiro said that his expert, the noted forensic pathologist Dr. Henry Lee, says that between one and three hairs are necessary to make effective comparisons. Judge Kennedy-Powell initially ruled that the prosecution could get no more than 10 hairs from Simpson's heady, head, head. When Clark objected, the judge told her that if the prosecution needs more than 10 hairs, then bring in a hair analysis expert to prove it. Later, Clark would prove that between 30 and 100 hairs were needed. Her expert? A page from a book written by none other than Simpson expert witness Dr. Henry Lee.

The first witness called to the stand was Michele Kestler, the assistant director of the LAPD's criminalistics lab. Kestler, who is married to an LAPD detective, explained that the role of a criminalist was to collect and preserve all evidence found at the crime scene. Was there enough blood-spot evidence collected, for example, so that the defense could get enough to do its own independent analysis? Shapiro asked. "There's never any guarantee that you have enough evidence to analyze," Kestler testified. This exchange, in my opinion, was a hint of things to come. The prosecution, through Kestler, was telling the court and the defense that they were not going to give up portions of their evidence for independent analysis easily. It didn't take long for my concerns to be realized.

Shapiro asked Clark about a list of items already recovered from various places, such as the Ford Bronco, the Rockingham estate and the Bundy Drive murder scene. "We have not received a list of those items," Shapiro told the judge. "We haven't received the list either," Clark shot back. "We should have had it," Shapiro countered. "The police have 10 days to file their report," Clark explained. Judge Kennedy-Powell ruled: "As soon as you get the report, Ms. Clark, get it to the defense." Sitting in the courtroom and hearing this exchange, Rose Brown, Linda Johnson Phillips' older sister and a fellow court watcher, opined: "Translation: What the judge is saying to the prosecution is 'Give it to the defense when you get good and damn ready.'"

During this phase, Shapiro showed that he can be both a master of wit and a penetrating examiner at the same time. Just before his cross-examination of Kestler, Shapiro asked for her resumé. "Do you need it?" Judge Kennedy-Powell asked. "We may want to contest her," Shapiro answered. "It could save time."

The request prompted a recess. And it gave Shapiro time to hold court with several print media reporters. He told us that his office was getting over 150 calls a day, so he took his work home with him "to get away from the madness." One of the deputy sheriffs sauntered over to warn Shapiro that he can't conduct a press conference in the aisle of the courtroom. Feigning hurt, Shapiro told the deputy as he held his hand over his heart, "I'm just talking with my friends." As the deputy left, Shapiro told us that he would always talk to members of the print media.

During this lovefest, I took the opportunity to ask Shapiro why he asked for Kestler's resume. "She's a criminalist, not a criminologist," he responded. "What's the difference?" I asked. To which Shapiro retorted, "the same as being an optometrist or an opthalmologist." Later with Kestler back on the stand, Shapiro proceeded to slice up her qualifications. How much experience did she have analyzing blood samples, hair samples? Had she written any articles or books? Kestler testified that she had only co-authored a 1982 article about "clandestine drug labs." She also admitted that she had never written on the subjects that "I am testifying to today."

As Shapiro peered over Kestler's "statement of qualifications," he pointed out that despite her lack of experience, she had testified in court 35 times on the subject of hair follicles. Further, Shapiro got her to say that on the subject of the preservation of blood samples for analysis, the last time she testified in court was "in either 1986 or 1988." Before that, Kestler said she testified more than 50 times in court. On the subject of DNA, Shapiro slit her throat. Kestler told the court that she had only taken an eight-hour course in DNA analysis, "but I get constant updates," she added. Updates aside, Kestler didn't know who discovered DNA nor had she read any of the discoverer's books. In fact, Kestler admitted, she hadn't been in a classroom of any kind since 1970.

Dr. Irwin Golden was a big farce for the prosecution. It was he who performed the autopsies on Nicole and Ron Goldman. He was uncooperative and he admitted under cross-examination that he had made several mistakes. Later on Chicago's WVON radio talk show, *World Objectives*, I joked with the audience that Dr. Golden was a graduate of the University of Illinois Medical School. "We are wondering here in Los Angeles," I quipped, "How in the hell did Golden get into the U of I medical school and, most importantly, how in the hell did he get out?"

Moving right along to one of the biggest hoaxes of the trial, the testimony of Allen Wattenberg and Jose Camacho, the co-owner, with his brother, and an employee of Ross Cutlery, respectively. Wattenberg testified that on May 3, 1994, he and Camacho were working in the store located at Third and Broadway. A film crew was working outside of the store that day. Simpson was on the set. The actor came into the store at least twice, Wattenberg testified. "We just let him browse around. I didn't bother him."

On his second visit, Simpson began looking at several items, Wattenberg remembered, and he sent Camacho over to assist him. Then Simpson came over to Wattenberg. "He had an interest in some knives." One in particular, a 15-inch (when opened) German stiletto with a stag antler handle and a shiny steel blade. Price: $74.98. Simpson went back out to get the money and when he returned, Wattenberg said that Camacho brought the knife back saying that Simpson "wished to have it sharpened."

Camacho, who actually made the sale and had spent the most time with Simpson, testified that he was about to get screwed. After detectives came to the store on June 14, 1994, word leaked to the news media that he had sold Simpson a knife. Then his boss, Wattenberg, signed an agreement with the *National Enquirer* for the rights to the story. In the end, Camacho, who rightfully should have gotten all the money, split the $12,500 three ways with the Wattenberg brothers.

Poor guy. Camacho said that after he initially testified before the grand jury, he was deluged with calls and visits from reporters. "They came to the store," Camacho remembers. "Channel 5, Channel 4, *Hard Copy*, so many. And they're very tricky people, those reporters. They force you to talk." Talk he did. When they signed the deal with the *Enquirer*, his bosses gangstered him out of two-thirds of the money. Further, the prosecution got pissed off because he talked to the media in the first place. Needless to say, the knife that Simpson purchased from Ross Cutlery was not the knife used in the double murder.

But Camacho said that "somebody named Patti" in the DA's office told him he could talk to the press if he wanted to. The "Patti" he was referring to was the victim's advocate Patti Jo Fairbanks, cruelly known as "Fatty Jo." She had also told Jill Shively the same thing, according to Shively's attorney, Eric Davis. Shively testified before the grand jury that she was nearly run off the road by Simpson on the night of the murders. But the prosecution opted not to call her to the stand because she, too, had sold her story to a tabloid TV show.

On Tuesday, July 5, Allan Park, the limousine driver, came to the stand. He had an order to pick up Simpson at 10:45 p.m. on Sunday, June 12. Park said he arrived early about 10:25 p.m. and parked at the corner of Rockingham and Ashford, across from Simpson's estate. He said he never saw or "noticed" if there was a white Ford Bronco at the side of the house.

After smoking a cigarette, Park said he pulled up to the gate at 10:40 p.m. and began ringing the intercom. The time is important here because all-news radio station KFWB had been broadcasting all day that Park began ringing the intercom at 10:25 p.m. That was simply not true. "I rang the intercom," Park told the court. "And there was no answer." He said he noticed that one light was on upstairs. None on downstairs. He called his boss at 10:50 p.m. "Mr. Simpson is always running late," Park says his boss told him, "Just wait until 11:15 p.m."

Park then says he saw a white male (Kato Kaelin) come out from behind the Ashford side of the house. "Almost simultaneously, when I saw him, I saw someone black cross the driveway and go into the house." The person was over six feet tall and weighed over 200 pounds, Park said. "I couldn't tell who it was, whether it was a male or a female."

Park rang the buzzer again, and this time "I got an answer from a person who I believed was Mr. Simpson. He told me that he had overslept and that he just got out of the shower and he'd be down in a few minutes." Kato let Park in the gate and after he parked the limo, Kato asked the driver whether he had felt an earthquake. Park said he hadn't. The driver then began petting Simpson's dog until O.J. came out with his bags.

Park said that when he was told about the three bumps on the back of Kaelin's bungalow, there was some discussion among the three men about checking it out. Then O.J. said, "We gotta go."

"Did he look nervous?" Park was asked about O.J. "I've never met him before so he seemed O.K. to me." Park also said he hadn't noticed any scars on Simpson's hands nor whether his hair was wet.

Park said they arrived at the airport at 11:35 p.m. He popped the trunk open, retrieved Simpson's bags and that was the end of that.

Kaelin was an interesting witness. No one could really pin him down. He said he first met Nicole Simpson in Aspen, Colorado in 1992. He saw her again at a party at her former house in Brentwood. While at the party, Kato noticed the vacant guest house behind Nicole's Gretna Green house and asked if he could move in if he cleaned it up. "The rent was $500," Kato said. "But she would deduct stuff, for instance, if I took care of the kids."

When Nicole moved to Bundy, Kato said that O.J. offered to let him move into one of his vacant bungalows—rent-free. "He said it would be better if I moved there with him because it wouldn't look right to have me moving inside Nicole's condo." Kato also mentioned that Simpson told him "in a passing conversation" that the relationship between Nicole and him was over.

On the day of the murders, Kato said he saw Simpson for the first time at about 2:30 p.m. O.J. had told him that he had a good golf game and that he had also played cards. Simpson also told him he was to attend a recital for daughter Sydney at 5:30 p.m. That night, O.J. came to Kato to get some smaller bills so he could tip the skycap at the airport. All he had was $100 dollar bills. O.J. also told him that he was going to McDonald's. Kato asked if he could go along. They took the Rolls Royce. At McDonald's, they ordered through the drive-thru window and took the food home. During this exchange, Marcia Clark kept asking Kato whether or not he saw any bruises on O.J.'s hand. He hadn't.

When they returned from McDonald's, Kato said he went to his room to eat and to telephone friends including one Rachel Ferraro. That's when he heard the loud thumping on his wall—at around 10:40 p.m. Kato said to Rachel, "I think we just had an earthquake. Did we have an earthquake?" Rachel said, "No!" Kato said he picked up a flashlight to go check behind the bungalow, "but the dog wouldn't go with me," he said. The courtroom chuckled. That's when he saw Park and then Simpson.

Another significant witness was LAPD Detective Mark Fuhrman, who testified that he received a call at his home at approximately 1:05 a.m. on June 13 to go to 875 North Bundy. He and another detective arrived at 2:10 a.m. He said he walked through the house and saw no disturbance. While on the balcony, however, Fuhrman said he saw a knit cap, a leather glove and footprints going westward in blood puddles. He also saw coins lying on the ground.

Later, he, Vannatter and Detectives Lange and Phillips went to the Rockingham house. When he checked the Ford Bronco parked outside the gate, Fuhrman said he noticed a small red stain near the door handle. At that point, after no one answered the intercom, Fuhrman was instructed by Vannatter to scale the wall. Once inside, he knocked on Kato's door, "engaged him in conversation" and checked both the immediate premises and Kato's clothes lying on the floor. Fuhrman said that Kato told him about the thumps. When the detective went behind the bungalow, he testified that he found "a glove that was similar to the one I observed at Bundy." He described it as sticky and two of the glove's fingers were stuck together "with some form of liquid."

At approximately 8 a.m., well over two hours after the detectives had rummaged through Simpson's house, the house was sealed and Vannatter called in for a search warrant. By then, cops had already eaten up Simpson's food, played his football tapes on the VCR and God knows what else. All this before they obtained a search warrant. When asked why he gave the order to scale Simpson's wall without a search warrant, Vannatter testified that he felt that someone might have been in the house bleeding or being held hostage. "Did you enter with guns drawn?" he was asked. "No, we didn't," was his reply. Vannatter also danced around the question: Did it take four detectives to inform Mr. Simpson that his ex-wife was murdered and that his children were being cared for at the West Los Angeles station? He hemmed and hawed on that one.

Uelmen, the lead attorney on these exchanges, moved to strike most of the evidence found at Simpson's estate due to a violation of the Constitutional right guarding against unlawful search and seizure. Judge Kennedy-Powell denied that motion. Tom Elias, my colleague, says that the prosecution's insistence on admitting the illegal search and seizure was a "tactical error." Had the judge thrown out the evidence seized at Simpson's place, that would have eliminated Fuhrman as a witness. I reminded him, of course, that it was Fuhrman who spotted the blood on the Bronco door handle. That happened outside of the estate. But Elias countered that they could have "lied" and said that any one of them had found the blood spot. You mean the police might have lied about the evidence they found? But, of course, the police would never do a thing like that. Or would they?

CHAPTER 4
THE JURY

TOM ELIAS

An Omen That Didn't Lie Meets a Jury That Did

Pulling the first numbered slip of paper at random from a large bowl as he began jury selection on Sept. 26, 1994, Judge Lance Ito did a double-take. He had chosen number 32—the same number O.J. Simpson wore as an All-American running back at the University of Southern California and as an all-star professional with the Buffalo Bills.

"I don't know if this is an omen," Ito observed wryly to the roomful of prospective jurors. As the judge spoke, Simpson smiled and slowly nodded his head. Sotto voce, the defendant began singing, "It's a New Day Coming."

Both Ito's joke and Simpson's song would eventually evolve into truth. If he'd had a panel full of jurors wearing number 32 jerseys, Simpson couldn't have found a jury more malleable to the persuasions of his large corps of attorneys. This was no accident. Rather, it developed from a combination of shrewd defense planning and the fateful decision by Los Angeles County District Attorney Gil Garcetti to move Simpson's trial downtown.

The jury that eventually acquitted Simpson never came near to reflecting the ethnic mix in Los Angeles County, where Simpson lived and where his ex-wife Nicole and her friend Ronald Goldman were murdered. At the time the verdicts came down, the demographic makeup of America's most populous county was 41 percent Caucasian, 37 percent Latino, 14 percent black and 6 percent Asian, with just 2 percent from other ethnic groups. But the final jury was composed of nine African Americans, two Caucasians and one Latino.

This came about via a four-step process starting with Garcetti's first major decision in the case—to gun for a grand jury indictment, thus avoiding a preliminary hearing on the evidence.

Once the D.A. involved the grand jury, a downtown location was assured for the trial—even though the grand jury was quickly tossed off the case. When jury selection began, blacks made up just over 21 percent of the population pool from which jurors could be chosen in downtown Los Angeles. This was a substantially higher percentage than is normal when jurors are summoned in Santa Monica, where cases from the Brentwood district are normally heard. Garcetti's move all but guaranteed that Simpson's jury would feature at least a few blacks.

Step two in getting a mostly minority jury was the hardship questionnaire administered by Ito. It eliminated anyone whose employer would not continue paying wages for the unlimited time required in the Simpson case. It meant jurors would likely be government employees, postal workers or persons employed by large corporations that could afford to share the cost of civic duty. With jurors in Los Angeles County receiving just $5 per day plus carfare, workers whose employers normally refuse to continue paying full wages would have to be eliminated. And because the percentage of minority personnel employed by governments and large corporations in Los Angeles is far higher than the percentage of minorities among workers at small firms, the pool became skewed even before defense attorneys said a single word.

These realities also left room for retirees; there were to be three among the final 14 jurors and alternates. Ito's six hardship-related questions quickly eliminated 91 of the 219 persons who filled out his form on the first day of jury selection. Another 63 were immediately placed into an uncertain category and never questioned again. That left just 65 able to serve. Similar proportions held up through the other groups of candidates who were summoned. Jury prospects listed a wide variety of disqualifying hardships, from hearing difficulties and a broken tailbone to child-care and elder-care problems.

The third step toward a mostly-black jury was an intensive questioning process that began when potential jurors not eliminated by hardship filled out a 294-entry questionnaire designed by lawyers and consultants for both sides. Ito's aim was to weed out anyone with a hidden agenda in the case. He succeeded in eliminating some obvious problem jurors, like a former fireman who had been briefly accused of arson in one of the deadly brush fires that ravaged parts of Southern California in 1992.

Ito and lawyers for the two sides spent more than two months cross-examining potential jurors. The judge excused any who admitted knowing much about Simpson or his case, along with all who admitted having experience with domestic abuse and those who said they would dislike being sequestered. This meant that anyone with a high degree of literacy was bound to be bounced, because it was impossible in the months leading up to the trial to read any newspaper or magazine without learning something about the case. And the end result proved the process a failure anyway. Neither oral nor written questioning could ferret out everyone seeking to make money or prove a point by becoming a Simpson juror. In the end, the result demonstrated that Ito's carefully crafted elimination process was a dismal failure. In large part because it demanded that jurors be either ill-informed or untruthful.

The final selection step allowed peremptory challenges, when lawyers summarily and without needing to provide explanation dismissed 34 potential jurors and alternates who had survived the questioning process. Race became a major and obvious factor in the trial only during the last two steps of jury selection. Defense lawyer Robert Shapiro had promised publicly that race would not be an issue in this case, yet it was he who raised the issue after four weeks of detailed questioning of potential jurors. He claimed that prosecutors systematically asked African Americans different and more leading questions than they were feeding whites and Latinos. "It implies an insidious effort to try to get black jurors removed for cause because they are black and because they have black heroes and O.J. Simpson is one of them," Shapiro charged.

"This appears to be the latest in a series of efforts by the defense to manipulate public opinion," replied Deputy District Attorney William Hodgman, then the co-lead prosecutor on the case. "We are proceeding very, very carefully with jury selection." But prosecutors clearly were not careful enough. While defense lawyers paid close attention to the advice of jury consultant Jo-Ellan Dimitrius of the firm Forensic Technologies, prosecutors gave little heed to their consultant Donald Vinson, from a firm called DecisionQuest. Dimitrius was in court each day of jury selection, often huddling with Simpson, Shapiro and Johnnie Cochran, but Vinson was almost never visible. No juror was dismissed or accepted by the Simpson team without advice from Dimitrius, but prosecutors preferred to work essentially without Vinson's help.

They may have been lulled by the nature of the *voir dire* questioning of potential jurors, which often verged on the absurd. In one exchange, prospective juror number 1797, a 29-year-old black man whose name was never made known, revealed under defense questioning that his brother had been stabbed fatally in 1988. He also opined that murderers commonly lie about their crimes. But he was not disqualified until he told prosecutor Marcia Clark that he believed Philip Vannatter, a key detective in the case, wore a toupee. Clark said this was not so, then moved to have him dismissed, presumably because his interest in Vannatter's hair indicated that he had watched closely during television coverage of the preliminary hearing.

Juror number 32, whose designation initially intrigued Ito and amused Simpson, didn't wait to be dismissed. She asked to be excused, but not before her *voir dire* had revealed how far afield the process could go. A 31-year-old divorced white woman with a college degree in industrial engineering, she said the person she admired most in all the world was Elizabeth Dole, the onetime Bush administration Secretary of Transportation. Why? "She's focused, committed and she puts up with Bob," the woman responded. She also opined that the 911 tapes of Nicole Simpson's desperate calls to police "were adapted for media propaganda."

Potential juror number 98—who became Juror number 9 and eventually voted to acquit Simpson in both ballots taken by the jury—expressed the opinion that "racial prejudice sometimes can enter a jury." The 52-year-old black woman, a postal clerk, said she thought athletes in contact sports are more aggressive than most other people. "If you do something every day, it becomes part of you," she said. She said she also believed that domestic violence "should be handled privately." Like most of the rest of the potential panelists, she denied either having seen much of the

June 17 chase that preceded Simpson's arrest or watching more than a few minutes of the preliminary hearing. This constant refrain of unlikely answers eventually made both sides skeptical of their entire jury pool.

Shapiro was the first lawyer to express those misgivings openly, questioning the veracity of jury prospects during a closed hearing on Oct. 19, 1994. "We have 300 people begging to be on the case of the century who will give you any answer you want, unfortunately," he observed. Moments later, Clark agreed. "Those 300 jurors that sit there and say they can be fair...they all want to sit on the case of the century," she said. "Many if not most are lying to the detriment of the people because they are sitting there as fans of this defendant saying, 'We want to get on this jury because we want to turn a blind eye to your evidence and a deaf ear to the testimony so we can acquit this man, no matter what.'" My colleague Dennis Schatzman suggests most whites were eliminated from the jury because they were "stupid" and gave honest answers. Maybe most of the whites—like the majority of blacks who were also eliminated—were up against a selection system that penalized them for being honest.

Later events were to prove both Clark and Shapiro correct in their assessment that many of the potential jurors did not tell the whole truth. There was Jeanette Harris, who sat in seat 10 in the jury box for almost four months before her dismissal in early April 1995. On the questionnaire she filled out when she began her jury service, Harris didn't respond to the query asking whether she had ever been involved in domestic violence. Months later, Ito would learn that in 1988 she filed a complaint against her husband, accusing him of pushing her, threatening her and forcing her to have sex with him. After Ito tossed her off the jury, she told reporters she didn't consider such conduct true domestic violence. But in her 1988 complaint, she wrote on an application for a restraining order, "I'm afraid the pushing will stop any day now and he'll begin to beat me." Explained Harris after leaving the jury, "Anybody has a relationship with anybody, there are times when things get difficult..."

Then there was Tracy Kennedy, the white-haired half-Caucasian, half-Native American suburbanite who sat for almost three months in seat number 3. He was dismissed after bailiffs found the journal he had denied keeping. And there was Francine Florio-Buntin, the 39-year-old white woman dismissed after spending almost six months on the jury. She, too, kept a diary, but was dismissed because Ito, in response to his constant efforts to root out jury misconduct, felt she was not truthful about whether she and fellow juror Farron Chavarria, a 28-year-old Latina, had passed notes back and forth. Chavarria would also be dismissed days later. And those were merely the ones Ito caught.

If jurors prevaricated while serving on the jury, why believe they and their colleagues were telling the truth when they gave preposterous answers to *voir dire* questions about how much they knew and whether they had discussed the case? Knowing they would say anything to get on the jury, why should anyone believe what they said after delivering their verdicts in near-record time?

While prosecutors never admitted asking different questions of black prospects, their actions in the final phase of jury selection made it plain that they distrusted black jurors more than whites. This was true despite Garcetti's constant assertion that "black jurors convict plenty of black defendants. I have as much faith in them as I do in white jurors." Conversely, defense attorneys plainly had it in for anyone who wasn't black.

Once peremptory challenges began, neither side could disguise its racial preferences any longer, regardless of their rhetoric. Both camps were obvious in their efforts to get the sort of racial mix that would favor them. The first round of peremptories saw all pretense disappear as defense lawyers and prosecutors played a game of ethnic chess. The defense excused five whites, two Native Americans, one Hispanic, one person of mixed race and just one African American. Prosecutors dismissed eight blacks and just two whites. Before settling on the original 12 alternates, prosecutors eliminated six African Americans and just one white. Defense lawyers, meanwhile, blackballed two whites, three Latinos, one Asian-American and just one black.

Among those sworn in after both sides agreed on the original panel was a 48-year-old black man who had worked 25 years in quality control for the Hertz Corporation, but denied ever meeting company pitchman O.J. Simpson during that time. He was eventually dismissed when his denial turned out to be false. The fate of the lone Asian American best revealed the defense aims in jury selection. The prospective alternate, a 28-year-old Japanese American, identified himself as a graduate student in biochemistry at UCLA, specializing in DNA analysis. When his number came up, amused and cynical reporters listening to the process via closed circuit in a small room three floors up immediately began making informal book on how long he would last. I guessed the defense would ding him within twelve seconds. That was wrong. He was gone after just seven. With him went the last hope for a jury that would include even one person with a rudimentary understanding of DNA, which plainly was to be a major part of the prosecution case. In fact several jurors and alternates who survived the selection process voiced open skepticism or disdain for scientific laboratories and the results they obtain.

Schatzman says the entire process targeted blacks for exclusion. That's ridiculous. The final jury was dominated by African Americans. The pool of 42 potential jurors available before peremptory challenges began included 26 blacks. The 44 possible alternates still eligible before those peremptories included 25 blacks. There's no way this could have happened *twice* if Ito or his process had aimed at eliminating African Americans.

But it did eliminate anyone with significant respect for science or scientific evidence. This was clearly reflected in the jurors' behavior once the trial began. Day after day, several appeared to have difficulty staying awake, especially during the prosecution's almost two-month-long presentation of DNA blood evidence. Others seemed almost never to pay attention to any of the voluminous scientific evidence presented by prosecutors. And the feelings of most panelists toward some of the lawyers who went before them daily soon became transparent. Their facial expressions made it clear that several disliked Clark from the first moment they saw her. And virtually all the jurors seemed to dread the days when prosecutor Brian Kelberg appeared. His lengthy presentations drew eye-rollings and silently-mouthed groans, even when he was dramatically re-enacting the murders with Coroner Lakshemanan Sathyavagiswaran holding a ruler to his throat.

A typical day was February 28, 1995, when detective Tom Lange testified at length about finding small drops of Simpson's blood beside the red footprints leading away from the murder scene. As Lange answered questions, Tracy S. Hampton, the 26-year-old flight attendant who would be dismissed at her own request five weeks later—only to turn up as a *Playboy* model—stared at her shoes. No matter what Lange or anyone else said, no matter which grisly pictures were placed on the huge curved screen above the witness stand, Hampton seemed to rarely look up. "She's exactly the kind of juror I love," longtime criminal defense lawyer Frank King told me a few days later. "When it comes time for final arguments, I can tell her almost anything, and she has to believe it because she hasn't paid much attention."

But Hampton wasn't alone in her seeming inattention. The juror in seat number 9, the 52-year-old postal clerk, was occupied much of the day with removing snags from her long, beaded necklace. When she wasn't untying knots, she leaned her chin on an open hand, eyes closed, giving no indication that she had any idea what was transpiring around her. Juror number 6, on the other hand—marketing representative Lionel Cryer, a 43-year-old black man—was much more attentive. His eyes darted back and forth from witness to lawyers while he made no notes for 30 minutes or more, then wrote furiously for three or four minutes.

Behind him, juror number 12, the 54-year-old Willie Cravin, a postal operations manager who would cry racism when he was dismissed months later for supposedly intimidating other jurors, fixed every lawyer and witness with a laser-like glare. Each of these behavior traits meant something, jury consultants assured me. But no two experts agreed on what the meaning was. Of Cravin, the San Francisco-based consultant Ronald Beaton said, "He's either paying close attention or he's trying like mad to stay awake."

But the jury's most significant behavior was the obvious lying engaged in by some who wound up on the final panel and by many who were eliminated earlier. Their hidden agendas, which for some included making a quick killing on book or magazine contracts at trial's end and for others may have included a desire to turn the trial into a racial statement, ensured they would be amenable when Cochran suggested in his closing argument that they ignore some or all of the evidence before them during deliberations.

Eight months-plus of sequestration also contributed to their malleability. Kept away from their families except for brief visits three times a week, given only censored newspapers and magazines to read, and denied even the right to make unmonitored telephone calls some jurors by the end were clearly ready to accede to almost anything so long as they got away quickly.

William Zamora knew the feeling well. He was sequestered for more than seven months as a juror in the 1971 trial of mass murderer Charles Manson. Like the Simpson jurors, the Manson panel was closeted in a hotel in downtown Los Angeles, subjected to much the same rules and enjoyed similar entertainment and group outings. "I really regretted being sequestered," Zamora told me. "But I was an ideal juror because I had been out of the country when Manson was arrested. It really got to me. I even tried to escape once, but the deputies caught me. I would have done almost anything to end it."

When the Simpson jury finally began deliberating, its first vote was 10-2 in favor of acquittal. Anise Aschenbach, a 60-year-old divorcee and retired gas company employee, was one of the two who initially wanted to convict. On her questionnaire, she said that while serving on an earlier jury, she had been the only one wishing to convict on the first vote. But she held out and by the time a verdict was rendered, she recalled, she had turned all her colleagues around.

Aschenbach made no such heroic effort this time. After many months of sequestration, she was apparently too tired, or too despairing, to convince anyone of her point of view. And she didn't want to be part of a hung jury. "I thought of all the months, all the money, this case not being resolved..." she mused later. She also said, "I think he probably did it and that's the pits...Chances are good he did it, and that's a shame." But she switched her vote and Simpson walked away a free man. "It doesn't make me feel very good," she said later. "But on the other hand, (Simpson is) not a serial killer." There's a rationalization sure to promote respect for the jury system!

None of the nine African Americans on the jury felt at all similarly at the time, but at least two expressed misgivings after hearing some of the information that was withheld from them while they were serving. Their performance, in particular the speed with which they returned their verdicts, made me think of what the distinguished Wyoming defense lawyer Gerry Spence told me early in the trial: "You always have to remember that these jurors will have to go back and live in the (black) community after this is over. If they convict O.J., everyone around them will know they did it."

The instant verdict demonstrated that there wasn't much consideration of the trial's voluminous evidence during whatever deliberations went on. "Really and truly, I believe Nicole and Ron were killed by someone connected to drugs," former juror number 12, 72-year-old Beatrice Wilson, said afterward to a reporter. "I heard Ron knew martial arts," she added. "So he should have been able to fight off O.J. Ron was a young man."

Cochran and Shapiro first floated the drug-dealer theory during the fall of 1994—while jury candidates were under strict orders from Ito to stay away from all coverage of the Simpson case, whether in newspapers, magazines, radio, television or books. Wilson, like all the other jurors, piously assured Ito on repeated occasions that she was living by his rules. Once the trial began, Ito specifically forbade any mention of the supposed drug connection theory by defense lawyers. So, except in Cochran's rambling opening statement, the drug dealer theory was never voiced in the jury's presence.

Nor was there more than a slight hint offered in the courtroom about any Goldman interest in martial arts like judo and karate. The question is: Where did Wilson hear this information, whether it was true or not? One possibility is that it came to her during unsupervised family visits, during which any talk about the trial was supposed to be strictly forbidden. Another possibility is that other jurors, supposedly operating under the same strictures, clued her in. A third is that Wilson and the other jurors simply wanted to free Simpson and cast about for reasons only later, after they had done it.

Wilson's comments make it clear that the jurors, who early on convinced lawyers on both sides they were a pack of liars, eagerly adopted the stance Cochran pushed during his final argument: The rest of the facts didn't matter; all that counted was that detective Mark Fuhrman was a racist liar and that O.J., the veteran actor, made it seem as if he were having difficulty donning the bloody gloves from the murder scene.

Cochran's critics called his appeal an attempt at jury nullification, in which juries sometimes give some other considerations higher priority than the evidence they've seen and heard. If that's what they did, and only the jurors know for sure whether they thought about the evidence at all during their ultra-brief deliberations, they needed to hear the words of the 19th Century black abolitionist Frederick Douglass: "I know of no rights of race superior to the rights of man." If the primary right of all persons is the right to life, then these jurors had a duty at least to consider and debate all the evidence indicating that Simpson deprived two persons of that most fundamental right.

DENNIS SCHATZMAN

Was It a Question of Black and White?

"If selected as a juror in this case, the Court will instruct you as follows:
A defendant in a criminal action is presumed to be innocent until the contrary is proved, and in case of a reasonable doubt whether his guilt is satisfactorily shown, he is entitled to a verdict of not guilty. The presumption places upon the People the burden of proving him guilty beyond a reasonable doubt."

The O.J. Simpson Juror Questionnaire

I didn't get to see much of the actual jury selection process up close and personal. On August 16, 1994, I was thrown out of the courtroom by sheriff's deputies, an action later sanctioned by Superior Court Judge Lance Ito. I didn't get back into the courtroom until mid-October, about the time the Simpson juror questionnaire was released to the public.

This is what happened to me. I was sitting in Judge Ito's courtroom with 25 other reporters when the judge called a mid-morning recess. I approached the railing to call Johnnie Cochran over for a brief chat. That's when Sergeant George Smith told me to step out of the courtroom. I asked him why I had to leave when other reporters didn't have to leave.

"Because I said so!"

"Because you said so?" I asked.

"Let's go," he ordered.

Outside the courtroom, Smith pointed me out to two deputies, one male, one female, who asked me to step into one of the back hallways. I went, reluctantly.

"Gimme your credentials," the big guy demanded. I refused.

Snatch. I was down on the floor and handcuffed before I knew what hit me. Then I saw Sergeant Smith coming around the corner with the LAPD press pass that I had exchanged for my court pass.

"Is this you?" he asked.

I asked back, "Am I under arrest?"

The sarge said, "No."

"Then am I free to leave?"

"Not exactly," he said.

"Then gimme my press pass and let me get out of here," I demanded.

"No! I'm gonna turn this (my press pass) over to the LAPD."

Oh, shit, I thought to myself. Knowing that I wasn't on the LAPD's Christmas card list, I figured that if they got my press pass, I'd never get it back. So I started pitching a bitch: "Either take me to jail or give me my press pass."

Other reporters by now had gotten wind that I was in some back hallway with two sheriff's goons. Linda Johnson Phillips thought I was getting my ass kicked, so she called the *Sentinel*. Jennifer Thomas, the paper's airhead chief financial officer and the publisher's wife, sent my colleague James Bolden down to the courtroom.

While all this was going on, Sergeant Smith took me into his office and Jerrianne Hayslett, the court's public information officer, tried to calm me down. She told me that this was all a mix-up. "They didn't know that you were a reporter," she explained. "What do you mean they didn't know? I have press credentials on. What is that shit supposed to mean?" I asked. Hayslett never answered that question. Though I was expelled from the courtroom for the rest of the day, I got my press pass back.

Later, as I was watching the proceedings on a television monitor on the 11th floor, Sergeant Smith came up to me and said he wanted to speak to me. "What did I do now?" I inquired. Nothing, the sarge said. But since I was handcuffed and taken to the floor, he must take a statement from me. "That's OK, no harm, no foul," I said, trying to be a good sport. "But I must insist," Smith demanded mildly. This time I just went along quietly. I told Smith I didn't want to press charges. They didn't hurt me. They were just doing their jobs. I sounded like a freaking politician. And that was the end of that. For the next two months, however, Bolden handled the courtroom activities and I wrote stories on the trial from the outside.

The racial makeup of the jury had always been a concern of everyone's, from the media to the prosecution to the white community and of, course, to the black community. Would the prosecution try to keep blacks off the jury; would the defense try to load down the jury with several of O.J. Simpson's "peers"?

I hadn't had much experience with juries. When I was on the magisterial bench in Pittsburgh, I was the judge *and* the jury—the Roy Bean of Pittsburgh's largest black community. So I looked to the *Los Angeles Daily Journal*'s Mike Harris for advice.

I had always had a good relationship with reporters on the *Daily Journal*, the city's legal publication. Scribes like Jean Guccione and Martin Berg had always helped me out with photos of judges and bios, things like that. I, in turn, would share information with them. It was the best relationship I had with reporters from another publication.

Harris, a fellow Pennsylvanian who covered the criminal courts for the *Journal*, turned out to be no different from his colleagues. He turned me on to a story he wrote on June 30,1994, in which he queried various jury consultants on the importance of the jury questionnaire. And for good measure, Harris threw in an advance copy of the juror questionnaire. What a guy!

The jury pool initially started off with about 1,000 prospective jurors. It was pared down to 304 ethnically diverse men and women. This is when the questionnaire became relevant, according to Harris' experts. "The questionnaire is important for a couple of reasons," noted Terry Walker, a jury consultant from Oakland, California. "Number one," she said, "prospective jurors have been exposed to so much media information about the case. As a result, what the questionnaire will do is give the court and the lawyers some feel for the amount of information that people are bringing to the jury selection." Walker said the questionnaire was also important because it would provide insights into prospective jurors' attitudes toward such sensitive related issues as domestic violence and race.

Many prospective jurors, mostly whites, didn't need their answers on the questionnaire to get them thrown out of the jury pool. One of Judge Ito's charges to the pool was that they abstain from watching television or reading newspapers. Apparently, the white folks weren't paying too much attention to that order. Whites were getting thrown off in droves. One parent was kicked off for watching Mickey Mouse on TV with his kids. Others were relieved from jury service for watching the news. I found that real funny, since this happened about the same time that Charles Murray's book *The Bell Curve* was getting big media play. Murray's best-seller argued that the African American was intellectually inferior to the white man. Apparently, Murray hadn't interviewed these stupid white jurors.

My concern right from the very beginning was how they were able to segregate blacks from the rest of the potential jury pool. My analysis of the 294-question document showed that the authors of the questionnaire—Jo-Ellan Dimitrius for the defense and Donald Vinson for the prosecution—were not only brazen in their attempt to weed out potential black jurors, they were using the *Los Angeles Sentinel*, the area's leading black-owned "specialized medium," to do it.

For example, in question number 247, jurors were asked: "What magazines and newspapers, if any, do you subscribe to?" Ten publications were listed: *Time, U.S. News and World Report, Newsweek, People, New Yorker, Los Angeles, The Daily News, The Los Angeles Times, USA Today* and the *Sentinel*. Of that group, only the *Sentinel* is targeted toward a specialized audience—African Americans. Specialized media like the *Sentinel, Korea Times, Rafu Shimpu* (Japanese), *La Opinion* (Spanish language), the *Jewish Journal* and a few others are geared toward certain ethnic and/or religious groups. Although each of the above-mentioned specialized media, other than the *Sentinel* and the *Jewish Journal*, are daily publications, only the *Sentinel* was listed in the questionnaire.

It was of particular interest to me that question 247 specifically asked prospective jurors about publications to which they "subscribe." Although the *Sentinel* is read by a respectable number of non-African Americans, outside of some non-black controlled institutions and businesses with a particular interest in the black community, it is usually blacks who plunk down the $25 *per annum* subscription fee. All others purchase the publication over store counters or at newsstands.

Answers to question 247 were set up by question 245: "Do you read a newspaper on a regular basis?" Again, the *Sentinel*, a weekly publication, stands apart from the three daily publications listed: the *Los Angeles Times*, the *Daily News* and *USA Today*. Once again, no mention of the *Korea Times*, *La Opinion* (which would eventually get a permanent seat in the courtroom) or *Rafu Shimpu*. "That's because the court, the attorneys and the high-priced jury consultants are not expressly interested in the views and habits of Latinos, Koreans, Japanese or any other racial group," Celes King, III, owner of the state's largest bail bond agency and state chairman of the Congress of Racial Equality, told me at the time. "They're only interested in the views and opinions of blacks."

On the subject of DNA blood testing, prospective jurors were asked, in question 197, where they received their news and information. Again, the *Sentinel* was the only specialized medium listed among the 20 publications, television and radio stations from which potential panelists could choose.

The process of targeting the reading and viewing habits of prospective black jurors began with question 80: "If you have learned about this case from television, radio, newspapers or magazines, please check all areas listed below which describe your exposure to each." The answers to this question can tell you a lot about a person. Let's say a person checks the *Sentinel*, KCRW-FM (public radio), the *Los Angeles Times* and the *New Yorker*. That person is probably black, and a professional. Whereas if the person selected only the *Sentinel* and KTLA-TV, that person might be a member of the working poor or unemployed. And he or she probably picked up the *Sentinel* at their parents' house.

There were other questions aimed at getting some back door answers that gave hints to one's ethnicity and economic status. Question 10 asked in what part of Los Angeles County one resides and "what is your zip code?" Question 16: "Is English your first language?" Question 22: "Do you have the authority to hire and fire employees?" If the answer is "yes," you are more than likely looking at a white person. Question 23 asks: "If not currently employed outside the home, please check the category that applies to your employment status." If the person checks "Unemployed, not looking for work," that person might very well have a criminal record.

In California, all a person has to do to obtain a police record is to be arrested. Not convicted of a crime, mind you. Just *arrested*. In the black community, young black males in particular are often hassled and arrested by police if they see them standing on the corner in the summertime. Many stand on the corners because it's too hot inside their houses. Most blacks and browns living in South Central Los Angeles, for example, don't have air conditioning. They often get picked up, taken to the station and released later. When they begin looking for jobs, they're asked if they've ever been arrested. If they answer truthfully, they are eliminated right off the bat. If they lie, and it's found out later, then the person is fired for lying on his job application. That's the way it is in Southern California.

Here's an interesting question. Number 32 asks: "If you attended one or more high schools for any length of time, please give the name of each high school and the city in which each is located." If a person lists Locke, Fremont and Jordan High Schools, that person is probably black or Latino and was probably kicked out of at least two of the schools. Or their parents moved around a lot. Which means they couldn't pay the rent and had to break camp quick, fast and in a hurry.

So now that we've gotten the picture about how blacks were "targeted," let's move on briefly to the actual jury. In the beginning, there were 24 men and women selected. Twelve jurors and 12 alternates. Eventually, this group would be cut down to 12 jurors and two alternates. Among the first group to go were a couple of white jurors who had been accused of planning to write books about their jury experiences.

One black woman, Jeanette Harris, was thrown off because she lied on her questionnaire about domestic violence. She said her husband never touched her. But Cheryl Tillman, a former co-worker of mine at the *Sentinel*, told me that was pure horsepucky. Tillman lived next door to that juror and used to lie awake at night listening to her husband throw her against the wall. Tillman told me that she once confronted the husband about it out by the garbage cans, "and he told me to mind my own business."

Another black juror, Willie "Bobo" Cravin, a postal supervisor, was kicked off the jury because one of the white women claimed that he intimidated her. Getting rid of him was apparently a big coup. Just before his dismissal was announced in open court, Marcia Clark emerged from Judge Ito's chambers grinning and giving the thumbs up sign. Michael Knox, another black juror—the one we called "Country GQ"—was kicked off because he dared to wear a San Francisco Forty-Niners cap to Simpson's estate during their jury visit. And he stared too long at the photos on Simpson's wall. We called him "Country GQ" because he dressed like a country bumpkin. Red suit, red socks, red shoes, shit like that. Then another black juror, a black female, wanted to get off and she got her wish. Later she spent some time in the hospital for stress, but apparently recovered enough to ink a deal to pose *au natural* for *Playboy* magazine.

These panelists, once seated, were not the kind of people you would want to play poker with. They gave very little indication as to what they were thinking at any time. There were times, however, when they unified to make a statement. Once, when there were concerns about how the sheriff's deputies were treating them, three of the officers were taken off jury protection duty. Several of the jurors, however, objected to the dismissals and staged a protest that consisted of them all wearing black. Nonetheless, all the way to the end, the jurors rarely revealed their hands. That's probably the best jury one could ever get.

Following their verdict, white legal pundits, like former L.A. County District Attorney Robert Philibosian, ganged up on them. Philibosian accused the jury of being mesmerized by Simpson's "celebrity," and not the "mountain of evidence" that was presented in the case. On a pilot news program hosted by Leslie Abramson, I chumped Philibosian off. When he made that statement on camera, I shook my head in disgust. Abramson saw it right away and asked, "Mr. Schatzman, do you have a comment?"

"Let us assume," I started off innocently enough, "for the sake of argument, that Mr. Philibosian graduated from an *accredited* law school where they teach the rules of evidence. And had he been paying attention in class, he would know that there is a big difference between best evidence and circumstantial evidence." Out of the corner of my eye, I could see Bob turning several different shades of red. Johnnie Cochran just sat there laughing his ass off.

In the end, the jury seemed to understand that distinction better than all the pundits: Obeying the judge's instructions about reasonable doubt, they unanimously found O.J. Simpson "not guilty."

The rub against all of Africa America has been particularly insulting, especially since it comes from learned lawyers and law professors nationwide—all of them white, mind you! The fact that they are white presumably gives them license to insult a whole race of people on national television without penalty. This is galling because blacks like we are are generally powerless to defend ourselves against these sick accusations because we rarely get invited onto talk shows where we could set the record straight.

CHAPTER 5
DOMESTIC VIOLENCE

TOM ELIAS

No Big Deal
(But It Should Have Been)

N icole Brown Simpson's voice rang loudly from beyond the
grave for all in the courtroom to hear on the last day of
O.J. Simpson's trial for her murder. "He's going to beat
the shit out of me!" were her panic-stricken words, recorded on
an October night in 1993 as she watched her ex-husband beating
down her back door.

Her words were even stronger in the early morning hours of
New Year's Day, 1989, when Detective John Edwards, then a
patrol training officer, answered a 911 emergency call placed from
the Simpsons' ivy-covered mansion on North Rockingham
Avenue. "He's gonna kill me! He's gonna kill me," Nicole
screamed, then whimpered to the policeman and his trainee
Patricia Milwiski that night. When Edwards arrived at the estate's
gate on Ashford Street, he told the jury that he saw Nicole running toward him across the lawn, alternately yelling and sobbing
about Simpson's malevolent intentions. She wore only a bra and
muddy sweat pants in the chill mid-winter night's misty air, as she
quickly pushed a button to open the gate, then clung to the
policeman. Her fresh bruises were readily visible under Edwards'
flashlight and later to the Polaroid camera in the West Los
Angeles Division station house. So was the large hand-imprint
squeezed into the left side of her neck.

The soft-spoken Edwards described her graphically. "She collapsed onto me. She was wet, she was shivering, she was cold. I
could feel her bones. And she was beat up." Edwards wrapped
Nicole in a police jacket and sat her in the rear of his patrol car as
his trainee tried to calm her. Then Simpson appeared, wearing
briefs and an open bathrobe, veins angrily popping out on his
forehead. He asked Edwards why they were "making a big deal

out of this" when other officers had been out on similar calls and done nothing. As Nicole sat in the back of Edwards' black-and-white squad car, Simpson pointed directly at her and declared, "I don't want that woman in my bed anymore. I got two other women."

Acting charitably toward a well-known celebrity, Edwards didn't arrest and handcuff Simpson on the spot, even though Nicole said he had slammed her with his fist, slapped her, kicked her and pulled her around the house by the hair. Instead, the cop told the former football star to go back inside his house and get dressed. Then, he told Simpson, he would have to make an arrest because Nicole had "obvious injuries."

Simpson, however, did not comply. About 90 seconds after being told he was going to be arrested and booked, he had dressed and Edwards watched helplessly as he left the grounds and sped south on Rockingham in his Bentley Turbo-Rocket. That was when Nicole told Edwards, "You guys never do anything about him. You've been out here eight other times." Five prowl cars soon scoured the neighborhood, but police didn't catch Simpson that night and he was never penalized for running away. He attended the Rose Bowl football game the next day, then turned himself in, but was never physically booked or fingerprinted. Instead, he was to plead no contest to spousal abuse charges several weeks later. His penalty, imposed by Judge Ronald Schoenberg: a few telephone therapy sessions and some hours of community service.

One meaning Simpson could draw from this treatment was that society agreed with his assessment that the battering he administered to Nicole was "No big deal." Another was that his celebrity status counted for far more than his race, so he would never be subjected to the kind of beatings Los Angeles police were sometimes known to inflict on black crime suspects. But Nicole clearly thought the incident was a big deal. In a list of her husband's abusive acts prepared for her divorce lawyer, she described Simpson "chasing me through (the) house into (the) office, into (the) backyard, into (the) housekeeper's room. (He) beat me on the bed. (He) kept beating me until police came."

Later, she would say in a letter written but never delivered to Simpson that "I called the cops (that night) to save my life...I've never loved you since or been the same. It made me take a look at my life with you—my wonderful life with the Superstar, that wonderful man O.J. Simpson, the father of my kids—that husband of that terribly insecure girl—the girl with no self-esteem or self-worth—and certainly no one would be envious of that life."

This incident, and more, was fresh in the minds of the jury when Simpson was acquitted. Yet it seemed not to make a dent in the panel's consciousness. "This was not a domestic abuse trial," insisted former juror Brenda Moran the morning after she helped free O.J. Simpson. "If you wanted a domestic abuse trial, go in another courtroom." There was only one reason Moran could have made that statement, when she and the rest of the jury knew Simpson often beat and humiliated his ex-wife over their seventeen years together: The Simpson prosecutors didn't effectively use his history of wife-beating and other forms of abuse. They failed in this key task partly because of a series of rulings by Judge Lance Ito. He refused to allow murder victim Nicole's diary into evidence. He only allowed the jury to hear about relatively few wife-battering episodes. That made it easy for jurors like Moran to shrug their shoulders and say domestic violence wasn't a factor in Nicole's murder.

But Simpson's prosecutors made it plain they believed it was a factor, just as Nicole predicted it would be. Her cries to police showed that, at least in times of domestic crisis, she was convinced Simpson would eventually murder her. The only question was when. Nicole knew that Simpson's abusive behavior didn't begin with the New Year's episode or end with her 1993 call to 911 from the home she rented on Gretna Green Way after she left him. She knew his battering began almost with the beginning of their relationship, as far back as 1978, when she was just eighteen and he was still a professional football player. That was the year he berated her loudly on a New York street corner, then beat her while having sex later the same evening. In her log of such episodes, Nicole wrote, "1st time, after Louis & Nunie Marx anniversary party. Street corner of N.Y. 5th Ave. Called (my) mother (a) whore. Hit me while fucking me. Continued to beat me for hours as I kept crawling for the door."

The beatings may actually have started even before that. In her divorce memo, Nicole reported that in late 1977, during her first months as Simpson's girlfriend, she found an earring in the bed in the apartment they shared and "accused O.J. of sleeping with someone (else)…He threw a fit, chased me, grabbed me, threw me into walls. Threw all my clothes out the window… Bruised me." That episode was overheard by neighbors Connie and Steven Goode, who said they heard Simpson throw Nicole against a bedroom wall adjoining their apartment while screaming ugly names at her. Mrs. Goode later saw Nicole sporting two black eyes in the building's elevator.

The jury never heard about those two incidents. Too far in the remote past, Simpson's lawyers argued. Ito agreed, partly in the interests of cutting the trial's length. Jurors never saw Nicole's divorce memo or her diary. Ito ruled they were strictly hearsay because defense attorneys couldn't cross-examine the deceased Mrs. Simpson. The judge was obviously and justifiably disturbed at having to exclude the diaries from the trial. In his written ruling, he declared: "To the man or woman on the street, the relevance… of such evidence is both obvious and compelling, especially those statements made just days before the homicide. It seems only just and right that a crime victim's own words be heard, especially in the court where the facts and circumstances of her demise are to be presented."

But only a few of Nicole's words were ever presented. And the jury learned about few of the episodes in which Simpson tortured her. The combination of Ito's ruling and the prosecutors' fear of alienating the jury minimized the role of domestic violence throughout the trial. The prosecutors' original plan was to open and close their case with domestic abuse. But that strategy shifted as the proceedings dragged on through months of blood, hair and fiber evidence and the jurors became restive in their sequestration. Neither side wanted to be seen by jurors as responsible for making the trial run on and on.

"Whenever you have a long trial, one that is so blocked, almost with separate trials on separate areas, it is hard to weave things together," lamented Deputy District Attorney Scott Gordon, the prosecution specialist on domestic violence cases, after the trial. So a trial that began and ended with Deputy District Attorney Christopher Darden stressing the abusive side of Simpson's personality eventually fizzled into a welter of technical debates. Conditions in the Los Angeles police crime laboratory became more central to the outcome than Simpson's motives or his pattern of behavior.

Darden outlined those motives in his opening statement, saying Simpson's friendly and open public persona hid a controlling and domineering man who was determined that if he could not have Nicole, neither would anyone else. "She left him," Darden said. "She was no longer in his control. He could not stand to lose her. And so he killed her."

To prove that charge, prosecutors would need to catalog scores of abusive events over the seventeen years Simpson knew his ex-wife. But this they did not even attempt. There was testimony from her sister Denise about the time Simpson humiliated Nicole in the Red Onion restaurant in Malibu, grabbing her crotch and saying to a group of friends in a restaurant, "This is mine. This is where my babies come from." There was testimony from Officer Edwards and others about the 1989 New Year's incident. There was testimony from 911 operators about the 1993 door-breaking episode. But the entire catalog—even the limited list authorized by Ito—was never presented. Nor was there any effort to prove Simpson was a determined stalker of his wife. Time was the only reason for this glaring omission, which allowed some jurors to conclude that, as the former juror number 6 did, "He never hit her after the 1989 incident."

Said Gordon, "There was so much evidence, we had to make choices." So for the sake of shortening the trial, prosecutors forsook some of the most compelling details of the Simpsons' often sordid life together. To assuage the jury's understandable desire to go home, Nicole's mother never testified. Juditha Brown, the last known person with whom Nicole spoke before her murder, was billed at one point as the final prosecution witness. Her name even went up on the handwritten witness list the district attorney's publicists posted on one door of the print press room. Her task would have been to detail her final telephone conversation with Nicole, just minutes before the murders, and to repeat some of the obsessive remarks she told investigators Simpson frequently made to her.

"The only woman I want in my life—and I can't have—is your daughter," he supposedly told her in March 1994. "I can't let her go," he had told the mother two years earlier. But Juditha Brown never took the witness stand, and prosecutors never presented expert testimony about how those statements were typical declarations by abusive husbands and ex-husbands.

The jury also never heard how Simpson supposedly told fellow actor Eddie Reynosa on the set of *Naked Gun 2½* that if he saw one of Nicole's boyfriends driving the white Ferrari she got as part of their divorce settlement, he "would cut his fucking head off." Or how Simpson flung his wife's clothes down the stairs of his house in 1982, then physically threw her on top of them. Or how in 1986, Nicole was treated in St. John's Hospital in Santa Monica for injuries supposedly suffered in a bicycle accident. The physician who treated her reported the injuries, including a large head wound, were not consistent with a cycling accident. The jury never saw Nicole's handwritten note saying that the couple fabricated the cycling story.

They also didn't hear about a 1986 incident in which Simpson beat Nicole, then locked her into a wine cabinet and went off to watch a football game on television, returning several times over a two-hour period to beat her again and again. Or from two limousine drivers who were prepared to testify about seeing Simpson beat or slap Nicole in the back seats of their cars. Or from a football fan who said he saw Simpson beat a woman, presumably Nicole, on the beach near his Orange County condominium. Most telling, the jury didn't hear about Nicole's call to the Sojourn Domestic Violence Shelter in Santa Monica just five days before her death, in which she complained that Simpson was stalking her and she feared for her life.

Defense lawyers never bothered even to try denying any of these incidents, either the ones the jury heard or those it didn't. Some of them, including the call to Sojourn, were omitted because Ito ruled them hearsay and refused to allow them as evidence. The prosecutors simply skipped most others. Ito almost allowed usage of the Sojourn telephone records, which could have been among the most damaging domestic abuse evidence against Simpson. "I find them material to the issues in this case," he said on January 11, 1995. But, eventually, Ito acceded to defense demands that Sojourn's records be branded hearsay, again because Nicole couldn't be summoned back from the dead for cross-examination.

The most glaring omissions among the incidents that prosecutors could have used are the stalking episodes that led to Mrs. Simpson's sad call to Sojourn. Her onetime lover Keith Zlomsowitch, manager of the restaurant where she ate her last meal, testified about some of them in the abortive grand jury sessions that preceded the preliminary hearing. He told of dinners in swank Brentwood and Beverly Hills restaurants where Simpson would suddenly turn up and either stare at him and Nicole from a nearby table or walk up and declare, "She's still my wife." Zlomsowitch also told of a time when Simpson observed from a spot in the bushes outside the living room of Nicole's rented house on Gretna Green Way as he and Nicole engaged in a sex act on the couch. Had Juditha Brown testified, she could have detailed some of the stories her daughter told her about Simpson turning up unexpectedly as she pumped gasoline into the Ferrari or her Jeep Cherokee and about his following her as she ran errands around Santa Monica and the west side of Los Angeles.

There was no discernible reason other than time constraints for the district attorney's failure to call Mrs. Brown. Zlomsowitch, however, could have posed problems, because Simpson saw him after the peeping-tom incident and told him, "No hard feelings." Defense lawyers could have used this in trying to show Simpson was neither violent nor vindictive. Similarly, prosecutors didn't call Nicole's best friend and biographer Faye Resnick, even though Resnick wrote that Nicole told her several times she believed Simpson would kill her. Resnick's admitted history of drug use, they feared, might bolster the defense claim that the murders were drug-related, with admitted former cocaine user Resnick as the real target.

But overall, the picture of O.J. Simpson as a long-term wife batterer dwarfs what is known about any other modern athlete who has committed similar acts. When quarterback and television football analyst Warren Moon beat his wife, there was no evidence that it was more than a one-time occurrence and he quickly entered therapy. Ditto for Bobby Cox, manager of baseball's Atlanta Braves.

Yet Simpson consistently tried to downplay his violent episodes. When police talked with him during the New Year's incident, he told them a domestic quarrel had simply "gotten a little bit out of hand. I didn't hit her. I just pushed her out of the bed...This is a family matter. You've been out here eight times before and now you're going to arrest me for this?" When prosecutors first sought to introduce Simpson's history as evidence, his lawyers didn't just refuse to call it battering. They didn't even want it labeled with a generic term like violence. Their pet euphemism was "domestic discord," as if these were mere verbal arguments.

Schatzman likes to compare Simpson's long history of abusing Nicole with incidents he handled while a judge in Pittsburgh. But without exception he describes one-time episodes. He suggests Nicole "used to kick a little ass herself." But Simpson's abuse went on for almost 20 years, establishing a pattern of violence and obsession. And no one, not defense lawyers or O.J. buddies or even Schatzman, ever presented even one piece of credible evidence that Nicole ever assaulted Simpson. If Simpson was provoked to violence, we must then conclude, his motive was jealousy, possessiveness or insecurity, not retaliation.

Like Schatzman, defense attorney Gerald Uelmen, harking back to the concern for Simpson's image that governed defense strategy in the preliminary hearing, often tried to downplay Simpson's violent history. "The label prosecutors want to put on this case is that this is a domestic violence case involving murder, not a murder case involving domestic violence," he said. "They seek to transform this from an investigation of who killed Nicole Brown Simpson and Ronald Goldman and force the defendant to justify 17 entire years of his life. We are concerned about...Mr. Simpson's reputation."

But neither Uelmen nor any other defense lawyer ever

denied that any of the abusive incidents actually occurred. Instead, Uelmen said only, "We need to avoid putting (him) in the position of defending himself against uncharged offenses." Rather than denying the truth of any of the 59 episodes prosecutors listed in one document, Uelman noted that "the statute of limitations has run out" on most of them. And he in effect threatened Ito with an interminable trial if the judge allowed many incidents into evidence. "Each incident will require a mini-trial," he said.

But the defense never made good on that threat. Nor did they present promised testimony from psychologist Lenore Walker, a pioneer in research on battered women's syndrome, who had examined Simpson in jail. "I didn't see any of those mini-trials," said Gordon. "Where was Lenore Walker? We never saw the tests Cochran promised, tests that supposedly showed Simpson was not a classic batterer."

The defense didn't have to do any of that because prosecutors allowed the jury to virtually forget about the whole issue. What's more, defense lawyers could see that the jury was not receptive to domestic violence as an issue when prosecutors did bring it up. Said Gordon, "My experience is that people discount crimes against women. And people make judgments about the victims. This is true in rapes, domestic violence and other sex crimes. We always have to convince the jury that the victim is a worthy person."

The crux of the defense claim that domestic violence was irrelevant came in Uelmen's claim of a "total lack of similarity between this case and any of the earlier incidents." If he meant that the earlier incidents didn't result in murder, he was correct. But if he meant that Simpson never used an implement or tool when venting his anger on Nicole, he was dead wrong. There were at least two such incidents. One was a 1978 episode in which Nicole reported that Simpson hit her with a wine bottle. The other was the 1985 incident when Mark Fuhrman, then a patrol cop, arrived at Rockingham to find Simpson smashing the windshield of his wife's car with a baseball bat.

Amazingly, even Schatzman, who challenges virtually every part of the case against Simpson, can say nothing to deny this long history of battering. Instead, he implies that because prosecutor Christopher Darden was rumored—only rumored—to be a batterer himself, battering is not a big deal. "Exhibiting such behavior doesn't categorically mean that someone killed someone," Dennis says. But patterns of behavior do mean something. And when Simpson's long history of abuse is combined with his blood at the murder scene, the victims' blood in his car and his contradictory alibis, the reasonable conclusion is obvious. Obvious, as New York columnist Jimmy Breslin put it, to anyone who is not a cabbage.

Meanwhile, the papered-over descriptions Simpson's lawyers tried to apply to his violent outbursts conflicted sharply with the victim's versions. Said Uelmen, "Few of these instances involve blows. Where there were blows, they involve slaps." This fits only some of the descriptions given by Nicole—whose narrative wasn't intended either to convict or exonerate anyone of murder charges. And it directly conflicts with other descriptions she wrote. In both the wine cellar and wine-bottle incidents, she said Simpson used fists and a bottle against her. In the New Year's incident, she said he punched her with a clenched fist.

It was left to the pleasant, round-faced Gordon, who bears a striking resemblance to politician Newt Gingrich, to sum up the import of all this. He performed this task eloquently, but out of earshot of the jury. No other prosecutor was to attempt anything similar.

"The events that lead up to a spousal homicide are inextricably linked," Gordon told Ito, while arguing that the wife-battering evidence wasn't just relevant, but crucial. "The pattern of abuse that leads up to the death of a spouse cannot be torn away from the final act of abuse…Women that are killed are primarily killed by intimates—their boyfriends and husbands. Control is at the heart of domestic violence. The beatings have one design in mind. They are mechanisms to keep this woman within his control. Estrangement is the leading motive of spousal murder. The second-leading cause is involvement with another person… These themes are very strong in this case. Nicole Brown Simpson all through her relationship echoed her abuse and her fears and left a trail."

Gordon's eloquence helped get Ito to admit incidents that occurred as early as twelve years before Nicole's murder. But once they won the right to use that history, prosecutors didn't exercise it vigorously. They didn't call top researchers on Battered Women's Syndrome to testify about whether Simpson's behavior was typical of abusive husbands who later murder their wives, or whether Nicole's behavior was typical of abused wives who eventually become murder victims. Some authorities, like sociology professor Lynn M. Appleton of Florida Atlantic University, are convinced that both were archetypal.

Perhaps prosecutors were cowed because Simpson's money had bought the services of feminist Walker, the Denver-based psychologist who originated the concept of Battered Women's Syndrome. Perhaps they felt the jury would simply be bored with academic studies. They consistently declined to answer questions about why they used so little of the domestic violence information available to them. Instead, prosecutors focused on only a few incidents, clearly believed these had not played very well with the jury, and then all but abandoned the entire subject area until the trial's very end.

It was only then, during Darden's final summation, that they seemed to realize how crucial was their need to link Simpson's abusiveness with Nicole's murder. So Darden introduced the notion of the "long fuse" gradually burning down to June 12, 1994. Ignoring the issue for months, while jurors and others focused on myriad other types of evidence, blunted the power of Simpson's history as a batterer. If they had emphasized that background on virtually every day of the trial, as they first hinted they might, jurors like Brenda Moran and Lionel Cryer probably could not have dismissed domestic violence so blithely.

Was race a factor in any of this? Probably not. Black women are battered as often as whites. White athletes are just as likely to beat their wives as blacks are. The police decision not to arrest Simpson in any episode other than the New Year's beating indicates that he was treated more like a celebrity than a typical batterer of any race. And the decision to use only some wife-beating evidence, while discarding domestic violence as the underlying, ongoing theme of the case, also was not race-based. But it was another of the major miscalculations that disillusioned many of the millions who watched the trial and allowed O.J. Simpson to leave court a free man. It was Simpson who called his wife-beating "no big deal." And that's what it was in his trial. But it could and should have been a very big deal indeed.

DENNIS SCHATZMAN

The Domestic Violence Case That Never Was

"An additional consideration regarding the requested release of the (1989 incident) photographs is the fact that it has not yet been determined if they will become relevant in the current murder investigation. Notwithstanding the provisions of ss 6254 (f), in an abundance of caution, the release of these photographs could impact the defendant's and the People's right to a fair trial...

"With Regard to any 911 calls concerning the murder of Nicole Brown Simpson: It has been previously stated that the murder investigation of Ms. Simpson and Mr. Goldman is continuing...in consultation with those involved in the investigation and prosecution of these individuals, that premature disclosure of the information that may be contained in any 911 calls would endanger the successful completion of the murder investigation."

Deputy City Attorney Donna Weisz Jones'
"To whom it may concern"
denying requests to release
the above-referenced information
June 22, 1994

Weeks later, both the tapes and the alleged domestic violence photos of "the beautiful, blond Nicole" hit the airwaves and filled up the television screens. I asked myself what was the purpose of this "lie-then-leak" strategy? To engage in an act of preliminary embracery, I answered myself.

Preliminary embracery? Actually, it's a legal term I made up. Embracery is the common-law misdemeanor of attempting to bribe or corruptly influence a juror. "It is immaterial," says *Barron's Law Dictionary*, "that the influence might be in the direction of a just or proper verdict since the crime is the impermissible interference with the jury function." Thus, preliminary embracery, loosely translated for my purposes, is the act of using the media to influence the potential jury pool one way or another long before the trial begins.

I'm figuring that it didn't take Gil Garcetti, his assistant D.A. minions, the cops or even my media colleagues long to figure out that about the only "hard evidence" they could exploit was Simpson's past history of domestic abuse. In my opinion, there was no doubt that this pre-trial leakage of non-germane yet sensitive information would give cause for concern to fair-trial proponents like yours truly.

In fact, I felt strongly that Simpson's right to a fair trial had been seriously jeopardized. Even Judge Ito faked like he was as concerned as I was. "The all pervasive and invasive news media coverage had exceeded that of previous high-profile trials," Ito's August 12, 1994, order read. "Most of the media accounts have been factual; however, there are glaring examples of rank rumor and speculation, prurient sensationalism and outright fabrication that are the result of competitive commercial journalism."

Not surprising to me, however, is that Ito overlooked the fact that much of what he described as "rumor," "speculation" and "outright fabrication" came as a result of leaked information from sources close to the case. Ito, a Democrat, in my learned opinion was secretly on the prosecution's side. I honestly believe that he wanted to get in good with Garcetti so that, in the future, Ito might get the D.A.'s nod to run for state Supreme Court or Attorney General.

Now, at the time, I was still considered to be somewhat of a minstrel sideshow by virtually all of my white colleagues, and a no-account scribe by the district attorney's office. I got some attention when I published an article entitled "Did He Have to be Handcuffed?" on June 16, 1994. But after that, the white boys and girls pretty much ignored me.

That is, until I wrote another article in which I quoted from several cases that went to the question of pre-trial publicity. One, *Shepard v. Maxwell (384 U.S. 1966)* had U.S. Supreme Court Justice Tom Clark saying point-blank that "there is a trial-by-media problem in America." In overturning the conviction of Dr. Sam Shepard, the high court ruled in an 8-1 opinion that Shepard had been deprived of a fair trial in his 1954 conviction of 2nd degree murder of his second wife. Press coverage, Justice Clark continued, "created a Roman holiday atmosphere."

Ditto the case *Irvin v. Dowd (366 U.S. 717 1961)*, in which the high court set aside a state murder conviction because "newspaper publicity prevented a fair trial." Charges that the defendant had confessed to six previous murders had been widely publicized. Thus, he was indicted and convicted of murder. "With his life at stake," the high court ruled, "it is not requiring too much that petitioner be tried in an atmosphere undisturbed by so huge a wave of public passion and by a jury other than one in which two-thirds of the members admit, before hearing the testimony, to possessing a belief of his guilt."

From then on, my colleagues slowly but surely began to realize that I was not just some nigger journalist writing for a nigger newspaper, but that more often than not, I knew what I was talking about. The article did not set well, however, with those in Garcetti's office. Suzanne Childs, *Jurassic Park* author Michael Crichton's ex-woman, Garcetti's public information officer and, some say, current woman, spoke to me for the first time when she called and expressed concern "about the tone" of my articles. "Oh?" I responded. "Well, *you* never leaked anything to *me*." So kiss my ass, I said to myself. And besides, I continued in my mind, now that I have you guys' attention, fuck you!

Anyway, the road is now paved for a critical trip toward the issue of domestic violence as it related to this double murder case. The case for Simpson's violent streak was made largely by Nicole Brown Simpson herself in her writings and through her friends and by the psychiatrist whom she allegedly told of Simpson's vicious propensities.

"This trial is a search for the truth," the prosecution opened in their brief seeking to respond to the defendant's motion to exclude evidence of domestic violence. The People argued that to eliminate the domestic violence issue would unfairly deprive the jury "of relevant facts surrounding the victim's murder."

The brief, written by attorney Scott Gordon, by far the nicest and most accessible prosecutor in the team, made the point that Nicole Brown Simpson's murder was the "terminal point in a connected, progressive chain of events. In order to honestly and truthfully render a verdict in this case, the jury must hear the entire truth, including those facts which illuminate defendant's motive, intent, identity and the facts that portray the murder as a part of a common plan or scheme."

The People claimed that Simpson beat on Nicole because she was suffering from "learned helplessness." I took this to mean that she couldn't help but stand there and get her ass kicked. I found that interesting, since it had been mildly reported that Nicole used to kick a little ass herself. Not only O.J.'s, but also the maid's.

My critics, like NOW's Tammy Bruce, would say, "So what? You're not supposed to hit a woman." My good friend, Los Angeles bondsman Celes King, III, said the same thing. I, however, have a different view. As a rule, I will take one slap from a woman. One. I figure that if a woman is brazen enough to slap me, I probably deserve it. But, I repeat, she's only getting one "bite out of the apple." After that, she takes her physical well-being into her own hands.

Here's why. You see, if one starts letting someone, male or female, take combination swings at you, one risks getting one's glasses broken, one's lip busted and one's hard-earned clothes torn off one's torso. Fuck that. You hit me twice, I'm defending myself. It's as simple as that, girlfriend. One slap per customer.

Of the 3,000 or so cases I adjudicated as a magistrate in Pittsburgh, roughly 100 were what could be called domestic-violence cases. Only in Pennsylvania they were called "harassment" cases. And they were summary offenses, charges that draw even less of a sentence and/or fine than a misdemeanor: up to 90 days in jail and no more than a $300 fine per offense.

Many of those cases fit the scenario I just described. "I began dating another woman," one defendant testified before me. "This woman sitting over there comes through my bedroom window one night, jumps on the both of us (the other woman). So I threw her back through the window."

"Does that explain why she has those bandages on her arms and legs?" I asked.

"Well, I guess so, Your Honor."

"Could you venture to explain what would possess her to come through your bedroom window in the middle of the night?"

"She is the mother of my son. But we couldn't get along, so I broke off the relationship," he told me. "But I still pay my child support and I come and pick him up every week." I guess he threw that in to get some mercy from the court.

Since I held public hearings, I told both parties to approach the bench. "Young lady," I said to her. "Do you know how dangerous it is to come through someone's window in this neighborhood? You could get yourself shot." Was the dick that good?

Apparently, it was. Even though I found the defendant "not guilty," they were back before me several months later on charges that *he* filed. This time, she used a more conventional entrance into his abode. But she exited pretty much the same way. Girlfriend rang the doorbell at about 6:00 a.m. Defendant goes to the door. His current paramour is in the bedroom. Girlfriend gains entrance by alluding that something is wrong with their little son. Once she's in the apartment, girlfriend starts talking about "Why can't we get back together?"

Defendant tries to see her to the door. She does the "Spiderman" routine. You know, when the woman grabs the doorway with both her hands and her feet and you can't budge her. Defendant then reaches for the telephone to call "911." Girlfriend pulls the phone out of the kitchen wall. Defendant picks her up and throws her out the front door and locks it. About an hour later, defendant leaves for work at a local steel mill. As he gets into the car, Spiderwoman jumps out of nowhere and onto the defendant's car hood.

I wish I could have personally seen what the defendant and his witnesses say happened next. He's driving down the street with Spiderwoman hanging onto the hood of his car, like she's Keanu Reeves or something. Finally, Ms. Keanu falls off the car, drags herself back to the apartment, gets in her car and several traffic lights away, catches the defendant and rams the back of his automobile. "What do you have to say about these series of events?" I asked, trying to keep a straight face. I don't even remember what she said, it was so fucked up. But I gave her a break and fined her $100. He was pissed. "If you don't like it," I said to him, "appeal!"

This was not a typical case, however. Some were really gruesome. One guy fashioned himself to be a pimp. But he traveled by bus. How are you going to be a pimp and ride the bus? I asked myself. Anyway, this guy used to brutalize his girls. One he beat up in her apartment parking lot and then pulled out a pair of scissors and cut off all her pretty, long black hair. The neighbors were sitting there watching. Another woman, he just flat-out beat the shit out of her.

Like most criminals, this guy was really stupid. He ran all the way to the end of the county. I called the local police and they picked him up "on information" and brought him before me. I arraigned him and set bail at $5,000 straight, no percentage. Since he had outstanding warrants, he sat in jail for a long, long time. When he finally came before me, this clown was unremorseful. "You gotta keep 'em in line," he told me in open court. Back to jail he went, all 5'3" and 120 pounds of him.

A couple years later, when I was off the bench and serving as the Pittsburgh Public Schools' deputy controller, this guy saw me coming down the street and walked out of the McDonald's parking lot to "confront" me. "I didn't like the way you treated me in your court," he said. Without another word, I sucker-punched him because I figured he was going to haul off on me. That chump got off the sidewalk and went back to the parking lot. Punk-ass, sugar-pimp motherfucker.

Those are just two examples of battery cases that came before me, representing both sides of the spectrum. In the case at hand, the People brought largely hearsay evidence into court, and got away with it. Ito was responding to the growing public outcry over spousal abuse that erupted because of this case. So he let all kinds of shit in. For example, the People contended that shortly after Simpson and Brown were married in 1978, the couple, while in New York, engaged in an argument and Simpson beat up on her, even "while he fucked me" in the hotel.

This according to her friend Betsy Rockett, who told prosecutors that the argument started when Simpson accused Brown of responding to a bar patron's flirtatious musings. My question was always, "Who is Betsy Rockett and where was she on the night of the alleged beatings?"

The same question applies to Wayne Hughes, who told prosecutors that the victim told him Simpson hit her. On another occasion, Nicole wrote, presumably in a diary of some kind, that while she was in her Rockingham home, Simpson beat her badly and locked her in the wine closet while he watched television and she pleaded to be released.

This issue of domestic violence touched home even in the district attorney's office. I spoke to nine women who work for the D.A., and they all told me that Christopher Darden was a constant abuser of his former live-in girlfriend and fellow D.A. employee, Bea Williams. I figured that since the media could dredge up stories about Johnnie Cochran abusing his first wife, why not do the same with Darden? After all, fair's fair. The district attorney, however, didn't think so. He dispatched Suzanne Childs to bat her eyelashes at Ken Thomas, publisher of the *Sentinel*, and the story was killed. Later, when I was in Childs' office on another matter, she threw that in my face. Even though she wasn't smiling, she was sure as hell gloating, like she had put some nigger in his place in his own backyard.

Childs shouldn't have done that. On my next appearance on the Michael Jackson talk show, I pulled the covers off Darden on the air. And I did it again on NBC and on WVON in Chicago and on KXL in Portland. When Darden got wind of what I did, he quit speaking to me. Even in public settings where the bitterest enemies are supposed to be cordial, he would ignore my greetings. Once when I spoke to him in a crowded elevator, he wouldn't acknowledge me. People were looking around at each other, and I said, "What's the matter, homeboy? Ain't you gonna speak? Is it my breath?" You could see the steam rising off his bald head.

Many celebrities have been abusers. Recently, it was learned that pipsqueak actor Dudley Moore was a wife beater. Actress Loni Anderson told the whole world that her former husband, Burt Reynolds, used to kick her ass around the estate. Even mild-mannered Minnesota Vikings quarterback Warren Moon slapped his wife around. Now, there's no excuse for that kind of behavior. But—and this is a big *but*—that kind of behavior doesn't make you a murderer. None of the people I mentioned killed their wives, and according to a jury of his peers, neither did O.J. Simpson.

CHAPTER 6
THE JUDGE
AND
THE JUDICIAL SYSTEM

TOM ELIAS

Lance Ito Meets a Case He Can't Control

The entire defense team lined up neatly behind the counsel tables in Judge Lance Ito's courtroom an hour or so after the jury delivered the verdicts that freed O.J. Simpson. Johnnie Cochran was crowing. Simpson's son Jason read a smarmy, self-serving victory note from his father. Robert Shapiro and Carl Douglas sat quietly and smirked. Simpson's sisters and mother grinned as they sat in the single row facing the 58 reporters allowed in for this epilogue to the Simpson trial. The erstwhile defendant's relatives filled the jury box.

What in the world is this? I asked myself after running the gauntlet of sheriff's deputies providing security at taxpayer expense. Since when do judges turn over their courtrooms to the families of wife-beaters and murder defendants? When did court publicists start running press conferences for private attorneys? But I suppose I should have expected something like this. If there was one thing Ito loved about presiding over the Simpson case, it was the fact that the trial made him a celebrity. This was a judge who was never available to the working press that covered his courtroom every day. But when ABC's Diane Sawyer showed up, bailiffs quickly whisked her into chambers. When talk-show host Larry King appeared during one mid-morning break, the recess was extended an additional half-hour while he and Ito schmoozed. Everyone else, of course, cooled their heels in the hallway outside.

The sole interview Ito gave during the trial went to Los Angeles TV reporter Tritia Toyota, like him a Japanese American. Toyota never covered a minute of the trial, but she and Ito were old friends. Their session aired over five days in November 1994 on the CBS station in Los Angeles, making Ito feel uneasy. Even though he never said a word about Simpson while answering the fat softball questions tossed up by Toyota, his comments bordered on violating Rule 6 of the California Code of Judicial Conduct, which forbids jurists from speaking about cases ongoing before them. The close call in the interview came when Ito recalled how Delbert Wong, a retired judge he sent out to retrieve some evidence from Simpson's office, had been his childhood Cub Scoutmaster.

Just as he did on the last day of the trial, Ito gave Simpson celebrity treatment many other times. One notable occasion came on a day in February 1995 when he turned over his courtroom to Simpson and the full corps of defense lawyers at day's end so that Simpson could dress down all his employees at once. The defendant's bellowed complaints could be heard in the hallway through the closed doors. It was the first time I had heard of a judge turning his courtroom over to a murder defendant. The explanation: The attorneys' visiting room in the county jail wasn't big enough.

Celebrity treatment for Simpson continued to trial's end, when Ito failed to cut off Simpson's long-winded and clearly out-of-order declaration of innocence. But Ito topped himself in celebrity sycophancy after the verdicts when he again let the defense use his courtroom as they wished, rather than relegating them to the lobby area where Simpson's lawyers had given all their previous formal press conferences. My question: Why should taxpayers provide both the security and the facility for a self-serving private function?

It wasn't the first time I had questioned Ito's tactics and practices. There was the way he handled the press all through the trial. There was the way he let lawyers blather on month after month, only rarely reminding them they were being repetitious. And there was his frequent inconsistency, first taking a firm action and then often rescinding it a day or so later. This was a new Lance Ito, only a little like the man I had watched just two years earlier, when for more than four months in 1991 and '92 I went to work almost daily in his courtroom, covering the trial of savings and loan swindler Charles H. Keating Jr. The judge I saw then seemed a very different Ito from the man America saw every day in the Simpson trial.

The old Ito delivered few small witticisms calculated to show how bright and informed he was. He offered no tidbits of pop culture. His parents never visited the courtroom as they did for opening statements in the Simpson trial. There were no visiting celebrities. And competing lawyers did not parade constantly to sidebar. Every important issue in Keating's trial was settled in public, as they should have been in Simpson's.

There was also no large media crowd, only a small contingent of four newspaper and wire service reporters who attended almost every day. Court TV's camera showed up only occasionally. The Simpson case was different in almost every area. Remote-controlled television and still cameras hung permanently over the shoulders of the jury, positioned on the west wall of the courtroom where it would be difficult for them to capture the images of any jurors. The longer I watched Ito, the more I realized television's presence was warping his personality and conduct.

Through both trials, only one thing remained constant about the judge: At every point, Ito left little doubt that he wanted the prosecution to win. His sentencing message to Keating spelled out why he agreed with the jury that convicted the former thrift owner and manipulator: "The magnitude of the crime, the vulnerability of the victims, the fact that (the defendant) took advantage of trust...the court finds these are aggravating factors. The callousness, the planning and sophistication required for this crime prompt me to sentence (the defendant) to the maximum term permitted by law."

Despite Ito's extreme awareness of Simpson's celebrity, I knew from the moment he took over the case that he craved another opportunity to speak words like those, which could have suited Simpson as well as they did Keating. Ito would have loved another chance to throw the book at a high-profile defendant, even one he treated with deference during the trial. I had seen the satisfaction on his face when he gave Keating the maximum sentence of nine years and eight months after treating him respectfully while listening to the litany of Keating's schemes and misdeeds. "You have to have a desire that things come out right," he once said in an interview. That sentiment suited me just fine as I went into the Simpson trial, but it was about the only part of

Ito I liked. And I liked it only because I wanted to see Simpson convicted.

Ito's pro-prosecution bias was no accident. A onetime county prosecutor, he was married to Captain Margaret (Peggy) York, the highest-ranking female officer in the Los Angeles Police Department. He had been appointed to the bench by George Deukmejian, a Republican governor of California who often said his primary mission was to create a strongly anti-crime judiciary. If so, Ito was his man. He consistently gave tough sentences to minor drug offenders and gang-bangers. He rejected the idea of probation for Keating, even though the swindler had no prior criminal record and his lawyer, Stephen Neal, begged that he be allowed to "use the rest of his life productively."

Ito's bias became more obvious with almost every motion the Simpson defense filed. When Robert Shapiro objected early on to the prosecutors' sending blood samples to more than one DNA analysis laboratory, Ito let him talk as long as he wanted, but quickly ruled for the state after he finished. When Shapiro complained that the defense wasn't getting access to all the blood evidence, Ito asked for an inventory and then told prosecutors to give portions of each blood sample to defense experts as soon as possible. Translation: Whenever you're ready.

When defense attorneys objected to evidence collected from Simpson's house before police had a search warrant—and they voiced this objection many times—Ito always came down quickly on the prosecution side. So it was no surprise to me that Ito was sorely disappointed with the verdicts. He neither confirmed nor denied reports that he and his wife wept together in his chambers after the verdicts were read. For sure, he didn't give the Simpson jury the same effusive sendoff he gave the Keating jurors, whom he thanked profusely for their months of service.

Ito may have favored the prosecution at every legitimate opportunity, but he also gave defense lawyers every conceivable chance to argue their case. His goal: to make any verdict reached in his courtroom virtually appeal-proof. Knowing that Ito didn't like to cut any lawyer short, I was sure from the moment he got the case that we'd be in for a long trial. All through the Keating case, I had watched impatiently as Ito allowed lawyers to blather on almost without limit. No matter how repetitive their questions, no matter how long-winded their arguments, no matter how many conferences they wanted in his chambers, he was going to allow it. "I want the lawyers to be precise and concise, but I'm also an exceptionally patient person," he once said.

I also knew that we reporters would not receive the best of treatment. Ito acted as if he considered reporters little more than pests during the Keating trial. With the media contingent increased exponentially for Simpson, there had to be trouble. The judge ran his courtroom like a martinet all through what he called "the Keating matter," and for Simpson things were to be different only in the technology available to him. He had to depend on his own eyes and ears to discern what went on in his courtroom as he tried Keating. This time he had not only the Court TV pool camera, which occasionally panned the audience, but also his own private television camera and monitor. Ito happily controlled it with the aptly named joystick mounted behind his bench, and its sole purpose was to check out what was happening in the courtroom audience.

There was also the locked courtroom door. All through Keating's trial, even after one of the swindler's victims slapped his face with a wig in the hallway outside, Ito's courtroom was open whenever court was in session and often when it wasn't. It even stayed open after one of Keating's elderly female victims ran in and began pounding on him—outside the jury's presence. Observers could come and go at will. But not for Simpson. Just as they had for Keating, sheriff's deputies checked every person and package arriving on the ninth floor with X-rays and a metal detector. But Ito kept his courtroom door firmly locked except when the audience was coming in or going out. Anyone not inside by the time court was called to order wasn't getting in. Anyone who left for any reason was staying out until the next break. Except the lawyers. Ito said this was for "security reasons." But where's the security risk if a reporter leaves for a few moments to place a phone call and then returns? What's the risk if a family member visits the restroom and returns? This wasn't about security; it was about control.

Ito had never liked anyone to eat in his courtroom, not even small candies or breath fresheners. For Simpson he posted "No gum chewing" signs every few feet on the backs of the courtroom benches. And when his secret camera, hanging from the ceiling in a brown plastic bubble, caught the occasional reporter or spectator chomping away, he'd sometimes call the perpetrator into chambers for a dressing down. No whispering was tolerated, either. Two reporters who whispered only slightly one day in the spring of 1995—Gale Holland of *USA Today* and Kristin Jeanette-Meyers of Court TV—were banned for the duration of the trial. This episode sparked a group protest letter from other reporters and an individual one from my colleague Dennis Schatzman, the only journalist with the chutzpah to tell Ito his "death penalty" was grossly out of synch with the reporters' alleged offense.

The seeds of Ito's anti-media bias first became visible during the Keating trial. Reporters there were frustrated when they brought portable computers to court, hoping to compose stories during the proceedings so they could be transmitted immediately at day's end. Ito objected to the faint clicking of the keys and his bailiffs threatened to confiscate my machine at least twice. Ito also consistently refused to grant interviews to reporters, though he was not averse to the occasional brief conversation during chance encounters.

But that's as far as he went in Keating's trial. He took much firmer control almost from the moment Simpson arrived in his courtroom. Press seating was regulated. The slightest noise resulted in expulsion. Even dozing was banned. When Schatzman briefly dropped off one day because of his anti-cancer medication, Ito immediately spotted the infraction on his private monitor and bounced the reporter.

But his treatment of reporters was insignificant compared with his consistent disregard for the public's right to know. By allowing cameras into his courtroom, Ito created the illusion of full disclosure. With television recording every move by anyone other than the jurors, viewers believed they were seeing everything of significance in the case. But the public was left out of the critical sidebar conferences, where lawyers often debated the scope and subject matter of the questions they would ask witnesses. And proceedings frequently stopped for hours, with reporters waiting in the hallway, analysts vamping on TV and viewers not knowing when live action would return, while Ito staged private meetings in his chambers.

These sessions could decide everything from the makeup of the jury to the content of the poster boards both sides continually used while questioning witnesses. In one closed session, lawyers argued for an hour over whether the jury should see gruesome autopsy photos of Nicole Simpson and her friend Ronald Goldman. When I asked several law professors why this should have been debated in private, they could find no answer. Ito liked to say the televised proceedings were an ideal chance to educate the public on the Constitution. But from the beginning, his secret meetings trampled on the public's right to know even as he publicly said he was furthering it.

Meanwhile, he made his anti-press feelings public by calling reporters "jackals" and claiming that much of the jury pool was "poisoned" by the press. He even censored the jury portraits drawn by television artists. After deciding some were "too accurate," he demanded that no drawings be shown on TV without first being submitted to him and literally receiving his stamp of approval, which came in the form of a red circular seal. Artists had to comply with his censorship or their networks and stations risked permanently losing access to the courtroom. Ito's successful censorship offended me more than all the ridiculous strictures he placed on me and my colleagues. For if he could get away with this mild and innocuous-seeming form of prior restraint, what else might he or some other judge try next?

Ito implied with all this that giving accurate information to the public might somehow damage someone. Consistent with that conviction, Ito had his bailiffs expel all reporters from his courtroom at the beginning of jury selection, later allowing a small pool in only when media attorneys deluged him with a barrage of briefs demonstrating that his action was blatantly illegal. Even so, the mass of reporters was consigned to listen to jury selection via closed circuit audio in a small room three floors up, with the public totally excluded. Ito stationed a bailiff outside that room to make sure no reporter carried a tape recorder in, lest a single word of the proceedings be recorded. He even banned word processors after learning that some laptops could make short voice recordings.

But that was nothing compared with the tirades he occasionally spluttered into when television made errors. One came just after opening statements, at a time when the case still had eleven alternate jurors and two were seated in swivel chairs in front of the jury box. A wide-angle shot from the wall-mounted camera caught the image of one alternate for about three seconds, a transgression Ito spotted immediately.

Instantly, he shut down the camera for the rest of that day and threatened to ban it for good. "I can't begin to tell you my concern and my disappointment with…the inability of the news media to follow a basic rule," Ito said. There he went again, generalizing about the media. Because the *National Enquirer* and the *Globe*, both supermarket tabloids, printed gory photographs, he branded all media as "jackals." Because one cameraman made a small error, all media were at fault, even those who didn't use the camera. It was the same kind of tarring with one brush he engaged in when making the rules for press seating. If a seat went unoccupied without prior notice for two days—any two days, not two in a row—all its occupants would lose their places in the courtroom, said Ito's rules. That made me responsible for my seatmates' presence, and they for mine. This rule never changed, but Ito's concern about exposing jurors to the camera was assuaged when a narrower-angle lens was installed before the next day's session. A similar intemperate outburst came months later, when a juror appeared in a TV picture for less than one second as the camera panned over a poster board. That time, Ito cut off both the video and audio feeds from the courtroom, even though radio stations using only audio had no relation to the brief offense.

The judge's hottest outburst of the entire trial, however, was not directed at the camera but at KNBC, the NBC-owned Los Angeles station that aired a story about Simpson's bloody socks in September 1994. The station reported DNA tests of blood on socks found by police in Simpson's bedroom pointed to Nicole as the source of the blood. In fact, the prosecution would later try to make this a strong element of its case, and the defense would spend days claiming that Nicole's blood had been planted on the socks. But when KNBC reporter Tracie Savage aired the report, the blood had not yet been subjected to DNA analysis.

Ito first warned the station its information was incorrect, but when KNBC expanded on the initial report that evening, he became furious: "This news operation was put on notice...that this was incorrect information," Ito thundered. "They have chosen not only to republish it but to embellish upon it. This is fundamentally unfair. It's also fundamentally wrong." Then he threatened to remove the TV camera from his courtroom, relenting only after media lawyer Kelli Sager convinced him that the courtroom camera had nothing to do with the socks report.

I and other reporters who had seen Ito work in the Keating trial could recall no similar outbursts from him. "I don't know if it was the TV camera that changed him or not," observed Jerry Kammer, who covered Keating for the *Arizona Republic*. "But in the Simpson trial, I saw somebody who appeared to enjoy the spotlight and was playing to the camera. In Keating, he enjoyed the complexity of the case, but he didn't do any grandstanding." Said E. Scott Reckard, who covered Keating for the Associated Press, "It certainly looked as though he went over the top. This bizarre secret camera to keep track of the audience seemed extraordinary."

I agreed with both. From the start I thought the TV camera created a different Ito. He swiftly became the most-recognized judge in America, eclipsing even Joseph Wapner, the retired Los Angeles judge who went on to fame on *The People's Court*. Ito always denied his fame could ever match Wapner's. "Joe Wapner will always have the title of 'most watched,'" he said smilingly in the one interview he gave during the trial. "I'm just a flash in the pan compared to him." Despite that disclaimer, Ito was an instant celebrity and soon began to act like one. When reporters asked for interviews, they were treated with disdain. "Where did you come from?" court publicist Jerrianne Hayslett responded when I made one such request. "Did you just fall off the turnip truck?" The real question was where did she and Ito get off treating the working press that way?

Ito's inner need to control everything about his trials was the likely reason he was so tight in his attempts to regulate the press. But this effort was doomed from the first. For no one can really control the press. Ito might be able to keep his hand at our collective throat while we're in his courtroom, but neither he nor any other judge could decide what we did anywhere else. Said Douglas Mirell, the American Civil Liberties Union lawyer who often helped reporters fend off Ito's attempts to exclude the press and public, "Experience teaches that a free press either will or will not behave responsibly. But it is the public, not Ito, that has the capacity to reward or punish media irresponsibility."

In his desire to control the press and other details, micromanager Ito lost control of the lawyers and the case itself. One retired Los Angeles judge observed that he "lost control of the courtroom early on, and when he tried to get it back, he did it in petty, silly ways, like throwing out a reporter for chewing gum." An active colleague on the Los Angeles Superior Court said, "He let these lawyers repeat themselves over and over and over. He was a disaster. He made what should have been a six-week case into a yearlong nightmare. He says he's patient, but he gives patience a whole new meaning."

By reversing himself on rulings that ranged from fines assessed against lawyers to evidence and the camera's presence, Ito added to his control problems. "If you change your mind all the time, you are sending a message that the last one that whines to you gets his way," said another judge. "That's what Ito did continually." Ito's steady waffling combined with the outcome to make American justice a laughingstock around the world. Newspapers from Taiwan and Singapore to London and Dublin deplored both the verdicts and the conduct of the trial. They were correct on both counts.

So Ito's efforts at control failed miserably. Still, his desire to direct everything about the proceeding never abated, extending all the way down to camera angles. He sometimes offered the rotating camera operators advice on where to focus. But it was his own focus that was less than sharp almost from the beginning. The camera's presence and his constant awareness of it likely had a lot to do with that. In his first interview after the trial, Ito defended his decision to allow it in.

"The problem with not having a camera is that one must trust the evaluation and analysis of a reporter who's telling you what occurred in the courtroom," Ito said in the interview given to a journalism student at California State University at

Northridge. There was that thought again: Reporters aren't trustworthy, Ito implied. "Any time you allow somebody to report an event, you have to take into consideration the filtering effect of that person's own biases. Whereas, if you have a camera in the courtroom, there's no filtering." Except when you make key decisions in private.

The camera also can highlight some qualities of the major characters it shows, especially if they constantly play to it. They may not even know how they're being revealed. That's what happened to Ito, and it quickly became apparent to most of the lawyers in his courtroom. "He was obviously enamored with the…celebrity," observed defense DNA specialist Peter Neufeld after the verdicts. "There were a number of times…when his conduct was inconsistent with what one expects from someone presiding over a murder trial."

Nevertheless, there was one way Ito might have positively controlled the outcome of the trial: jury selection. But as activist as he tried to be in many other areas, Ito was passive in this key arena. He and the lawyers for both sides consistently eliminated anyone who said he had even the most remote knowledge of the case. These potential jurors were said to be "poisoned" or "polluted" because they'd been exposed to media reports, which were sometimes mistaken. But this meant that the brightest, best informed prospects were all taken off the case before it began in earnest. That's the opposite of what should have happened. The jury should have been peopled with members who cared about the case enough to inform themselves. It would have helped if the only known DNA expert in the pool had not been summarily dismissed.

Under today's system, the best educated and informed potential jurors can be systematically excluded—not only from high-profile cases like Simpson's, but also from routine assaults and purse-snatchings. This can leave juries extremely susceptible to demagoguery. One reason this system, which exists in most parts of America, is tolerated may be that some judges and lawyers think the process makes juries easier to control. The only jury reform actively under consideration in most parts of America in the '90s has been a proposed move away from unanimous juries.

"That would be a very unfortunate thing," Cochran told me one day in the courthouse hallway. "We've had this unanimous-vote system for 600 years and it's worked fine. To change just because people don't understand this one case would be a terrible thing." It was yet another distortion of fact by Cochran. For the unanimous jury requirement has been a thing of the past in England, where the idea originated, since the late 1960s. And two American states—Oregon and Louisiana—also allow less-than-unanimous verdicts in anything other than capital cases. The most powerful push for expanding the move away from the unanimous-vote tradition now comes in California, where the district attorneys' association wants the same 10-2 vote now accepted in the United Kingdom. Fred Goldman, father of murder victim Ronald Goldman, joined the campaign for a ballot initiative embodying this concept as his first civic endeavor after the Simpson trial.

"Something needs to be done about a system that is broken, badly broken," Goldman said. "I found (in the trial) that we were in a system that condoned dishonesty, unfairness, manipulation of the truth and, least of all, justice." The executive director of the district attorneys' association told me, "This change has been needed for more than 30 years. And we think that if we act in California, there will be a national movement." He may be right, but non-unanimous juries could still be chosen in the same almost imbecilic manner as the Simpson panel—a process that rewarded ignorance and discouraged curiosity.

Through it all, Ito learned the hard way that neither *voir dire* nor any written regulations can assure a judge control of anything about the cases he hears. Only the judge's own firm, reasoned behavior can do that. Ito lost control of press, jury and lawyers because his behavior wasn't always firm and it wasn't always fair or reasonable. He tried to control everything, even areas where judges have no business, and so he ended up in control of nothing—not the press or the lawyers or the jury and especially not the verdict.

DENNIS SCHATZMAN

I Got Lance in My Pants, Oh Yeah

One of the reasons I was a more astute reporter with respect to this trial than most of the others who covered it is that, although I wasn't an attorney, I spent three years as a magistrate in Pittsburgh, Pennsylvania, the nation's oldest unified judicial system. If a murder was committed in my jurisdiction of Homewood-Brushton, the arraignment and preliminary hearing was held in my courtroom. So I felt confident about being able to understand the judicial temperament in the Simpson trial. Which brings us to Lance Ito, the Superior Court judge who selected himself to hear the Simpson case. Why do I say that he selected himself? I refer you to the May 1994 article in *California Lawyer* by Jean Guccione, then of the *Los Angeles Daily Journal*. In that article, Guccione writes that Ito is one of two Superior Court judges who select which judges will hear high-profile cases. Ito told Guccione it is important for judges in high-profile cases not to embarrass the judiciary by, for instance, picking their noses in front of the camera. Among the cases in which he had a hand in selecting the judges were the first Menendez brothers double-murder trial, the first Rodney King beating trial and the trial of the men who beat trucker Reginald Denny at the start of the Los Angeles rebellion in April 1992. Thus, based upon Guccione's excellent article, I concluded that Ito knew what he was getting into.

Was I wrong! As events would later confirm in my mind, Ito was in way over his head. Not only that, he was more than unapologetic in his penchant for being pro-prosecution in virtually all of his rulings. Ito also displayed early and often an intense dislike for the news media. It was here where he showed his greatest chutzpah. In many instances, he would throw reporters out for nodding off during boring testimony about DNA or passing mints amongst each other or whispering during breaks in the testimony.

To me, that was chicken-shit. And because of it, I have no sympathy for him.

On August 16, 1994, for example, during the first few days that Ito had the case, sheriff's deputies threw me out of the courtroom because they didn't think I was a reporter. Once that situation was straightened out, Ito had aide Jerrianne Hayslett write my boss and complain about my behavior. Here I am, a reporter with credentials having to prove that I'm a qualified reporter, when no one else—no one *white*—had to prove *they* were reporters. And everyone wondered why I got pissed off. So he was on my shitlist from then on.

Another incident that ticked me off with respect to his treatment of my colleagues was when Ito threw out the wife of retired Superior Court Judge Burton Katz, who was whispering to a friend during a lull in the testimony. Now let's think about this for a minute: Everyone in the room is an adult. Virtually everyone in the room is a professional. You cannot expect these people to sit there like little kindergarten kids and not whisper to each other as long as it doesn't disturb the court. But Ito, who is younger than virtually everybody in the room—not yet 45, and certainly a lot shorter (he stands 5'6")—wants to treat people like children.

Then there was the time that Ito threw two of my female colleagues—one from *USA Today* and the other from Court TV—out of the courtroom for the rest of the trial because they chose to whisper something in clear earshot of one of the jurors. Now I don't agree with their being Chatty Cathies during an important trial, but their crime was no worse than the one committed by one male television reporter whom Ito caught reading a magazine with O.J.'s picture on the cover during a motions hearing. Ito called him by name and asked him to put away the magazine. Therefore, in my opinion, Ito could have just slapped the two females on the wrist, maybe suspended them for a week at the most, and let them go on and do their work. Instead, what he did has probably put a black mark on their careers.

Many of my colleagues were incensed by Ito's outrageous action. But not outraged enough to write individual letters. Most of them, led by Andrea Ford of the *Los Angeles Times*, wrote him a joint letter. But I was so pissed off that I wrote my own letter, and this is what I said: I told Ito that he who is without sin was not in the room. I reminded him that when he pointed out that one of the jurors had caught a baseball at a recent Dodgers-Pittsburgh Pirates game, he had pretty much exposed that juror to being identified. I explained that in this day and age, many people videotape those games and, when people catch foul balls, they usually appear on camera. It doesn't take a rocket scientist to go back and figure out which one of the one or two people who caught a foul ball that day was a juror—and maybe the five or six people sitting around him were jurors, too. I also reminded Ito that I had also once sat high and looked low and I understood the role of a judicial officer, as well as the power that he holds. If there's one thing I learned, it is that it's dangerous to abuse that power. And it's especially dangerous when you abuse the power against people who buy ink by the barrel. Very soon, he will be repaid, as he's being repaid right now.

One of the things I did like about Ito was his quick wit and his ability to retain all the information that was thrown his way by both the prosecution and the defense. I was really impressed when he would often correct attorneys about incorrect minutiae found in their own documents. I'm sure his parents were very proud of their bright little Lance. But he showed extreme sissiness when he cried or choked back tears on several occasions in front of the cameras. Once, when one of his bailiffs was shot and killed near his home and another time when he heard that Mark Fuhrman claimed that Ito's wife, Margaret York, had "slept her way to the top." Those scenes were reminiscent of when, in 1972, crying about something negative somebody had said about his wife took Senator Edmund Muskie of Maine out of the presidential race. We all have feelings, but when you're presiding over a courtroom, you have to keep your emotions in check. Even Richard Nixon waited till he got on the plane on August 9, 1974, before he started bawling like a baby.

Let's talk about Ito as the prosecution's best friend. I asked Carl Douglas, Simpson's lead motions man and a partner in the firm of Johnnie Cochran, how many times he thought Ito ruled against the defense and he said he couldn't remember. I asked him if he could pull out all the motions the defense submitted that were struck down by Ito, and he said it was just too much. It was no secret that Ito was a prosecuting attorney before he was appointed to the bench by former Governor George Deukmejian. So all he knew from a lawyer's standpoint was how to put people in jail. This is important to understand because, in my opinion, in order to be an effective and impartial finder of fact, you have to understand that defendants have the same rights as the prosecution. Especially when it's a well-known fact that defendants—all defendants—operate at a great disadvantage when it comes to defending themselves against the state.

Prosecutors, however, don't care about the rights of the defendant. All they want to do is put you in jail. Period. End of discussion. They will do whatever it takes to send a defendant up the river. If it means that they have to get a jailhouse snitch to testify against the defendant, they'll do it. If it means that they'll jack up the charge and force a defendant to plea bargain, they'll do that, too. They don't care. It's not their money; it's not their life. Unfortunately, this doesn't happen just to guilty parties. This happens to people who are often innocent and to people who might have happened to be at the scene of a crime. Ito comes out of that school of thought.

Which brings us to Ito's relationship with lead prosecutor Marcia Clark. I'm not suggesting that there was anything complicit in their relationship, but it seemed rather odd that virtually every time Ito would threaten to rule favorably on a motion offered by the defense, Clark would bat her eyelashes the next morning and Ito would switch around and reverse the decision he had hinted at making the day before. This happened so often it became very noticeable to everyone in the press corps. On a few occasions, some of this was offset by Chris Darden's sophomoric outbursts, but those occasions were very few indeed.

There are stories about how Lance used to go to cocktail parties and show off the little snub-nosed .38 that he carried on him all the time. I remember as a magistrate that the county sheriff would routinely grant each judge a license to carry a revolver. And all of them did—except me. To me, if you perform your job on the bench honestly and fairly, you don't need a gun. And my jurisdiction was considered the worst magisterial district in the entire Commonwealth of Pennsylvania. But I walked back and forth to work. I never at any time felt that I needed to carry a gun. The point is this: It's not the job that you have, it's not the title you have, it's how you perform your duties. And Ito's little gun-toting history is a case in point about how judges who, unlike me, live in places far from their judicial districts, walk in fear. I believe it's because of the way they treat people, especially black and brown people.

Now, one of the things I learned in judiciary school, which was held at Wilson College in Chambersvania, Pennsylvania, is that you must always control your courtroom. That doesn't mean you have to be a tyrant. But you outline the rules of the court at the outset and you make sure that everyone adheres to it. When you're talking, no one else talks. When a witness is talking, no one else talks. And that's that. Ito violated that rule almost every day. The sumbitch just let everybody in the courtroom run over him—except for the journalists, of course, and we weren't trying to.

On many occasions, for example, Johnnie Cochran and Chris Darden would engage in childish arguments in open court and Ito would let them get away with it. He should have fined them straight up and down, instead of just threatening to fine them. Ito was good at threatening, but very rarely would he put his foot down. Same thing with Barry Scheck. Scheck would keep picking and picking and picking and picking with Ito over some legal issue and when Ito said he'd heard enough, Scheck just kept on talking and talking and talking. When the judge says he's heard enough, that's what the hell he means. I find it hard to believe that Scheck would get away with that back in Manhattan Borough Courthouse. He would have been sitting downstairs in a holding cell eating cheese sandwiches on a contempt charge. But Ito was always nice, much too nice, to these attorneys.

I remember on several occasions during my judicial tenure when I had to lay down the law to those who didn't obey my order in court. You see, the judge's decision is final. At least it should be. And for those who don't like it, their only recourse is to appeal. Now in Pittsburgh's Homewood-Brushton district, when I told somebody that if they don't obey me, I'm sending them "downtown," that meant to the predominantly black residents who lived in my jurisdiction that I'm sending them down before a white judge. The only way to overturn an indirect contempt charge leveled by me would be for them to go before a Common Pleas Court judge, similar to a California Superior Court judge. Like in Los Angeles County, virtually all of them are white.

I was hearing a truancy case once when the father of a 15-year-old student kept getting up and interrupting me. I asked him politely, as I always did, to wait until it was his turn to talk, and I would call on him. I operated under the same philosophy as actor Patrick Swayze did in *Roadhouse*. Swayze, who played a celebrated bouncer at a bar, told his staff to "be nice until it's time not to be nice." In this instance, I was nice until I had to not be nice. Then I sent his black ass downtown.

I remember a grandmother kept chiming in every time a defendant who was accused of beating her granddaughter was testifying. She would say things like "Oh, my lord!" Or "Jeeesus Christ!" Or "The boy's lyin'." Her large derriere got sent downtown, too. If you're gonna be a judge, you've got to be an equal-opportunity judge. When I said you're goin' downtown, I meant everybody's goin' downtown. No favorites. Apparently, Ito didn't agree with that. What he should have done, early on, is instead of showing everybody how witty he was—with comments like "Shipp happens"—he should have laid down the law and kicked some ass at the outset and the trial would have run much more smoothly.

One of the worst moments in the trial occurred when Ito allowed only two excerpts of Mark Fuhrman's hideous comments to be introduced to the jury. I say that because he let the 911 tapes in, which, in my opinion, said absolutely nothing. He allowed all the autopsy photos to be set up on display, which also said absolutely nothing about who committed the murders. But he only let the two excerpts in from Fuhrman's racist ramblings. His reasoning was that he didn't want to unduly influence the jury with respect to the N-word. So what did he think the releasing of the 911 tapes and the photos were designed to do? Were they meant to give the jurors a warm and fuzzy feeling inside? No, they were meant to influence the jury. If there's one thing I can't stand about non-blacks, it's that when it comes to the N-word and any other forms of racism, they become embarrassed and feel that black people can't handle it. That's bullshit. All it tells me is that

Ito has as much of a guilty conscience as most of these white folks out here. Like they ain't heard or told a nigger joke before. Like they had never used the word or been in the company of people who routinely used the word.

I wondered out loud and in print why Ito refused to admit Fuhrman's comments about planting evidence on black men, especially those he found in the company of white women. If the 911 tapes were germane, then why in the hell weren't Fuhrman's comments about planting evidence germane? Explain that one to me. I firmly believe that if Ito had had the courage to be fair on the Fuhrman issue, the jury would have stayed out about 20 minutes instead of four hours. That is, if he still used the same jury rules that he gave the jury before they went into deliberations.

Another one of Ito's weak points was his penchant for being a stargazer. On a couple of occasions, he allowed nationally-known journalists like Barbara Walters, Larry King, Diane Sawyer and Geraldo Rivera to come into his chambers and have private audiences with him. That shit really pissed me off, because on one occasion I wrote him a letter asking if I could bring in ten journalists from foreign countries who were here in California courtesy of the World Press Institute to see him. He allowed the journalists to sit in on a few sessions, but he wouldn't see them privately and he wouldn't allow me to introduce them to him. I'm in court every day, and Ito lets Barbara Walters and Geraldo Rivera come in and stroke his ego. Ditto, actors Richard Dreyfuss and James Woods. Although they didn't go into chambers that I know of, these guys were let into the courtroom before we were. Maybe if I had a star on the Hollywood Walk of Fame, I could have sat up there on the bench with him.

As I write this chapter, I find it hard to believe that my esteemed colleague Tom Elias and I disagree very little about Judge Ito. I'm sure that we're not the only ones who picked up on his *faux pas*, his egotism and his blatant prosecution bias. But as I said earlier, in the interests of fairness, he must be given points for knowing the law. But, see, it's the smart judges who are the most dangerous of them all. They know where to find the appropriate case law they can hang their hats on to advance themselves. To me, that's Ito in a nutshell: a little man in a big chair.

CHAPTER 7
FUHRMAN AND THE N-WORD

TOM ELIAS

Fuhrman Injects the Race Card, Cochran Plays it

Race is not and will not be an issue in this defense.
— Robert Shapiro, July 18, 1994

S hapiro was never more wrong about anything he said during the entire O.J. Simpson trial. Once Detective Mark Fuhrman emerged as a major witness, race was bound to be an issue. The only question was whether it would dominate the trial.

That question was decided in early January 1995 after Johnnie Cochran and Christopher Darden staged the most impassioned debate of the entire trial, arguing about whether black jurors could be rational once they heard the word "nigger." Carefully tip-toeing around use of the word itself, the two black lawyers debated whether defense attorneys would be permitted to cross-examine Fuhrman about his supposed past use of the racist term, which came to be known as "the N-word."

Their debate was the result of a failed motion by prosecutor Cheri Lewis, who argued to Judge Lance Ito that Fuhrman's use of the N-word was not relevant because the only supposed instances of Fuhrman using the term had come no fewer than eight years earlier. Ito responded by saying only that he would protect Fuhrman against harassment, thus leaving the field wide open for argument about the N-word.

"It is the dirtiest, filthiest, nastiest word in the English language. It was created and used for one reason only—to demean people and strip them of their dignity," Darden asserted in a twenty-minute speech that built gradually to a crescendo of emotion. "It is not a word I allow to be used in my household. It is so prejudicial and so inflammatory that to use it in any context will evoke an emotional response from every black person. It'll upset the black jurors. It'll be a test, and the test will be: 'Whose side are you on, the side of the white prosecutors and the white policemen, or are you on the side of the black defendant and his very prominent and capable black lawyer?' That's what it's going to do. Either you're with the man, or you're with the brothers...When you mention that word to this jury or to any African American, it blinds people. It will blind the jury."

In short, Darden was telling Ito, let in the N-word and you effectively give this case to the defense. Said the prosecutor, "Mr. Cochran wants to play the ace of spades and play the race card, but this isn't a race case. You shouldn't allow him to play the race card...It's the prosecution's position that if you allow Mr. Cochran to use this word and play this race card, not only does the direction of the case change, but the entire complexion of the case changes. It's a race case then. It's white versus black, African American versus Caucasian, us versus them, us versus the system. It's not an issue of simple guilt or innocence, or proof beyond a reasonable doubt. It becomes an issue of color. Who's the blackest man up here?"

While Darden spoke, defendant O.J. Simpson swiveled his chair to face him directly, first shaking his head and then turning to look at each black person in the courtroom audience.

Then Cochran took the lectern, calling Darden's speech "perhaps the most incredible remarks I've heard in a court of law in the 32 years I've been practicing. I want...to apologize to African Americans across this country," he added, playing to the TV camera. "It's demeaning to our jurors to say that African Americans who have lived under oppression for 200-plus years in this country cannot work within the mainstream, cannot hear these offensive words. African Americans live with offensive words, offensive looks, offensive treatment every day of their lives. But yet they still believe in this country. To say they can't be fair is absolutely outrageous."

Both lawyers also talked about Fuhrman, with Darden saying the detective had returned from a tour of duty with the Marines in Vietnam just before joining the Los Angeles Police Department. "He was suffering from stress, and it has to be stressful to be a police officer in the city of L.A.," Darden insisted.

To which Cochran answered, "I am ashamed Mr. Darden

would allow himself to become an apologist for this man...Being a police officer is tough...it doesn't make you use racist terms. You can't justify that in a civilized society...Nobody wants to introduce race into this case, but...race plays a part of everything in America."

Of course, Cochran really did want to introduce race. It was crucial to his chances of winning and he had predicted even before he joined the team of Simpson lawyers that it would be, so long as Fuhrman was a key figure. "As much as I don't want to see race brought into this case, if this person has a feeling against minorities, his credibility becomes very much at issue," Cochran told a reporter on July 18, 1994. "It could be a very powerful issue...I think you'll see the defense really seek to exploit it." And so the defense did, with Cochran leading the way.

His emotionally-charged exchange with Darden, the most emotional debate I have ever seen in any courtroom, had a profound, immediate and unexpected effect on me. When Darden pronounced the N-word the "dirtiest, filthiest, nastiest word in the English language," I had to shake my head. Thinking I was talking under my breath and only to myself, I said "Bullshit!"

As Darden spoke, I had flashed immediately on several other words I consider just as offensive: kike, wop, spic, nip, chink and others. But my sotto voce comment was to lead to my most bitter confrontation of the entire trial. After the court session, as I walked from the 12th floor press room to the snack bar one floor up, I was accosted and upbraided by Andrea Ford, veteran reporter for the *Los Angeles Times* and a black woman. "I heard what you said down there!" she snapped. "That's the single most racist thing I've heard from a reporter during this whole trial!"

"Andrea," I tried to explain, "I wasn't saying that's not a horrible word. I was only saying others are just as bad." I felt torn inside. To be labeled a racist by a respected colleague was the most upsetting thing that had happened to me during a most disturbing trial. I instantly remembered my parents, both now dead, and how they had been forced to flee from country to country to country to escape the racist genocide of Adolf Hitler. I though about my freshman year at Atlanta's Emory University, when I was arrested for sitting in with black students from Morehouse College at a segregated lunch counter. And I remembered my years as a checker and conciliator for the Westside Fair Housing Council in Los Angeles, with landlords occasionally pulling pistols on me when I confronted them with evidence of their discrimination against blacks, Chinese, Latinos and others.

But Andrea wasn't listening. She simply wasn't interested. "You just don't understand. It's the whole black experience," she said. "You just can't understand what that word means." I thought I could talk to her, and I desperately wanted to free myself of her odious accusation. But she was having no part of it, walking away angrily after venting at me, leaving me with nothing to do but shrug my shoulders and go back to work.

If merely debating about the N-word could have that impact on two experienced reporters who had not only heard the word often before, but were supposed to be objective observers of the trial, I could only imagine the effect it might have on the jurors. Fuhrman's use of the N-word and his lying about it essentially turned the Simpson case around. With the entry of Fuhrman's past racial epithets, the trial became a race case. Once it did, the prosecution was probably doomed.

Ito realized this. He tried hard—more than once—to limit the use defense lawyers could make of Fuhrman's racist expressions. His first attempt at setting limits came shortly after the Darden-Cochran exchange when he ruled that Fuhrman could not be questioned about racist remarks he made in a failed 1981 attempt to get an LAPD pension. Too far in the past, Ito said. But the judge gave the defense a chance to show that remarks Fuhrman made about five years later to real estate broker Kathleen Bell were relevant. Once they convinced him of this, he had to allow her to testify about her contacts with the detective. "If the challenged racial epithet was used in a relevant incident, it will be heard in court," Ito ruled.

All this meant that much of Fuhrman's racist history would never be heard by the jury. In the pension case, Fuhrman told one psychiatrist examining his claim that he was "tired of having a bunch of Mexicans and niggers that should be in prison telling (him) they weren't going to do something." The jury never heard that.

ELIAS: Judge Ito called the media a pack of "jackals" that regularly "poisoned" the jury pool, but the real poison was the way he systematically dismissed the most informed potential jurors and did little to control the lawyers.

SCHATZMAN: Obviously, Ito agreed with me in that even well-read people aren't necessarily the smartest ones you could find to sit on a jury. After all, if they can't follow simple instructions, how smart can they really be?

ELIAS: Bill Hodgman wasn't sick yet, but daily confrontations like this early one with Johnnie Cochran almost killed him. The absence of his low-key, sensible reasoning at the finish allowed Cochran's histrionics to carry the day.

SCHATZMAN: Like Johnnie Cochran, Bill Hodgman wore nice ties and was generally an honorable man. But it wasn't Cochran who nearly killed him. It was D.A. Gil Garcetti's meddling that nearly sent him to the morgue.

ELIAS: Marcia Clark's aggressiveness never played well with the mostly female jury. Did they expect her to meekly submit to Cochran's machinations?

SCHATZMAN: Marcia Clark suffered from the same discrimination that black people suffer from—not being taken seriously. She was considered "bitchy," not tenacious. That wasn't fair. But it was the media, not the jury, that sold her short.

ELIAS: Ron Shipp seemed like a pretty reliable witness—to me and most white people. But his standing with the mostly black jury plainly dropped after Carl Douglas questioned him aggressively about his past alcoholism.

SCHATZMAN: Credibility my ass. Ron Shipp was a Simpson hanger-on, a freeloader and a drunk. But to white folks, he was talking their language. He's like the inarticulate Negro who television news camera crews seek out for interviews just to embarrass black people. Shipp was an embarrassment to all of us.

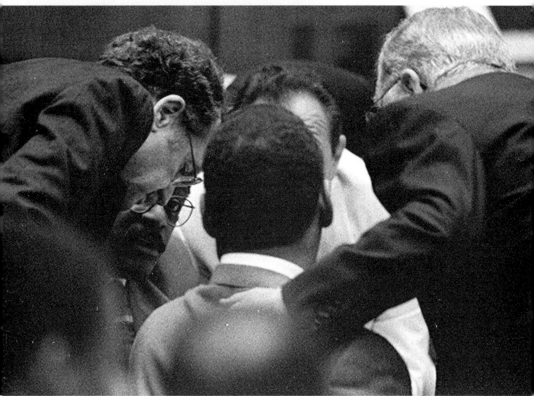

ELIAS: It quickly became obvious that O.J. Simpson was the quarterback of the defense team. Judge Ito even let him use the courtroom for a classic reaming of his key players.

SCHATZMAN: So what if Simpson was the quarterback of the defense team? After all, as the Dallas Cowboys' Jerry Jones would say: "It's my money." And he got his money's worth: They won the case for him.

ELIAS: Denise Brown's weeping wasn't enough to compensate for the prosecution's failure to exploit the full implications of the spousal abuse she described and the many other incidents that were simply ignored.

SCHATZMAN: There is no doubt that Denise Brown's sorrow was legitimate. Problem is, however, with respect to her distaste for Simpson's former life as a spousal abuser, she wasn't too distraught to ask Simpson for a $5,000 loan, which he gave her. By the way, Denise, did you ever pay the money back?

ELIAS: Dennis claims O.J.'s pigeon-toed walk proves he didn't leave the the bloody foot- prints. Is this a pigeon-toed walk? There was no sign of inward-pointing toes as Simpson led cops around his house.

SCHATZMAN: If Mary Ann Gerchas can't tell a Latino from an Anglo at 50 paces, how can you tell if O.J. Simpson is walking pigeon-toed from a side-view photo? What turnip truck do you think I fell off of?

ELIAS: Simpson, the un- sworn witness, showed the jury his unscarred middle finger, demon- strating that it had healed completely, but more than six months had passed since it was injured on the night of the murder. This didn't prove he cut it on a bro- ken glass in his Chicago hotel room, nor did it prove he had arthritis.

SCHATZMAN: The judge wouldn't allow the testi- mony of the American Airlines reservationist to explain how she heard Simpson break a glass in the hotel in Chicago. That's why there was no proof. Ito, the prosecu- tion's star witness, wouldn't allow it.

ELIAS: F. Lee Bailey completely destroyed the credibility of Detective Mark Fuhrman by digging up the tapes that revealed his racism in remarks to writer Laura Hart McKinny— knowledge the prosecution should have had before calling him as a witness.

SCHATZMAN: AARP members take note: F. Lee Bailey still has it when lawyers half his age are trying to figure out where the restrooms are in the courthouse. Be proud, seniors.

ELIAS: Barry Scheck demonstrated to the jury how small a milliliter of blood really is, but it was ridiculous to believe police could spread that tiny amount as far and wide as he claimed they did.

SCHATZMAN: Barry, Barry quite contrary. How does your status grow? Your critics hate you because you kicked the prosecution's ass. But as the late Roy Cohn said, "Don't blame me for your inadequacies."

ELIAS: The prosecution case began coming apart when criminalist Dennis Fung admitted to making many errors from the opening moments of the evidence collection process.

SCHATZMAN: Dennis Fung was, and still is, an honorable man. His problem was that he was the victim of his own fallibility. The defense took advantage of that by pointing out the flaws in his work. All's fair in love, war and murder trials.

ELIAS: Andrea Mazzola's upright posture never deserted her, but her bosses also never explained why they put a trainee on their biggest murder case in decades.

SCHATZMAN: Don't blame Andrea Mazzola for being assigned to the Simpson case. She was a trainee who apparently didn't do a bad job, but the prosecution was more than willing to see her thrown to the wolves.

ELIAS: Christopher Darden was right. The verdicts proved the accuracy of his passionate argument that introduction of the N-word into the trial—even once—would doom the prosecution.

SCHATZMAN: In court, Christopher Darden was a crybaby whenever he didn't get his way. And out of court he proved to be just as materialistic as the rest of us, arriving in a limousine at the Goldmans' dinner in the prosecution's honor.
How gauche.

ELIAS: The Louis Vuitton garment bag, completely stuffed when Simpson pal Robert Kardashian carried it away from Simpson's house the morning after the murders, turned up in court completely empty. What's missing?

SCHATZMAN: The bag, the bag, the bag. What's in the bag? Hell if I know. Cathy Randa says it was clothes. Is she not to be believed? I'd believe her before I believed Ron Shipp. Wouldn't you?

ELIAS: Jurors yawned through much of Coroner Lakshmanan Sathyavagiswaran's dramatic reenactment of the way Nicole Simpson's throat was slashed. Maybe they wished it was a real knife he'd been holding at the throat of prosecutor Brian Kelberg, whose long-winded presentations they always dreaded.

SCHATZMAN: Dr. Sathyavagiswaran's problem was that he never played a direct role in the autopsies. Dr. Irwin Golden did, and that's what led the jury and others like me to think long and hard about whether or not the prosecution and the good doctor were hiding something.

ELIAS: Simpson the actor tried to prove the glove didn't fit. But somehow he got it on. And TV pictures of him as a cold-weather football broadcaster showed the same sort of gloves in just as tight a fit.

SCHATZMAN: The glove didn't fit: It's as simple as that. He could never really get it on his hand. But to Tom, Simpson has gone from being Othello to Blackstone the magician—one who can make his hand grow bigger right in the courtroom.

ELIAS: If Laura Hart McKinny hadn't supplied evidence that Fuhrman often used the N-word, the jury might never have known he did, and they might have believed the rest of his testimony.

SCHATZMAN: Fuhrman was fingered not just by McKinny but by several other people who testified that they heard him use the N-word in front of them. And three of them were white.

ELIAS: Philip Vannatter lied—a little—when he finally swore out a search warrant. But you won't find evidence of any other untruths from him, certainly not enough to justify Cochran's final argument poster featuring "Vannatter's Big Lies."

SCHATZMAN: Once a liar always a liar. Leopards don't change their spots. Philip Vannatter didn't have to lie, but he did. Whose fault is that? As usual, Cochran was right on target.

ELIAS: If Mark Fuhrman hadn't found the glove, if the prosecution hadn't insisted on using the evidence he and other cops seized unconstitutionally at Simpson's house, he wouldn't have had to testify, then take the Fifth. With Fuhrman, they lost the case; without him, they'd have had a much better chance.

SCHATZMAN: As California jury instructions say, once you've caught a witness in a lie, you can presume that everything else he says could also be untrue.

ELIAS: During final arguments, Johnnie Cochran wore a stocking cap to demonstrate how common such hats are, and how easy it would have been for African American hairs to get on the one found near the bodies.

SCHATZMAN: Here we go again, picking on the nigger lawyer. White people are just going to have to live with the fact that Cochran did his job, and that's why he won. Isn't that what black America was told when Judge Joyce Karlin gave a convicted killer, Soon Ja Du, her "get-out-of-jail-free" papers after gunning down Latasha Harlins?

ELIAS: Like most white Americans, I was annoyed by Simpson's smirk when the not guilty verdicts were announced—but outraged and depressed by the jubilation with which his exoneration was received by most of black America.

SCHATZMAN: If you were found "not guilty" by a jury, what would you do—scowl? I reacted to the verdict with the same jubilation as millions of other African Americans, and I'm outraged by white America's self-righteous denunciation of that jury's final judgment.

But defense lawyers were determined that the jury would hear from Bell. Setting up her testimony, defense lawyer F. Lee Bailey staged one of the most dramatic encounters of the trial in his cross-examination of Fuhrman.

"You say under oath that you have not addressed any black person as a nigger or spoken about black people as niggers in the past 10 years, Detective Fuhrman?" Bailey asked.

"That's what I'm saying, sir," Fuhrman answered firmly.

"So that anyone who comes to this court and quotes you as using that word in dealing with African Americans would be a liar, would they not, Detective Fuhrman?" Bailey went on.

"Yes, they would," responded Fuhrman.

"All of them?" Bailey challenged, hinting there would be several.

"All of them," Fuhrman answered.

With that exchange, Bailey signaled that he intended to call multiple witnesses to contradict what Fuhrman said. It would be months before he got the chance, and by then, his task had become infinitely easier. The discovery in the summer of 1995 that Fuhrman had given a series of tape-recorded interviews to Laura Hart McKinny, an aspiring screenwriter who took the tapes with her when she moved to a teaching job in North Carolina, proved Fuhrman a perjurer at best and at worst an unabashed, braggadocious, violent, hateful racist. No matter how many of Fuhrman's friends and former patrol partners insisted that the tapes distorted his ideas and his personality, they couldn't deny what the man had said.

"Nigger drivin' a Porsche that doesn't look like he's got a $300 suit on, you always stop him," Fuhrman told McKinny in one interview, as she gathered information for a screenplay about Los Angeles police. "How do you intellectualize when you punch the hell out of a nigger?" he asked in another session. "When I came on the job, all my training officers were big guys and knowledgeable. Some nigger'd get in their face, they just spin 'em around, choke 'em out until they dropped," he said in a third meeting. "First thing, anything out of a nigger's mouth for the first five or six sentences is a fucking lie," he added in yet another session.

There were Fuhrman statements claiming that police routinely apply choke holds and kicks to blacks, but hold back in affluent white areas. "You have to be a switch hitter," he said. "You have to be able to look at your area and look at how you talk to people." Segments about brutality as a standard police practice led to wholesale questioning of the LAPD, not just Fuhrman.

Just as he had in January, once the tapes surfaced, Ito tried to minimize the impact of Fuhrman's racist rantings by allowing the defense to play only two references to the N-word for the jury. His ruling drew vituperative criticism from Cochran and other defense lawyers, who feared they might not be able to make their point about Fuhrman. But two was more than enough. The faces of the jurors lost their usual impassive mien when they heard the N-word. Several took on angry looks. Others looked grievously hurt.

The tapes clothed Bell and several other anti-Fuhrman defense witnesses in a new cloak of trustworthiness, as prosecutors could no longer credibly try to discredit them. They also eliminated any chance for a second Bailey-Fuhrman confrontation before the jury. When Fuhrman was hauled back into court after the tapes had been played, he was questioned by Gerald Uelmen with no jury present. "Was the testimony you gave at the preliminary hearing in this case completely truthful?" Uelmen asked. "Have you ever falsified a police report?" And "Did you plant or manufacture any evidence in this case?" After each question, Fuhrman consulted his lawyer, Darryl Mounger, then answered, "I wish to assert my Fifth Amendment privilege."

The tapes had already established that Fuhrman lied to Bailey and the jury about his use of the N-word. Now his refusal to answer created suspicion in the public mind about all the key evidence he found in the case: The bloody glove he picked up behind Simpson's guesthouse, the blood drop on the left front door of Simpson's car and blood drops on Simpson's driveway. Bailey suggested early in the trial that Fuhrman might have planted the glove, taking it from the crime scene—where the killer dropped a matching glove—and carrying it with him when he vaulted the ivy-covered stone wall of Simpson's estate.

Even if there was some question about the relevance of Fuhrman's use of racial epithets in the mid-1980s, there was no doubt about the relevance of the questions Uelmen asked

Fuhrman in that September 1995 repeat appearance. Nor was there much doubt about the importance of the letter that real estate agent Bell wrote defense attorneys in July 1994, detailing her mid-'80s encounter with Fuhrman in a Marine Corps recruiting station in the Los Angeles suburb of Redondo Beach. She testified that she wrote it only after seeing Fuhrman testify on TV during the preliminary hearing, implying that, if she hadn't seen his face, she wouldn't have been certain it was the same man who had spoken so offensively to her. Without TV, it's most likely that the Fuhrman tapes would never have surfaced either. They came to light when a cleaning woman left a message at Bailey's Boston office. Without the massive coverage, it's highly unlikely that she would have known the tapes had any significance.

In her letter, Bell said Fuhrman told her that whenever he stopped a car bearing a racially-mixed couple and they were doing nothing wrong, he would invent an offense. Jurors said later that statement, repeated under oath to the jury near the end of the defense case, had impacted heavily on them. It was relevant because Fuhrman knew for years that Simpson and the former Nicole Brown were a mixed couple. He had met them when he was summoned to the Rockingham mansion on the 1985 domestic-violence call in which Simpson shattered the windshield of Nicole's car with a baseball bat.

So Fuhrman's presence in the case ensured that race would be a critical issue from start to finish, no matter what disclaimers Shapiro issued. And once they had him testify in the preliminary hearing, prosecutors were stuck with him. If they hadn't called him as a witness, the defense would have. Fuhrman's racism and the one lie in which he was definitely caught created the single largest problem prosecutors encountered in the entire case: the question of police credibility. Even before the tapes were played, revealing the litany of alleged illegal police acts in which Fuhrman said he took part, his presence had raised the issue of whether the LAPD could be trusted.

As early as March 1995, just after Fuhrman's initial testimony, longtime prosecutors recognized this problem. "The prosecution's fear is that the eight black jurors (as the panel was then constituted) won't just squint at Fuhrman, but at all the police officer testimony," said Ira Reiner, a former two-term district attorney of Los Angeles County. "Fuhrman was the prosecution's best witness during the preliminary hearing, but if the racial stuff comes out, he's a goner." It came out.

Once it did, the credibility of all LAPD officers became an open issue. It was only because Fuhrman had established that some cops tell untruths that Cochran could credibly present a large poster entitled "(Philip) Vannatter's big lies" during his final argument, challenging most of the testimony of one of the two lead detectives on the case. Cochran even tried to join Vannatter with Fuhrman in the juror's minds, calling the two "twin devils of deception."

"You can't trust him," Cochran said of Vannatter in his closing argument. "You can't believe anything he says...When you are lying at the beginning, you will be lying at the end."

He attacked Vannatter for participating in the obviously orchestrated police story that Simpson was not considered a suspect when detectives went to his house on the night of the crimes. And he borrowed Ito's words later, saying Vannatter displayed a "reckless disregard for the truth" when he belatedly swore out a search warrant for Simpson's estate, saying Simpson had taken off on an unplanned trip to Chicago. The trip actually had been planned in advance and Vannatter knew it. Cochran also asked jurors to wonder why Vannatter brought a vial of Simpson's blood to the crime scene, suggesting that he or other officers may have sprinkled tiny amounts of that blood around in an effort to frame Simpson. This had a particular impact because the jury majority was black. "We're more familiar with the 'injustice' system than whites," my colleague Dennis Schatzman told me when it became clear many blacks did not trust the police. "We've seen how often they plant evidence and frame people."

All this might have had little impact if the defense had not first established that Fuhrman was a liar. But the repercussion from Fuhrman's tapes and untruths went far beyond the case itself. It spurred an internal investigation by the LAPD and an independent probe by the federal Justice Department's Civil Rights Division. It also aroused unprecedented public skepticism of the police department among parts of the citizenry that normally side with police. Everything from the department's evidence-gathering techniques to its training of new officers and the way it handles pension applications came under attack. So did the continuing presence on the force of at least three dozen cops who had been identified two years earlier as "problem officers" by the Christopher Commission, formed to investigate police practices in the wake of the 1992 riots and headed by Warren Christopher, who went on to become Secretary of State.

Schatzman writes, "The racism of one person is no big deal to white people unless it's exposed in an embarrassing way." But he's wrong when he tars all whites with that racist brush. White people joined blacks in the freedom rides of the 1960s. I know. I was arrested doing it. White people gave the Reverend Martin Luther King Jr. his Nobel Peace Prize. Without a white President named Lyndon Baines Johnson, there would be no Voting Rights Act. Warren Christopher, principal author of the Christopher Commission report, is also a white man. Plenty of whites have fought long and hard against racism.

It also makes no sense to suggest, as Schatzman does and Cochran did in his final argument, that the fact a racist cop like Fuhrman was involved in the early moments of the Simpson investigation should render all the evidence suspect. Fuhrman touched only a little bit of the evidence. He had nothing to do with the vast majority. If the fact that he liked to use the N-word caused the jury to ignore and distrust all the evidence Fuhrman never handled, then Darden was correct: The N-word alone was enough to blind the jurors and warp their judgment.

The race issue also quickly invaded the jury itself. When one-time juror Willie Cravin was tossed off the panel amid charges that he tried to intimidate another juror with harsh glares and that he deliberately brushed into her on an elevator, he cried racism. "It seems like the jury is on trial, not the Juice," he said just after his dismissal. He denied intimidating anyone. "Staring? Intimidating? What is that?" he asked. And he claimed later that "Any black man who does not grin and laugh becomes a menacing figure."

Another bounced black juror, Jeannette Harris, complained that white jurors got first choice in selecting videotaped movies to watch. White jurors also got a gym of their own at the Inter-

Continental Hotel, where the jury was quartered, she griped. Whites and Latins got better telephone privileges and, occasionally, longer shopping trips than blacks, she charged. She told of racial disputes on the jury, including one incident where a Latina juror and a white woman juror both hit a black male panelist as they walked behind him while he watched a movie.

Through all this, I continued to see the case as plain and simple murder. Yes, I believed, it was possible for the police to lie and for some cops to be racist, and for Simpson still to be guilty. But such distinctions were not part of Cochran's final statement to the jury, one that struck me as sheer demagoguery. Especially offensive to me as the son of Holocaust survivors was his comparison of Fuhrman to Adolf Hitler. Even if everything Fuhrman claimed he did on the McKinny tapes were true, he never approached being a Hitler. Cochran's defense of his remark was that Fuhrman's acts were like those of a fascist. But Hitler had followers and sought to take over first a nation and then the world. Fuhrman had no followers, never aspired to being a leader and wanted only a pension, so he could move away from the ethnics he so scorned. So as the Anti-Defamation League said immediately on hearing Cochran's speech, his Hitler metaphor trivialized a profound historical tragedy.

Cochran led into his Hitler comparison by noting that Fuhrman had told witness Bell, "If I had my way...all the niggers would be gathered together and burned." He suggested that this evoked images of the ovens in Nazi concentration camps and that unless someone stopped Fuhrman, he could develop into a Hitler-like scourge.

That argument sent the father of murder victim Ronald Goldman into a righteous rage. "This man (Cochran) is the worst kind of human being imaginable," Fred Goldman told reporters after hustling down to the first-floor press conference area during a break in Cochran's speech. "He's a sick man. He ought to be put away."

Even Shapiro spoke out later against parts of Cochran's closing argument. The man who had promised to keep race out of the trial now said his colleague had played "the race card from the bottom of the deck."

Ito could have stopped much of this, but stood by mute as it all happened. Much of Cochran's closing argument should probably have been ruled out of order and stricken from the record. It was a blatant attempt to persuade jurors to disregard the hard evidence before them and send a message about racism rather than judge the case itself. The jury's job, Cochran said, was to be a community watchdog. "You police the police," he said. "You police them by your verdict."

But the police were not on trial here. There was every possibility that Fuhrman, for one, might actually be put on trial later for the perjury the tapes revealed he committed. But it wasn't the jury's job to try him or the rest of the police force. It would take a different jury to try Fuhrman.

Ito knew all this and could have stopped Cochran at any time. But he didn't, and by failing to act, he essentially condoned the act of jury nullification Cochran asked for.

"If you don't speak out, if you don't stand up, if you don't do what's right, this kind of (police) conduct will continue on forever," Cochran thundered. But he never noted that if the jury didn't stand up, if the jury didn't do what was right with Simpson, the defendant's own vicious conduct might also be repeated. What's more, Cochran said, if jurors didn't do what he asked, "We will never have an ideal society." Did he mean that an ideal society is one in which O.J. Simpson is free to beat women and to murder again? Cochran put a heavy load on the twelve jurors when he invited them to ignore the evidence and allow race and Fuhrman's racism to become the deciding factors in a murder trial.

To me, that became the key point: The jury was not urged to find Simpson innocent on the basis of hard evidence. Instead, it was asked to free him as a message to society. And it did indeed send a message, the one Christopher Darden had predicted it might: Race and Mark Fuhrman's use of the word "nigger" had overwhelmed all other factors from the moment the N-word entered the case.

DENNIS SCHATZMAN

Eenie, Meenie, Miney, Moe, Catch A N...

Mr. Dennis Schatzman
C/O The Los Angeles Centinel (sic)
3800 Crenshaw Blvd.
Los Angeles, CA 90038

Re: Los Angeles Police Department
Detective Mark Fuhrman

Dear Mr. Schatzman:

The undersigned represents L.A.P.D. Detective Mark Fuhrman. It has come to my attention that you made the following statement on KFI Radio at approximately 3:30 p.m. on Monday, February 13, 1995 regarding Detective Fuhrman:

"He has a history of planting evidence."

When asked by the talk show host when Detective Fuhrman allegedly planted evidence in the past, you replied:

"Oh, it was a long time ago."

The purpose of this letter is to advise you that your statements were false and defamatory and tended to subject Detective Fuhrman up to scorn, ridicule and contempt amongst those who heard your outrageous and malicious comments.

Please be advised that demand is hereby made that you immediately make a public retraction of your aforementioned comments as well as issue a public apology to Detective Fuhrman. In this connection, please furnish us within forty-eight hours of the date of receipt by you of this letter with a tape recording of your public retraction and apology which, we also demand be made through the facilities of KFI Radio.

In the event you chose (sic) to ignore the demand for a public retraction and apology, you should understand that we intend to file an action in the Los Angeles County Superior Court against you for damages for defamation per se.

Very truly yours,
Robert H. Tourtelot

The above letter begins my up-close and personal relationship with former LAPD Detective Mark Fuhrman. Or rather, his ambulance-chasing lawyer Bob Tourtelot, who went from one anti-Simpson client to another in the course of the trial. What this letter indicates to me is two things: one, that this case was tangentially an issue about race, and two, that Mr. Fuhrman and his attorney must have had a guilty conscience about the issue of planting evidence.

Two days after I got that letter, on KFI, Tourtelot and I engaged in a battle of who will blink first. On the air, John and Ken, the station's afternoon sick-puppy talk-show hosts and in my opinion, unapologetic racists, called me at my office after Tourtelot refused to go on the air with me and asked me if I was going to retract my comments and apologize. My response was straight out of the TV sitcom "Alice:" "When donkeys fly."

Now let's go back to the beginning, when Fuhrman first testified during the preliminary hearing. Fuhrman claimed that at 5 o'clock in the morning after the murders, he spotted what he believed was a blood spot on Simpson's Ford Bronco the size of a large-headed pin. From there, he and his colleagues felt it necessary to violate all rules of search and seizure and scale the wall of Simpson's estate to save whoever was dying inside. No guns were drawn, mind you. But that's what they did. And the judge fell for that one. About a half hour later, Fuhrman rousted awake Kato Kaelin and searched his room. Stupid Kato did not have enough sense to tell this guy, "Get the fuck out of my room till you bring me a piece of paper with a judge's signature and seal on it." Had Kato said that, he would have been within his rights. But he also would have gotten his ass kicked. Because that's the way Mark Fuhrman is.

During his testimony at the preliminary hearing, Fuhrman said two things that sent up a red flag in my cranium. The first was, when he claimed that he found a bloody glove behind Kato's bungalow, he said he got a tremendous rush of adrenalin. The second was when he said that, back at the scene of the murders, he was standing on the balcony and saw "them"—meaning the gloves—lying in the foliage. Now, most people probably passed that last comment off as a slip. But judging from his past history and what we later learned to be his stated purpose in the LAPD— planting evidence on black men caught with white women—his comment was worth seriously noting. My colleague Tom Elias will go to his grave believing that this case had nothing to do with race. But the fact that a black man is accused of killing two white people, particularly a beautiful blonde white woman, automatically makes it a race case.

There is ample precedent for that, and anyone who doesn't agree with that is lying through his teeth. Let's go back to 1908 when Jack Johnson, the first black to win the heavyweight boxing title, married a white woman. Whites were outraged, and two years later Congress passed the Mann Act, named after an Illinois congressman, which prohibited the "transportation, coercion or enticement of females across state lines for the purpose of prostitution or immoral activities." The woman was his wife, so there's no way he was breaking any law, but since she was undeniably white, they decided not to recognize his marriage and used the law to run him out of the country or face prosecution and imprisonment.

In 1931, the famous case of the Scottsboro Boys again pointed out how the law could railroad black men who were accused of raping a white woman. Never mind the fact that these men had airtight alibis. They were placed in jail for upwards of eighteen years because everyone in the courtroom except them was white.

In 1954, two white men walked out of an Oxford, Mississippi, courtroom free as birds when an all-white jury acquitted them of killing fourteen-year-old Emmitt Till. Till's "crime" was that he whistled at a white woman and, in the still of the night, these courageous white boys dragged Till out of his grandfather's house and slaughtered him. So I say again, if there is anyone who doesn't think that this case, based on who was the defendant and who were the victims, doesn't touch the racial fibers in our bodies, they're full of shit.

Now before we get back to Fuhrman, let's deal with this issue of race. In the opening of his chapter on this subject, my colleague quotes Robert Shapiro's July 18, 1994 comment that "Race is not and will not be an issue in this defense." Now who did he think he was kidding? After all, it was Robert ("pure as the driven snow") Shapiro who first introduced the world to the real Mark Fuhrman. For it was he who leaked Fuhrman's Marine and LAPD psychological histories to Jeffrey Toobin of *The New Yorker* magazine. So I laughed my ass off when I saw Shapiro feigning embarrassment and shame because race had become a factor in the trial. Translation: What he meant to say was that since he is now going to be representing rich white boys in Beverly Hills, he needed to get his white-boy credentials in order.

One of the great highlights this facade produced came when Christopher Darden, playing the role of the classic black apologist, passionately got up before the court and literally begged Judge Ito not to let the N-word be interjected in this case. This led me to believe that Darden knew something about Fuhrman and possibly other cops involved in the case. Now I never claimed that Darden was a stupid man. What I claim is that he did some stupid things during the trial. And this was one of them.

Why? Because one of the things that a good lawyer learns is not to raise an issue like that, because when you do, you draw attention to it. So after he made those comments, everybody started thinking about it. Especially some of these do-gooder journalists and commentators who claimed to be covering this trial. What Darden should have done is what the late James Mason did in the movie *The Verdict*. When confronted with having to interview a black anesthesiologist, Mason, playing a lawyer who was defending a hospital accused of incapacitating a patient, told his charges, "Don't even raise the question of the doctor's blackness (read: inferiority)." What he did was just get a minor black rookie associate to sit at the table while the doctor was on the stand. Subtlety is everything.

But no. Darden had to go out and say that the mention of the N-word would be something that black people couldn't handle. But I don't remember anyone throwing up or getting woozy and sick behind hearing the N-word during the trial. Do you?

Indeed, the N-word was a part of the trial; but it was a part of the trial very subtly, before Fuhrman was exposed. Because, you see, let us not kid ourselves, black people are called niggers and everybody knows it. And when a nigger is accused of killing a white woman, his chances of gaining an acquittal become slim and none—unless he's rich and famous.

There is one notable exception in these here parts. Rock star Rick James went straight to jail, did not pass "go," when he and his white girlfriend were accused of torturing another white girl during a weekend of freebasing. The poor little girl told authorities how they burned her and forced her to have sex with both of them, but James said that the little woman was lovin' every minute of it until the drugs ran out. A judge set bail at one million dollars on a man who owns a mansion in the area, was gainfully employed and not a threat to run. One million dollars. That's ludicrous. The purpose of bail is to assure that a defendant will show up for all actions in court and that he is not a threat to his community. In my opinion, those kinds of unreasonable bonds are restricted only to blacks and browns. Because that's the way these judges are around here. So in that case, James' money didn't mean diddly.

As we said earlier, Fuhrman was the man who found a bloody glove on Simpson's property. He's also the man who bragged down through the years that if he saw a black man with a white woman, say in a car, he would pull them over and find some reason to arrest him. How far does his history go back? During the trial I was contacted by a retired black Seattle fireman who recognized Fuhrman as a man he had a confrontation with at the Seattle-Tacoma International Airport in 1975. At that time, the fireman was on duty at the airport doing inspections with three colleagues when a tall figure approached his three white associates to ask them about wood-burning stoves. The black fireman, a native of Oklahoma, knew something about wood-burning stoves and offered some advice. The man turned around with fire in his eyes and told the brother that he wasn't talking to him. For the next half hour, according to the fireman, the two engaged in heated arguments and the man told him that he was on his way to L.A. to be a police officer and he was going to put "niggers like you" in jail. And that if he ever caught his kind in the company of a white woman, he would beat them and then put them in jail. That man's name was Mark Fuhrman.

What bothered me about the laziness of my colleagues is that virtually none of them, with the exception of myself, ever bothered to look into Fuhrman's past. Now what am I to glean from that? Essentially, that the racism of a person is no big deal to white people unless it's exposed in an embarrassing way. So for eight months, the racist Mark Fuhrman was allowed to live the life of a hero because my white colleagues refused to believe or simply ignored the fact that the most important witness in this case was a hard-core racist. That thought sickened me.

Consider the remarks of *Washington Post* columnist Richard Cohen. During an appearance with me on NBC's morningshow "Today," Cohen expressed shock and dismay that Fuhrman would make the kind of racist comments that were revealed in Laura Hart McKinny's tapes. He claimed with a straight face that he had never heard anyone talk like that before. Bear in mind that this is the same Richard Cohen who started a firestorm in Washington, D.C., in 1988 when his paper introduced its *Washington Post Magazine.* In its premier issue, Cohen wrote an article agreeing that store owners should not allow young black men in their stores after dark. I waited seven years to get that biased white boy back. And I did by spanking him on national television. I asked him, "Why is it that you white people always express shock and outrage only when racism is exposed and not before?" He blabbered and blustered and stumbled until the interviewer jumped in and saved his ass.

Let's stay on this issue of motive. You remember the fact that O.J. Simpson was the evil, rotten, stupid son-of-a-bitch who beat his wife. The prosecution virtually labeled this an open-and-shut case because almost that and that alone—with the exception of the blood—made Simpson the murderer of Nicole Brown Simpson and Ronald Lyle Goldman. But Fuhrman, who bragged of wanting to plant evidence on black men with white women, was not judged by the same standards with respect to motive. And that's bullshit.

Just to show you how sick this motherfucker was, I refer you to the tapes of Professor McKinny. I'll just give you a few examples because it makes me mad just thinking about it.

Fuhrman: "Nigger driving a Porsche that doesn't look like he's got a $300 suit on, you always stop him.

Fuhrman: "And I want you to search them."

McKinny: "Why are you even talking to them?"

Fuhrman: "Because they're niggers. You stop them. You see who they are."

McKinny: "OK, do you have any probable cause or do you just want to talk to them?"

Fuhrman: "Probable cause? You're God."

McKinny: "What do you do if someone calls you a name? What do you do?"

Fuhrman: "Are there witnesses or are there not? Let's set the stage."

McKinny: "If there are witnesses, what do you do, say you are in front of the show telling people in line to move out of the street and it's kind of a minor situation. Somebody in line calls you a pig."

Fuhrman: "He goes to jail."

McKinny: "He goes to jail?"

Fuhrman: "Interfering. He was interfering with my duties. 148 of the penal code."

McKinny: "So you immediately take him to jail?"

Fuhrman: "Of course, he's so shocked that he immediately won't do (what I tell him), so he immediately gets thrown to the ground, so he immediately gets struck. I don't take anything in that uniform that I wouldn't take out of that uniform. Well, I'm sure he will have, because if he's got that attitude, he's probably gotten several tickets from policemen and he hasn't taken care of them. He's going to go to the station because he won't have any identification. Because he gives me his drivers license. I'll just rip the fucker up."

McKinny: "Have you done that before?"

Fuhrman: (Nods yes) "That's not falsifying a report. That's putting a criminal in jail. That's being a policeman."

These are some of the sage quotes that didn't make it to the jury. And there are some 39 others that they didn't hear either. Most people (read: white people) don't put much credibility in Mr. Fuhrman's beliefs with respect to black men, but this is a case involving a black man accused of killing a white woman for which he is a prime witness. To hear white people, we're supposed to shake this off and grin and bear it yet again. Why is it that we always have to grin and bear it and they don't? *Why?*

If one is to believe former LAPD Chief Daryl Gates, the Mark Fuhrmans of the force are just aberrations. "LAPD officers just don't do the things that Fuhrman brags about," Gates told a talk show audience. But that's not what black officers tell you. What are they, paranoid? Many of them have told me horror stories about how they've overheard white officers call suspects "niggers" right in front of their faces. And with no apologies.

The whole world remembers watching and hearing the tapes of the officers beating Rodney King to a bloody pulp and hearing in the background officers calling him "nigger." There was very little comment about that, was there? And even during this double murder trial, actor Brian Tyson, who played the role of O.J. Simpson in a Hollywood spoof called *Jury Duty*, was sitting in a car with his white girlfriend in the parking lot of a movie studio rehearsing some lines when two of LAPD's finest, from the North Hollywood division, snatched him out of the car and threw him up against the vehicle. Despite the protestations of his girlfriend, officer Jay Heccavarria ignored her denials and kept asking, "Did the nigger hit you? We don't want another Nicole on our hands."

When I called the station to find out whether they would investigate the situation or the incident, I was summarily ignored. Had I been with the *Los Angeles Times*, perhaps they would have halfheartedly looked into the matter. But I wasn't, so they didn't. When I told the story to the Police Protective League's Dennis Zine, he told me that it was preposterous and that LAPD officers don't use the N-word. He actually said that shit to me. Like, what kind of fool did he think I was? What offended me most was that I wrote a front-page article with a color picture of Tyson with Kato Kaelin in the *Sentinel* and no one at headquarters, including Chief Willie Williams, bothered to investigate. That was a big insult to me. And after that incident, and the one in which the chief publicly praised Mark Fuhrman after his February testimony, I wrote the chief off. He can go back to Philadelphia for all I care, and when they run his ass out of town, I won't lift a finger to help him. In my opinion, you're either with or against us on issues of racial prejudice. If you're not part of the solution, you *are* the problem.

I reiterate my learned opinion, and since I'm the only journalist covering this trial who ever sat on the bench and ruled on the admissibility of evidence, I say unequivocally that Fuhrman's comments about his planting evidence and performing racist acts against black men with white women is just as admissible as Ron Shipp's testimony that he heard Simpson say he once dreamed of killing Nicole. I rest my case.

CHAPTER 8
THE WITNESSES

TOM ELIAS

The Importance of the Non-witness

If the glove doesn't fit, you must acquit.
If the glove doesn't fit, you must acquit.

Johnnie Cochran,
Sept. 29, 1995

In plain English, the glove didn't fit.

Brenda Moran (formerly Juror No. 7),
Oct. 4, 1995

There were professional witnesses and witnesses who lied. There were neighbors who heard barking dogs on the night of the murders. There were family members, police and laboratory technicians. Prosecutors and defense attorneys paraded them all before the Simpson jury for more than eight months. But the two lines repeated by Cochran and Moran establish beyond much doubt that the single most important witness was one who never testified under oath: defendant O.J. Simpson.

Other witnesses debated the accuracy of DNA testing, described the precise nature of the wounds suffered by Nicole Brown Simpson and her friend Ronald Goldman and told of walking a veritable pack of dogs in Mrs. Simpson's neighborhood on the night of their murders. But in the end, the testimony that mattered most wasn't testimony at all; it was the way Simpson himself appeared to struggle as he pulled two extra-large Aris gloves onto his hands one day in late June 1995. Defense lawyers immediately recognized the exhibition for what it was: the seminal moment of the trial. "It's Cinderella," Alan Dershowitz told a reporter a short time later. "They tried to shove a slipper on a foot and it didn't fit."

Actually, Simpson's hands did fit into the gloves after a bit of worming and squirming, even though he also wore rubber gloves as he tried on the bloody leather ones found on the night of the murders at the crime scene and behind his house. But his words, spoken without being sworn in as a witness, reverberated across the rest of the trial. "They're too small....They're too tight," he told the jury. Simpson may have been an amateurish actor, but he remembered his lines when they counted most. And because he wasn't a sworn witness, he was never even questioned about the fit or anything else.

He was just one of many potential witnesses never called to the stand in his trial, but he was the only non-witness who actually gave testimony. His statement and demonstration were enough to convince Moran and the other jurors, even though they later saw photographs and videotapes of Simpson wearing either the same or similar gloves while announcing professional football games in wintry Eastern cities. They also heard a Bloomingdale's New York department store buyer named Brenda Vemich testify that she had sold the same or similar gloves to Nicole in 1990.

The fact that prosecutor Christopher Darden opted to try the demonstration before the jury without having tested it beforehand was a classic blunder. It violated one of the most basic rules for trial lawyers: Never even ask a question, let alone put on a demonstration, without knowing the outcome in advance. For months afterward, prosecutors were forced to backtrack, trying to prove that leather gloves can shrink after being bloodied or left out in damp, dewy areas. But those efforts were not enough. Without ever taking an oath, without ever risking perjuring himself, Simpson proved the key witness on his own behalf.

It wasn't his first obvious attempt to sway the jury with his hands. As early as February 1995, he walked from the defense table to the jury box to show off what purported to be an ailment of the middle knuckle on his left middle finger. His lawyers were trying to show that arthritis, not a knife cut, caused the swelling observed on that knuckle by Detective Philip Vannatter the day after the murders. The demonstration came during Robert Shapiro's hostile cross-examination of Vannatter, who said the injuries and cuts he observed on Simpson's hand reinforced his belief that he was questioning the correct suspect.

Earlier, during opening statements, Simpson had also walked to the jury box, limping noticeably, to display a knee scarred by football-related surgeries. Both demonstrations were designed to convince the jury and the television audience that Simpson was physically incapable of committing the murders. But this claim was to be undermined months later by one of his own witnesses, the doctor who examined Simpson during the week after the murders. That doctor, Robert Huizenga, expert on football injuries after years as a team physician for the former Los Angeles Raiders, was forced to conclude on the stand that Simpson was indeed physically capable.

My colleague Dennis Schatzman objects to my noting that Simpson limped only when he was trying to make a point to the jury. Schatzman says that when he's been sitting in a chair for long periods, his own limp becomes more pronounced. That's true for Dennis. I've seen it. But it wasn't true for O.J. in the courtroom. Simpson *never* limped except to make a point, no matter how long he'd been seated to listen to testimony. And no one, not even Schatzman or Johnnie Cochran, ever suggested that the murderer of Nicole Brown Simpson and Ronald Goldman was seated with his legs folded for any length of time before the murders. But Simpson, the actor, knew just when to limp and when not to.

Simpson's demonstrations raised other questions jurors should have wondered about, but which apparently never crossed their minds. One: If Simpson's hand bothered him every time he played golf, why was he out on his front lawn chipping golf balls at the time of the murders, as Cochran claimed in his opening statement? If he limped regularly because of his arthritic knee, why was there never a sign of this disability in either the exercise video he made just weeks before the murders or the home video showing him at his daughter's dance recital on the afternoon of the murders? And why did he never limp when he walked in front of TV cameras while working as a broadcaster? Jurors couldn't know, but reporters often laughed about the fact that Simpson never seemed to limp when entering or leaving the courtroom or the courthouse—except when the jury was watching.

These questions, of course, could have been raised if Simpson had testified. But he never did. The same questions could have been raised by prosecutors in their closing arguments, but they never were. Prosecutors explain their failure to raise these points by saying that time constrained them from using everything in their "mountain of evidence" against Simpson.

The Simpson decision not to testify therefore may have been almost as effective a move as his behavior when he was supposedly struggling to pull on the bloody gloves. For months, he wanted to take the stand. His close friend Lawrence Schiller, co-author of Simpson's jailhouse book *I Want to Tell You*, described Simpson's feelings to me several times in the hallway outside the courtroom. "Imagine how you'd feel if you had spent months listening to people vilify you. You'd want to get up and talk just for the sake of your mother. O.J. definitely does want to," Schiller said as the defense case got underway in July 1995. But Simpson never testified, and the main reason was his poor performance during a mock cross examination conducted by lawyer Christine Arguedas, imported from Emeryville, California, to impersonate prosecutor Marcia Clark. Known for a courtroom manner at least as aggressive as Clark's, Arguedas was said by some observers to have reduced Simpson to stuttering, fumbling and confusion. In later sessions, Simpson did better, but not well enough to convince Cochran and Shapiro that he should risk cross-examination. Cochran indicated for several weeks during the summer of 1995 that he wanted Simpson to testify, but after several other defense witnesses appeared to take some steam out of the prosecution case, the chief defense lawyer was chortling, not worrying. "It looked bad for a while," he told me in August 1995. "But I never leave a football game at halftime. When I try a case, always stick around to the very end."

That, of course, was said even before the jury heard detective Mark Fuhrman using the N-word and before Fuhrman took the Fifth Amendment when he was asked questions about planting evidence. But the witnesses who really delighted Cochran were microbiologist John Gerdes and statistician Terence Speed. Both professional witnesses in the sense that they testify often at trials and are well paid for their trouble, they cast doubts on key parts of the prosecution case.

Gerdes, clinical director of the Immunological Associates laboratory in Denver, told the jury the Los Angeles police crime lab "has a substantial contamination problem that is persistent...and chronic." His testimony, intended to back Cochran's opening statement claim that the crime lab is a "cesspool of contamination," aimed to discredit the prosecution's DNA evidence by casting doubt on the integrity of blood samples before they reached the DNA testing facilities. The Gerdes testimony was especially effective because police criminalists had already admitted under cross examination that their facility operates under far from ideal conditions.

Speed's testimony compounded the damage Gerdes did to the prosecution case. He attacked the statistics that had been presented with great fanfare by laboratory scientist Robin Cotton, director of the Cellmark Diagnostics testing center in Germantown, Maryland, where police first sent blood samples for DNA testing. Cotton had testified that some blood on a sock found in Simpson's bedroom almost certainly came from Nicole Simpson. She put the odds at one in 6.8 billion that the blood could have emanated from any other person. There are only about five billion persons on this planet.

But Speed, an expert from the University of California at Berkeley, testified that the statistics used by Cotton and Gary Sims, DNA expert from the California Department of Justice laboratory, could have been exaggerated. Together, the testimony of Gerdes and Speed left the DNA results in the realm of a quarrel among experts. This allowed some jurors to conclude that the scientific evidence may have been unreliable, or, as the former juror number 6, Lionel Cryer, later put it, "Garbage in, garbage out."

These two were soon followed to the stand by Dr. Henry Lee, the director of forensics for the Connecticut state police and an old friend of Shapiro's. Lee, involved in the case as early as the day of the slow-speed chase, testified engagingly in heavily-accented English about blood spots and spatters at the crime scene. His key line, the one that Cochran used in his closing argument and the one that jurors remembered later, was that there was "something wrong" with the prosecution analysis of the crime scene and the blood evidence. He never pinpointed what might have been wrong, but his manner and his catch-phrase reinforced the notion of "garbage in, garbage out."

That idea was first planted in jurors' minds during defense

attorney Barry Scheck's blistering cross-examination of criminalist Dennis Fung and his partner Peter Neufeld's grilling of Fung's trainee Andrea Mazzola. Fung and Mazzola repeatedly stumbled over details of how they collected blood from the crime scene and from the foyer and driveway at Simpson's home. Fung, for instance, admitted he left a vial of Simpson's blood in an unrefrigerated bag on a laboratory table the night of June 13, 1994, but insisted it had not been disturbed when he returned and found it the next morning. His testimony was later used to imply that the blood might have degenerated before it was used in DNA testing and that the lack of secure storage left open the possibility others might have taken a small amount from the vial and sprinkled it in key locations to frame Simpson. Neufeld also caught several minor inconsistencies between the testimony Mazzola gave at trial and what she said in a pretrial hearing months earlier. This led him to suggest she was trying to cover up for evidence tampering by other police in the case.

The "garbage-in, garbage-out" theory got further credence when prosecutors declined to use Deputy Medical Examiner Irwin Golden as a witness, even though he conducted the autopsies on both victims. Golden was caught in several errors during the preliminary hearing. Then a few weeks later, reacting to his nationally televised humiliation on the witness stand, he waved something that appeared to be a gun around the lobby of the coroner's office and made vague threats against lawyers. His apparent instability was one reason prosecutors called the county coroner himself, Lakshmanan Sathyavagiswaran, to testify about those autopsies and the exact way Nicole Brown Simpson and Ronald Goldman died.

Usually addressed as "Dr. Lakshmanan" because of his unpronounceable surname, the coroner conceded that there were "some mistakes" in the autopsies, beginning with Golden's failure to visit the crime scene. Among the mistakes: a failure to save the contents of Mrs. Simpson's stomach, which defense experts said might have helped pinpoint the time of death. Sathyavagiswaran dramatically reenacted his version of the murders over the course of two days, wielding a ruler at the neck of prosecutor Brian Kelberg in place of a knife. His analysis of the wounds on the two bodies indicated there had not been a fierce struggle, because both victims were taken by surprise and confined in a small area.

This testimony was challenged harshly by defense expert Michael Baden, former chief medical examiner of New York City. Baden, called into the case by Shapiro even before Simpson's arrest, testified that he believed both victims struggled mightily against their assailant, a scenario that might have left the killer's body covered with bruises. Simpson's torso was essentially free of bruises or wounds when it was photographed the day after the murders. Baden's testimony that Goldman may have struggled for 10 to 20 minutes also raised questions about the time-frame of the murders. The further defense lawyers could push back the time when the assailant fled the murder scene, the less likely it could have been Simpson.

So Baden, a professional witness like Lee, Cotton, Sims, Gerdes and Speed, furthered the "garbage-in, garbage-out" theory. So did the lengthy disputes between defense witnesses and FBI experts over blood on the socks found in Simpson's bedroom and blood found days after the crimes on the back gate of Mrs. Simpson's condo. Where FBI experts Roger Martz and Douglas Deedrick said blood on the sock and the gate had likely been splattered there at the time of the crimes, defense experts Herbert MacDonell and Fredric Rieders maintained that those claims were suspect. Rieders argued for days that the blood on the gate contained significant amounts of the preservative EDTA, indicating that the blood might have come from the reference vial police took from Simpson the day after the killings and apparently carried all over town. Prosecutors tried to show that the amounts were trivial and could have been present on the gate from normal cleanings. The claims of the witnesses brought in by both sides were so predictably sympathetic to whoever was signing their paychecks that they sometimes made me laugh. The implication: For enough money, it's possible to purchase an expert to say almost anything you want.

MacDonell was a classic hired gun. He used massively blown-up photos of the socks to claim that blood was smeared on them and not dropped from above, as would have been the case if Mrs.

Simpson's blood had dripped onto them during her murder. If the blood was smeared, MacDonell implied, police probably put it there. Of course, he didn't mention, nor did any prosecutor bring up the possibility, that the blood could have been smeared by an act as simple as Simpson scratching his ankle after committing the murders. Again, the dispute came down to paid expert versus paid expert, with the relatively uneducated jurors expected to choose between them. It soon became clear that the massive sums Simpson spent importing top experts were neutralizing the scientific testimony of many key prosecution witnesses.

This meant that the moments likely to prove most telling would be those featuring non-technical, unpaid witnesses. There were plenty of those. They didn't agree any more than the technical witnesses. Start with the friends and family members who surrounded Simpson in his home on the evening of June 13, 1994, less than 24 hours after the deaths of his ex-wife and her friend. Simpson's daughter Arnelle, his sister Carmelita Durio and his mother Eunice all took the witness stand as the defense began presenting its case. All claimed Simpson was distraught. Arnelle Simpson, who lived in a guesthouse near her father's swimming pool, said he was "very upset, emotional, confused" when told of Nicole's death. She described him sitting on a couch with his mother and muttering at a television set as it gave reports of the slayings. "He was numb," she reported. This testimony struck me as largely irrelevant and self-serving. No matter whether he committed the murders or not, Simpson could be expected to be confused, emotional, distraught and numb. Especially since he had not slept since his red-eye flight to Chicago the night before.

By contrast, Simpson friend Ronald Shipp, a former policeman who testified that for years he routinely brought other cops to Simpson's house to play tennis and enjoy other facilities, presented O.J. as a troubled man afraid to take a lie detector test. Shipp had counseled both him and Nicole after Simpson admitted beating his wife in 1989. He had no apparent ax to grind when he reported that he accompanied O.J. into his upstairs bedroom and listened while Simpson told of dreaming about murdering his wife. To me, Shipp looked like a solid witness. A former policeman who admitted he once had a drinking problem, he appeared to have no reason for turning on his old friend and benefactor. But my colleague Schatzman has chosen to emphasize that drinking problem, even though there was no evidence that it persisted beyond 1989.

He also finds it significant that Shipp several times brought women other than his wife to lounge with him in Simpson's jacuzzi. And Schatzman makes much of the fact that Shipp admitted under cross-examination that he had never attended sporting or entertainment events with Simpson. To which I say, "So what?" There was never a denial that Shipp knew Simpson well. Nor was it established that Simpson didn't confess his dream to Shipp.

Schatzman complains that whites "continue to believe that blacks are inferior to them in every field," and that simple racism is the reason most whites persist in believing Simpson is a murderer. Not so. Millions of whites work comfortably beside blacks and under African American bosses and managers. But whites didn't go into their observation of this case on the assumption that it was racially motivated. Most whites figured, like me, that this was a crime of passion committed by a jealous celebrity. So when a witness like Shipp appeared with no evidence to contradict his claim that he was a friend of Simpson's before the murders— enough of a friend that Simpson sought his advice after admitting he beat his wife—whites had no reason to doubt his word. Was it racist to believe the testimony of one black man about another, his former friend? I don't think so. If prejudice is at work here at all, it may be in Schatzman's refusal to believe that a onetime alcoholic can dry out to the point where he's capable of remembering a rather dramatic conversation. To Dennis, once a drunk, always a drunk. He doesn't trust Shipp, no matter how direct and intimate his contacts were with Simpson. Who's being unreasonable here?

Amazingly, aside from Simpson family members, Shipp was to be the only African American witness of any significance in the case. Defense lawyers brought on a few blacks to testify about the racism of Mark Fuhrman, and prosecutors called one African American detective who helped collect evidence. But for the most part, the corps of witnesses was lily white. This at times imparted a surreal quality to the case, with the fate of a black celebrity and the decision of a mostly black jury hinging on the word of dozens of Caucasians.

Nicole's sister Denise Brown, the only member of the victims' families called to the stand for substantial testimony, told how Simpson called Nicole a "fat pig" in her presence while Nicole was pregnant and said he behaved strangely at daughter Sydney's dance recital hours before the murders. As her testimony stretched over two days, Denise recalled how Simpson humiliated his wife in a Malibu restaurant, grabbing her crotch and insisting it belonged to him. Under questioning by Shapiro, she admitted she had a drinking problem and that she "had had a few drinks" on the night in the restaurant. But she made no such admission about the evening she reported that Simpson physically threw her and Nicole out of his house, shouting the "fat pig" epithet while Nicole was pregnant with son Justin. When Denise called Simpson's demeanor at the dance recital "frightening" and "spooky," Shapiro countered with a home video showing a smiling, gregarious Simpson leaving the recital. Again, Brown's testimony seemed to me to contain powerful ammunition for the prosecutors' domestic abuse campaign against Simpson. It wasn't her fault that this material wasn't properly exploited. But Schatzman focused on her alcoholism, and his paper's headline lumped her with Shipp as "two drunks."

A parade of police officers and detectives followed Shipp and Brown to the witness stand, after which it was the turn of Brian (Kato) Kaelin. The long-haired Kaelin, whose testimony for the prosecution during the preliminary hearing made him a celebrity, repeated his story of hearing thumps on the wall of his room beside Arnelle's around 10:45 p.m. on the night of the murders. He retold his story of accompanying Simpson in his Bentley on a hamburger run ending about 9:35 p.m. that night. Then, he said, he saw Simpson again at about 11 p.m., helping load his baggage into the limousine taking him to the airport for the flight to Chicago. Kaelin also mentioned a mysterious small black bag that Simpson didn't want him to handle. That bag never turned up again; it didn't appear after Simpson's return from Chicago.

But it was Kaelin's testimony about how Simpson treated Nicole that drew the most attention from lawyers in the case.

Under friendly cross-examination from Shapiro, he said that in more than two years of living at close quarters with both Simpsons, he never saw O.J. Simpson strike his ex-wife. He conceded he was present at least twice when they shouted and quarreled. One occasion was the 1993 incident when Nicole called 911 as Simpson battered down her back door. "He didn't hit her," Kaelin said. "There was no physical contact."

Prosecutor Clark also asked Kaelin about Simpson's complaint on the night of the murders that Nicole and her sisters wore tight mini-skirts and other sexy clothes at the recital and whether Simpson had been upset about it. At first, Kaelin said Simpson didn't appear agitated when he made those comments, but later he conceded in his trademark fractured syntax that there was "a degree of upset...It's such a hard thing to, being upset, uh. It wasn't throwing things. It wasn't like that." It was just as well that the jurors didn't ask for a readback of Kaelin's testimony during their ultra-brief deliberations. They wouldn't have understood him any better than anyone else did the first time.

Two months after Kaelin left the stand, writer Marc Eliot accused him of outright lying in his testimony, which Eliot said was calculated to paint Simpson in the most favorable light possible. Eliot had held months of taped conversations with Kaelin, aiming to ghost-write a book for Simpson's former houseguest. But when Kaelin backed out of the project, Eliot proceeded on his own with *Kato Kaelin: The Whole Truth*. Kato testified that he never saw O.J. upset, possessive or obsessed when it came to Nicole, wrote Eliot. "But in our taped conversations Kato clearly talks about O.J.'s rage at Nicole, his preoccupation with her sex life...his obsession with the provocative way Nicole dressed to go night-clubbing with her friends. By leaving this out of his testimony, Kato created a false impression not only about the relationship between O.J. and Nicole Simpson, but also about who they were, the kind of life they led and about events that happened immediately before and after the murders of Nicole and Ron Goldman."

Eliot's claims have never been rebutted by Kaelin or anyone else, which convinces me that Kaelin's stumbling and bumbling on the stand was part of an act calculated to prevent him from becoming the key witness against his longtime benefactor. His conduct was consistent with the promise that Eliot reports Kaelin made to Simpson when both attended Nicole's funeral. "I just want you to know I'll be there for you always, in any way I can," Kaelin said he told Simpson. By its finish, Kaelin's testimony gave no real advantage to either the prosecution or defense. His version of the evening left Simpson with a window of opportunity to commit the crime, but included no incriminating Simpson conduct. This did little to eliminate any doubts the jurors might have had about the prosecution case.

Almost as confusing as Kaelin were the many witnesses who testified that they walked their dogs or heard barking in the neighborhood of Nicole's condo on the night of the murders. An engaging group including a screenwriter, an auto detailer, a couple out on a date and a neighbor who often wears two wristwatches, they couldn't pinpoint the time of the murders beyond establishing that they occurred between 10:15 and 10:45 p.m. Screenwriter Pablo Fenjves, whose bedroom is mere steps from Nicole's home, testified he became aware of a loudly-barking dog "10 to 15 minutes into" the 10 o'clock news show he watches regularly. "It sounded like a very unhappy animal," he said. About an hour later, Nicole's Akita dog, also named Kato, turned up with bloody paws. The murder scene featured numerous bloody paw prints.

But Fenjves' testimony was disputed by several defense witnesses who said they walked in the neighborhood at about 10:15 or 10:20 that night and neither saw nor heard a barking dog. "I'm a stickler for time," said neighbor Denise Pilnak, wearing two watches on her left wrist. She heard no barking, she said, until 10:33 or 10:35. Neither did Sony Pictures employee Danny Mandel, walking his blind date Ellen Aaronson home that night. The couple reported that they walked past the murder scene shortly after 10:20, but heard no dog and saw no bodies or blood.

Then came car detailer Robert Heidstra, who testified that he was walking his own dogs near the crime scene at about 10:40 when he heard a dog begin to bark and the clang of a metal gate closing in the approximate direction of Nicole's condo. All the defense witnesses put the time substantially later than all the prosecution's. And the later the dog started barking, the less likely it is that Simpson could have committed the crime.

But Heidstra, who by coincidence regularly cleans the cars of Simpson's next-door neighbors, also turned into a potentially valuable and telling prosecution witness. He testified that he saw a white vehicle resembling Simpson's Ford Bronco leave the crime scene—but about 30 minutes after the time prosecutors set for the assault on the victims. His description of the vehicle and the manner in which it was driven would have been all the corroboration prosecutors needed to place Simpson at the scene—if they had called Jill Shively as a witness.

Shively, who lived nearby in Santa Monica, told the county grand jury just days after the murders that she was driving near the intersection of Bundy and San Vicente Boulevard on the night of the crimes, when a white Ford Bronco with a driver she identified as Simpson almost slammed into her. She said she clearly recognized him as he "turned around and glared at me" after the near collision. But she accepted $5,000 for telling her story to a TV show and was eliminated from the prosecution witness list. Did her willingness to sell her story render her less than reliable? If so, what does that make prosecutors Clark and Darden, both of whom signed large contracts to write books after the trial?

Shively was just one of many potentially important witnesses who didn't testify. The list, of course, starts with Simpson, who uttered key words in the case without ever having to take the witness stand. There was also Nicole's friend Faye Resnick, whose cocaine habit led defense lawyers to theorize that the murders may have been a drug hit gone wrong. In her book *Nicole Brown Simpson: The Private Diary of a Life Interrupted*, she claims Nicole told her that she feared for her life at Simpson's hands. Resnick said she badly wanted to tell her story in court. "The jury gets a very shallow view of Nicole," she said as the prosecution wrapped up its case without including her. "I don't think the jury has been introduced to Nicole yet."

There was also football star Marcus Allen, who succeeded Simpson as a Heisman Trophy winner at USC. Resnick's book reported that he had a torrid affair with Nicole before her death, but he resisted being called as a witness and was not required to appear. Defense lawyers had wanted him to testify that Simpson held no grudge against him because of the affair. There were also the two limousine drivers who claimed to have seen Simpson beat his wife in the back seats of their cars during the late 1980s. Neither Alfred Acosta nor Albert Aguilera were called, largely because of time constraints, prosecutors said.

One witness who was called but never heard by the jury was Rosa Lopez, housekeeper for Simpson's neighbors. Testifying on videotape in the midst of the prosecution case because of her determination to return to her native El Salvador, she tried to establish that Simpson's car was parked outside his house at the time of the murders. But her testimony became so garbled, so filled with "I don't remembers" and other inconsistencies, that her taped image simply disappeared about the same time she flew home to Central America.

Another potential key witness who evaporated after much ado was Kerry Mullis, Nobel Prize-winning chemist and inventor of the polymerase chain reaction (PCR) method of DNA analysis. The technique can differentiate the DNA of various individuals while using far smaller amounts than older, more accepted methods. Prosecutor Rockne Harmon, imported from the Alameda County district attorney's office in Oakland to deal with Mullis, promised to examine the scientist's surf-centered lifestyle, featuring a divorce and admitted use of LSD, if he ever took the stand in an effort to discredit the prosecution DNA evidence. Mullis attended several weeks of the trial, sitting with defense attorneys inside the bar, but never took the stand.

Afterward, he told a reporter he'd been prepared to attack "every single point" in the prosecution's scientific case. He insisted that "Too many people had a chance to mess with" the blood evidence against Simpson and said the DNA matches testified to by prosecution experts were less precise than needed for positive identification. Mullis also said he believed the defense claims of evidence tampering. "I could have held up pretty good, because in fact I don't have anything to be ashamed of," he said.

But prospective defense witness Mary Ann Gerchas plainly did have plenty to be ashamed of. Billed as a key eyewitness in Cochran's opening statement, she supposedly was apartment hunting in Nicole's neighborhood on the night of the crimes and saw four men, two whites and two Hispanics, hastily leaving the murder scene. She disappeared after being convicted of fraud in making false statements on a credit application. Defense lawyers claimed she was persecuted by the district attorney's office, which rarely prosecutes anyone for falsifying information on a credit document, but they opted not to call her. They wouldn't say, but maybe that was because they learned she had been sued at least 34 times in the past five years in cases where she allegedly defrauded the Marriott hotel chain, her relatives and suppliers and customers of her small jewelry store.

One more key witness could have been football-player-turned-minister Roosevelt Grier, whose Nov. 13, 1994, visit to Simpson in jail ended with Simpson shouting an exclamation clearly heard by a guard routinely stationed nearby. Over the strong objections of prosecutors, Grier was not required to testify about the exclamation, which some tabloid newspapers reported was "I did it!"—an admission of guilt. Grier insisted that he visited the jailhouse as a minister, not as a friend of Simpson and that "A minister hears a lot of things he keeps to himself." Ito did not force him to testify. He also ruled that Deputy Sheriff Jeff Stuart, the guard, could not repeat what he heard because it was privileged communication between a minister and one of his congregants.

And there was Simpson's lifelong friend and teammate Al Cowlings, who drove Simpson on his nationally-televised slow-speed chase. Prosecutors never called Cowlings to detail why Simpson took off from the home of his friend Robert Kardashian on the morning of June 17, 1994, rather than turning himself in as scheduled. Nor did they question Cowlings about conversations he and Simpson might have had in the car.

Each of these putative witnesses was in a position to contribute key facts or insights to the case. A Grier or a Stuart or a Cowlings or a Resnick could have provided enough information to sway at least some jurors to the side of conviction. A Mullis or a Gerchas might have raised some doubts in minds like mine.

Schatzman says I "blame the Negro" for the fact that Simpson as an unsworn witness was allowed to sway the jury without risking cross-examination. Not true. I don't blame anyone but the judge and the prosecutors who allowed it and the jury that fell for it. Yes, Dennis, that bugs me. Not because Simpson is black, but because I'm convinced he's a vicious murderer.

Schatzman also says Simpson "hadn't hit (Nicole) since 1989." But we don't know that. All we know for sure is that he wasn't convicted of beating her after that date. Even if he didn't hit her for those last five years of her life, we know he terrorized her, beating down her door, stalking her and threatening her. Was it racist to want him to answer for that? Was it racist to want him to explain with some consistency where he was when the murders occurred? Dennis suggests that since most other folks can't remember where they were the night of June 12, 1994, we shouldn't expect Simpson to do so either. But if you'd asked me on June 13 where I was the previous evening, I could have told you, and without giving two or three contradictory versions. To expect the same of Simpson is not racist; it's just reasonable.

But since the people who were in a position to know some of the most compelling facts of the case never testified, Simpson never had to answer any of the key questions he left open. Infuriatingly, that opened the way for Simpson to become his own most effective advocate, even though he never had to answer a single question.

DENNIS SCHATZMAN

Witness Credibility: Pipe Dream vs. Reality

First and foremost, as I've done in every one of my chapters for this book, I will explain why whites think so differently than African Americans on the Simpson double-murder trial. And I will also try to explain why whites are so way out in left field on most of the issues that it borders on fanaticism. There is no better issue on which to put this theory to the test than that of the perception of witness credibility.

Now, let us recap. Whites to this very moment continue to believe that blacks are inferior to them in virtually every field of human endeavor. With the exception of some major sports, entertainment and perhaps in the field of food preparation, whites consider it an affront to their integrity if a black defeats a white. And when they do, many whites take it personally and they usually plot to get them back. Anyone who doesn't think that's true can just look at how the civil cases against Simpson are viewed—as "wrongful death suits." Never mind that a jury found him innocent of the charges based upon the jury instructions and the lack of evidence, whites almost to a man and woman believe that this black man is guilty of murdering two white people. Thus, if there are witnesses who are called to support the prosecution's case, they are believed by whites. Those called by the defense? Well, they're just not credible. Period.

Consider, for example, the treatment given to the testimonies of former LAPD officer and self-described Simpson "friend" Ron Shipp, and Nicole's sister, Denise Brown. With virtually no exception, both witnesses were given rave media reviews for their on-camera assault on Simpson. The one exception I know of came from me. Shipp, the son of prominent Los Angeles black socialites, had been an LAPD officer for nearly 20 years. Then he quit.

Many have said that he was forced out because of his chronic drinking problems. Throughout the last ten years of his service, however, Shipp was a constant shadow of Simpson and often brought other "men in blue" over to the defendant's estate to play tennis on his courts, to swim in his pool and to help Shipp put a dent in Simpson's well-stocked liquor cabinet. On numerous occasions, Shipp, who also had a fondness for white women (he was or still is married to one), would bring over girlfriends to lounge in Simpson's Jacuzzi. We're told that he also occasionally long-stroked Simpson's secretary Cathy Randa and once after the murders banged on her door uninvited at one o'clock in the morning—stone drunk, of course. Now that's a paragon of virtue if there ever was one.

At least that's what most of my white colleagues thought. When Shipp testified that on the day after the murders he heard Simpson say that he had "once dreamed of killing Nicole," they damn near orgasmed all over themselves. "Oh, what credibility," they said almost in unison. "He's so trustworthy," they chimed. I didn't get it. Aside from being a cop, Shipp was an aspiring actor for whom Simpson was able to line up a few bit parts. But unlike Kato, who wallowed in work after the murders (and his testimony), Shipp's only appearance on the big screen came as a guest on a few talk shows playing the role of Simpson-basher. I guess he learned the hard way that try as he might to ingratiate himself with whites, he wasn't white and, thus, wouldn't be treated as well as Kato Kaelin.

Ditto Denise Brown. She too was labeled a pure-as-the-driven-snow witness. During her testimony, she and Chris Darden brought down the house one Friday afternoon when she tearfully described the drunken fight Simpson and Nicole had in her presence. As she (legitimately) sobbed in recalling the incident, Darden noted the time and smartly asked Ito to curtail the proceedings until Monday, giving the viewing audience the whole weekend to think about that pitiful sight.

Like Shipp, Brown admitted that she had "drinking problems." But in reality both downplayed the severity of the problem. In the minds of many, many, many people who claimed to know her well, Brown's drinking contributed mightily to her being an extremely loose woman. And when they say "loose," they're not talking about knocking boots of different sizes, shapes and colors every now and then. They're talking John Holmes X-rated-film type loose.

I called them both in print and on television and radio, "a couple of drunks." I never heard from Brown on the matter. I mean, what was she going to say? But she did come over to the Simpson family while I was standing in the hall one morning before court session began and shook my hand. It was the only time she ever spoke to me. Shipp, on the other hand, was reportedly incensed with me. Worse, his family was livid. Libby Clark, the *Sentinel's* longtime food editor and author of *The Plum Book*, black L.A.'s version of *The Blue Book*, stopped by my desk and told me how Shipp's parents were spearheading a drive to have other black Brahmins cancel their subscriptions in order to punish the paper. Of course, that threat came, and that threat went. The Shipps got five people to rescind their subscriptions; in the same period, I brought in over 600 new subscribers.

In short, both Brown and Shipp, in the minds of most of us in the African American community, were not the kind of people we'd walk across Temple Street with, let alone believe their testimony. The majority of whites, however, trusted the two "drunks." After all, they were out to get Simpson just as much as Denise Brown and Ron Shipp.

I've already given my impression on many of the key witnesses in other chapters. But there are several others to whom I will give the same credibility scrutiny as I have to Brown and Shipp. Dr. Robert Huizenga, the matinee-idol Beverly Hills doctor hired by former lead defense attorney Robert Shapiro to give Simpson the once-over two days after the double murders, was another legitimate witness who got raked over the coals. Huizenga testified that Simpson's old football injuries, especially to his knees, were so pervasive that they severely restricted his movement. The doctor also testified that Simpson's body was virtually free of scars and bruises one might get from, say, engaging in hand-to-hand combat with two very healthy (and younger) people. The only exception was that the scar found on Simpson's left hand came from broken glass rather than from a knife.

Prosecution attorneys, however, threw in the old back-door trick question. "Despite his injuries," Huizenga was asked, "could he have physically been able to commit the murders?" The doctor reluctantly answered in the affirmative. "Aha!" white America yelled in unison. What chickenshit. In reality, anyone is capable of killing anyone. Go to a women's prison and ask some 50-year-old, 4'11" Dr. Ruth lookalike what she's in there for. "Murder," she'll reply. Came across her daughter's 6'4" boyfriend kicking her child's ass and she decapitated him with a meat cleaver. Anything's possible. The question still remains, white America. Did O.J. Simpson, with his bad knees and after a physically taxing long day, kill two physically fit people all by himself? I don't think so. But more importantly, neither did the jury.

Since Plans A, B, C, D and E didn't work, my colleague Tom Elias shifted vainly to Plan F. Since we all saw Simpson walk calmly into the courtroom every day, how come when he approached the jury on two occasions, he showed a noticeable limp? "Aha! Part II." I love it when Tom leads with his chin. In this instance, I simply use myself as an example. Due to a series of accidents, my legs are all fucked up. I can't run, and I can't bend my left leg because of the Titanium alloy rods I have in it. But no one can notice it unless they watch me climbing steps or after I've sat in a chair for a long time. When I get up, my limp is very noticeable. Tom even pointed it out to me once at his home. That is the case, I suspect, with Simpson. On to Plan G, Tom.

Much has been said about the "expert" professional witnesses—Drs. Henry Lee, Michael Baden, Fredric Rieders, John Gerdes and Professor Herbert MacDonell—hired by the defense to refute various testimony and evidence presented by the prosecution witnesses. Since most of the critics couldn't intelligently refute their testimony, they shifted gears to criticize these defense witnesses because they were being paid. The logic the critics were trying to convey was that since they were drawing a check for their testimony, they couldn't be trusted.

Au contraire. To refute this, I again refer back to the movie, *The Verdict*, when Concannon (James Mason) the defense attorney tried to pull that one on the black doctor Paul Newman hired as an expert witness. "And you're being paid for your testimony, isn't that right?" Concannon, the confident slam-dunking lawyer asked the doctor in front of the jury. "Just as you are," the doctor low-bridged right back. It's interesting to note that even Newman, when he picked up the black doctor at the train station (he didn't know what he looked like), gave him one of those "oh no, a nigger!" looks. Even in the movies, we're still perceived as being inferior.

Of the expert witnesses, one witness' testimony is worth noting—that of Herbert MacDonell, a forensics expert who never earned his doctorate. Perhaps it was because he was so busy kicking ass in the field of blood-spatter work. MacDonell had become the world's leading expert in the area of blood spots as well as in other areas of blood work. Defense attorneys had gotten to him about a half-day before the prosecution did. I couldn't help but chuckle when "the People" tried to rake him over the coals on the stand.

MacDonell's testimony was damaging to the prosecution. He testified that Nicole's blood found on the socks which were in Simpson's bedroom had been applied directly "by compression" rather than being splattered on by someone walking through the blood puddles found at Bundy. That took the heart right out of their case and, worse, diverted attention away from the DNA evidence. Someone planted blood on the socks, so it's entirely possible that someone could have planted Simpson's blood at the scene of the crime. After all, didn't Detective Philip Vannatter drive around all day with the defendant's blood in his car instead of turning it right in? And didn't the people over at Piper Tech leave the door to the evidence room unlocked on occasion, possibly allowing someone to sneak in and take Simpson's blood and plant it? The answer to both questions is "Yes."

Let's look now at Candace Garvey. The strikingly beautiful blond friend of Nicole's, the wife of former wife-beater Steve Garvey, onetime first baseman for the Los Angeles Dodgers, testified that Nicole used to tell her about how Simpson would torment her. She never saw anything, mind you. And neither did any of Nicole's other friends who testified, and who were of the same ilk as Candace. Essentially, they got away with giving hearsay testimony. In my opinion, this group's testimony should be viewed no differently than one would treat the testimony of Simpson's relatives.

The people, led by Kathleen Bell, and Roderick Hodge—who heard Mark Fuhrman use the word "nigger" in their presence—now that's a different story. Their testimony wasn't hearsay. What critics said was that their testimony wasn't "relevant." That's bullshit. How could Garvey *et al's* testimony be relevant and Bell's and Hodge's not? That's the kind of white-boy logic that really pisses me off. First of all, it gets full play in the news media because the men and women who run that industry believe that shit too. It's not fair, and we African Americans don't get a chance to refute that crap because we are ignored by the media. Witness how many black commentators showcased their wares on these nightly talk shows compared to the number of white ones. But whites are the first to complain that all the problems in the nation are *our* fault. Just ask the Republicans. They've made an industry out of blaming the "nigger" for all our woes. Sorry. I just couldn't help that.

Let's now look at some of the men and women who didn't testify, for one reason or another. Jill Shively, the woman who told the Grand Jury that she had seen Simpson speeding away from the Bundy Drive scene on the night of the murders, was knocked off the prosecution's witness list after it was learned that she picked up a check from a tabloid TV show for her story. That excuse doesn't hold water with me because the men who sold Simpson a hunting knife back in May 1994 were also paid for their stories. What's the difference? I'll tell you what I think the difference is. I believe the district attorney's office found out she was lying. That's what I think.

Mary Ann Gerchas. Now there's a story for you. Gerchas claims to have been walking down Bundy Drive on the night of the murders when she says she saw four men dressed in dark clothing getting into a car and speeding away. She said they looked like cops. For the sake of argument, I'm going to say that Gerchas is prone to exaggeration. But the way the prosecution treated her raises a lot of questions about whether or not she was really telling the truth, stretching the truth or just out-and-out lying. The woman, a jeweler with a shop in West Los Angeles, had a history of juggling rubber checks, had a beef with a Beverly Hills hotel where she stayed for six months and presumably bounced a check for her stay. The government seized upon that, invoked the "speedy trial" concept, arrested her, found a sympathetic judge and hustled her off to jail. It was probably a civil matter, but the government figured "why quibble over minor details?"

Gerchas never testified. And she languished in jail, all because the government, in my opinion, feared that her testimony would further damage their case. If it wouldn't hurt their case, why would they go through all those gymnastics over a bounced-check case to keep her away from the Simpson jury? Remember, Dr. Henry Lee pointed out in court that there were other footprints found at the murder scene that were not the Size 12 Bruno Magli-type footprints the government claims were Simpson's.

Now we come to Faye Resnick, the Negro-look-a-like former drug addict who liked to pal around with Nicole Brown Simpson or anyone else who could help her satisfy her crack cocaine habit. After her boyfriend, Dr. Christian Reichardt, threw her out on her ass, she moved in with Nicole. She smoked "caine," presumably in the Bundy residence, because some of her drug paraphernalia was found in the room where she stayed. Now Simpson could be ridiculed for screaming at Nicole on the 911 tapes while the kids were in the house, but white America didn't have a damn thing to say about Faye smoking dope "with the kids in the house."

Anyway, Faye was well known as a druggie, according to "J.R." the onetime notorious "drug dealer of the stars." He wrote that she would do anything to get the drugs, especially when Reichardt cut off the funds. She never testified in the trial, but that didn't keep her from cashing in on the death of her "best friend" Nicole. The bitch didn't know Nicole but for only a couple of months. But her "credibility" was satisfactory enough to parlay into a bestseller, *The Private Diary of a Life Interrupted* (Dove Books). Worse, Faye, although she tells all about Nicole and her and their exploits, really lances Simpson. What I'm trying to figure out is whether or not Faye was of sound mind and body when she says what she says, or was she stoned out of her gourd.

Last, but certainly not least, let's talk about O.J. Simpson, the defendant. Tom Elias, agreeing with the Founding Fathers of this nation—who gave blacks, free or slave, no rights at all—and with the majority of whites following this case, believes that the Constitution doesn't apply to Simpson. He should have testified even though the nation's leading document says that he doesn't have to testify. Fuck that, says my colleague. "We wanted him to testify, and if that's what we in white America want, then so be it," I suspect he would say.

Elias cries foul because Simpson was able to "influence" the jury when he approached them to show scars on his knee and his arthritic knuckle on his left hand. It also pissed him off that "the glove didn't fit." Finally, it bugged him, I suspect, because Simpson was permitted to make a statement before the court. Bear in mind, it was Superior Court Judge Lance Ito who permitted these events to occur, not Simpson. It was the prosecution lawyers who also let it happen, not Simpson. It was Christopher Darden who wanted Simpson to try on the gloves in front of an international audience, not the defendant. But, as always, they blame the defendant, who "happens to be black," for their own inadequacies.

White America wanted Simpson to testify to the number of times he beat Nicole. Never mind the fact that he hadn't hit her since 1989 and even stipulated in his will that there would be severe financial consequences against him if he did. White America wanted Simpson to tell, under oath, where he was during the hours before and after the murders, never mind the fact that they can't remember where *they* were during the last two days of their own worthless, miserable lives. White America wanted Simpson to explain why he could not hold a hand of cards in a gin rummy game following a golf match but could muster the strength to hold two knives to kill his ex-wife and her friend. Here I refer back to the United States Constitution. A defendant doesn't have to testify in a court of law, in Los Angeles County or anywhere else. This also includes O.J. Simpson, despite what white America wants.

Postscript: There is a very tall black man named Edgar Richardson, a bodyguard and porno movie industry gadfly who occasionally did security work for Simpson and others in

Hollywood. Richardson came to my office early in the trial and gave me some startling information. After validating who he was and what he knew, he proceeded to tell me that he was in the vicinity of the Mezzaluna restaurant about 7:30 p.m. on the night of the murders and observed a black Mercedes 500 SL parked in front of the place. In it, Richardson says, were two men he claims were well know "hit men" for Colombian-affiliated drug dealers. Richardson says he called the police and told them about the incident and, of course, was politely ignored. I bring this up because, as one might expect, my colleagues thought that shit was funny. They scoffed at it. But Richardson, in my opinion, was as credible as, say, Ron Shipp. At least Richardson wasn't a drunk.

Well, credibility is as credibility does, to paraphrase Forrest Gump. It's in the eye of the beholder. Unfortunately for blacks, including part-time black Simpson, there are more of them than there are of us.

CHAPTER 9
THE EVIDENCE

TOM ELIAS

Not Quite the Perfect Murder

It was almost the perfect murder. There were no eyewitnesses when Nicole Brown Simpson and Ronald Goldman were slashed and mutilated on the walkway of her luxury condominium. No one besides her dog Kato even heard anything. But the operative word here is almost. For the murderer—or the man I and millions of others believe was the murderer—didn't quite get away unscathed. His left hand was cut. He dropped a glove. He left behind a navy blue wool cap complete with a few of his hairs. And he inadvertantly dropped a few fibers from the carpet of his car.

I have been convinced from the earliest days of the case that this was a carefully planned murder that went slightly awry when Nicole's mother Juditha Brown dropped her eyeglasses beside the curb outside the Mezzaluna restaurant near her daughter's home on the evening of June 12, 1994. If she hadn't dropped the spectacles, waiter Ron Goldman wouldn't have happened on the scene just as O.J. Simpson slashed the throat of his ex-wife, while their two small children slept nearby. If Goldman hadn't happened along, Simpson might have been questioned, but probably never would have been arrested or brought to trial. Even his red-eye flight to Chicago that night was planned as part of an alibi. But Goldman did turn up, so he had to be done away with too. Simpson caught him from behind and inflicted dozens of knife wounds on him while Goldman struggled to get away.

It was during the struggle that the right-handed Simpson dropped a glove and cut his left hand. As he fled, he didn't take time to wrap the wound in a handkerchief or anything else. So the largest wound he suffered in the brief fight with Goldman, near the knuckle of his left middle finger, dripped small amounts of blood for a while as he went. Simpson was probably unaware of this as he walked quickly to the alley behind the condo, got into his Ford Bronco and drove off, almost colliding with Jill Shively.

This is a tale written in blood, the key evidence in the Simpson case. Quite unconsciously, the murderer left a blood trail leading directly from the bodies to the alley to the door of the Bronco to the interior of the Bronco to the foyer of his house. Without that cut, without those blood drops, there would be little evidence that Simpson was anywhere near the murder scene. For some of the hairs and fibers linking him to the crime scene could conceivably have been deposited there on some other visit to Nicole and their kids.

These realities were the reasons defense attorneys spent months attacking the blood evidence gathered by criminalists in the hours before a police nurse drew a test tube of blood from Simpson's arm the next afternoon. They focused on the fact that police could never credibly account for about one cubic centimeter of the blood in that reference sample. The crucial fact that led to Simpson's arrest and trial was that most of the blood drops later found to be a match for the sample drawn from his arm were spotted and collected many hours before that sample was taken. Even if criminalists Dennis Fung and Andrea Mazzola were sloppy in collecting them, even if they failed to change their rubber gloves between each collection, even if someone had stepped on the blood drops—and there was no evidence of that—it wouldn't change the chemical characteristics that identified the blood as Simpson's.

For the blood found beside the killer's bloody footsteps leading to the alley was first identified as Simpson's type in conventional testing, then found to match his DNA. Scientists from the Cellmark and California Department of Justice laboratories put the odds at more than one in a billion that the blood came from anyone besides Simpson. The blood drop found just under the door handle of the Bronco was identified with similar certainty. So were most of the bloodstains inside the Bronco.

As I watched Barry Scheck and Peter Neufeld systematically assault this evidence over a period of more than two months, I grew more and more angry. For what they implied seemed completely preposterous and self-serving to me. I saw them as talented professionals prostituting themselves in the daily pushing of a blatant lie. I was ashamed they were Jews and sometimes feared that their performance would play into the hands of anti-Semites the world over.

They were arguing that because a tiny amount of blood was missing from Simpson's reference sample, jurors should believe police falsified every drop of blood in the case. Of course, police nurse Thano Peratis, who drew the blood, later testified that none was missing at all, but that he had mistakenly recorded taking slightly more blood from Simpson than he actually did. Also, for cops to do what Scheck and Neufeld charged, they would have had to run from site to site with a tiny eye-dropper, quickly depositing samples everywhere they went. Anything less precise and they'd have had to use far more than 1 cc. of blood. They would have had to carefully unwrap and rewrap each blood sample taken by criminalists and smear a small amount of reference-sample blood on the cotton swatches used to pick up blood from concrete and carpets. To plant Simpson's blood on the alley gate, where it was found about three weeks after the murders, they would have had to save and preserve that tiny bit of blood from the reference sample, then carefully place it on the gate in a random-appearing manner. They would have had to do this without anyone seeing them—unless every policeman in their city's most visible investigation ever was a co-conspirator. Anyone who planted even a single drop of blood would also be guilty of a felony and risk both his career and his pension.

For all this, we were told, the motive was race hatred. And yet, of dozens of police involved, only one—Detective Mark Fuhrman—was ever shown to be anything like a racist. One thing for sure: If there had been a shred of racism in the background of any other cop, Cochran would have trumpeted it over any microphone he could find.

So the entire defense scenario seemed too silly for rational consideration. But jurors had to believe all of it in order to discount the blood evidence against Simpson. Yes, there were problems with the way evidence was handled and stored. Blood wasn't refrigerated right away, risking the possibility that it might deteriorate. But when blood degenerates, its DNA content is not suddenly and mysteriously transmogrified into different DNA, like something from the imagination of the comic strip *Calvin and Hobbes*. Rather, it degenerates into useless particles whose contents cannot be analyzed. Most of the Simpson blood spots in this case didn't even degenerate that far. They remained usable in DNA testing.

Even my colleague Dennis Schatzman agrees that the blood, hair and fibers found at the crime scene were Simpson's. But he says the fact that Fuhrman lied about his racist vocabulary and that Vannatter lied about his reasons for getting a search warrant renders all that evidence invalid. For this to be true, you would have to believe that the same policemen we are asked to believe incompetent spent the afternoon after the murders spreading blood with extreme precision from the test tube Vannatter inexplicably and foolishly carried from police headquarters back to Simpson's mansion.

But even that wouldn't account for the blood found at the crime scene, on Simpson's driveway and on his car long *before* any sample was drawn from his arm. Schatzman says that the sloppy practices of the LAPD crime lab might have allowed Vannatter or some other plotter to put blood from the reference sample onto swatches collected at the crime scene. The problem, Dennis, is that if they'd done that, and if the original blood spots found on Nicole's condo walkway came from someone else, some other killer, the DNA tests on those swatches would have turned up blood mixtures. But that did not happen in three tests at two laboratories. Those spots contained DNA deriving purely from O.J. Simpson. So even if you believe the Schatzman-Scheck-Neufeld scenario of one tiny milliliter of blood—that may or may not have been missing—being spread all over Brentwood, you still haven't come close to clearing Simpson.

Yes, there were possible problems with other evidence. For instance, when Fuhrman reported finding a bloody glove behind Simpson's guesthouse matching the one left behind at the murder scene, there was no other blood around it. The leaves near the glove as it lay on a narrow walkway hadn't been disturbed, as they likely would have been if anyone had walked in that almost inaccessible area. The only plausible explanation for this might be that Simpson—seeing a limo waiting to take him to the airport—

walked through his neighbor's yard before entering his house, tossed a bag of bloody clothes including the glove over the fence and then walked up his driveway from the gate near which he parked the Bronco. The glove could have fallen out of the bag when it thumped against the back wall of Brian (Kato) Kaelin's guesthouse room and not been noticed when Simpson went out his back door, not visible from the street, moments later to retrieve the bag. Not a very likely story.

The bloodstains in Simpson's Bronco later found to come from Nicole and Ron Goldman were another potentially vulnerable piece of evidence. They weren't discovered until weeks after the crimes, long after reference blood samples had been taken from the dead bodies of the victims. In the meantime, the Bronco was entered or broken into several times. Police and prosecutors sometimes ran into almost laughable snafus when they tried to imply that other evidence might incriminate Simpson. One example was the plastic bag in the rear of the Bronco. At first portrayed as evidence that Simpson intended to carry off Nicole's body, the bag turned out to be standard equipment in Broncos, used to cover the spare tire.

There were also the bloody socks that were found in Simpson's bedroom the afternoon of the day after the murders. The socks didn't appear in the first police video of the bedroom, even though that tape clearly showed the spot from which they were later lifted. Were they planted? DNA tests revealed some of the blood on them was Nicole's. But defense expert Herbert MacDonell used highly magnified blow-up photos of fibers in the socks to show that Nicole's blood might have been smeared on them, rather than having spattered on them as it fell from her wounds. Of course, had Simpson done something as simple as scratch his ankle with a fingernail while driving home, those stains would also have taken on a smeared appearance.

But my thoughts kept returning to the blood trail. The drops beside the footprints were found by the first few policemen at the murder scene, none of whom had any prior connection to Simpson or Fuhrman. Houseguest Kaelin testified that when he was taken into the main house of Simpson's estate between 5:45 and 6:30 a.m. on the morning after the crimes, he saw blood drops in the foyer. He also saw blood drops on the driveway outside. DNA testing later revealed that those drops came from Simpson.

As for the blood on the Bronco, the drop near its door handle was also found in the pre-dawn hours, a time when Simpson was in Chicago. Even though Fuhrman found this drop, there was no way he could have planted it unless he was carrying a vial of Simpson's blood drawn on some prior occasion. That, of course, is nonsense. Not even Schatzman makes so absurd a claim.

There was also plenty of incriminating and unrefuted hair and fiber evidence. Cochran belittled the hairs, found in the wool cap left beside Goldman's body, by pulling a similar hat over his ears during his final argument, saying the one at the scene could have belonged to almost anyone. His act was designed to detract from the sober testimony of FBI agent Douglas Deedrick, who presented laboratory findings concluding many hairs in the cap "exhibit the same microscopic characteristics" as samples pulled from Simpson's head. Deedrick also said a single hair found on the back of Goldman's shirt closely resembled Simpson's and that he "wouldn't expect to find anything there if there was no physical contact." In short, the G-man was saying it was virtually impossible for Goldman's shirt to have picked up the hair from the ground, even if it had been left there on a previous Simpson visit. Deedrick also said a 12-inch hair with the same microscopic characteristics as Nicole's was stuck to the glove found at Simpson's estate.

No one claimed the hair evidence was nearly so precise as the blood evidence. But when you find both Simpson's blood and his hair at the murder scene, and when he has a wound at a spot that is a logical source for the blood, it's hard to conclude anything other than that he was present for and a participant in the murders. And there were the footprints. Etched in blood, they came from a pair of $325 Bruno Magli shoes comparable to ones Simpson owned. Schatzman makes much of the fact that Simpson ordinarily has a pigeon-toed walk and the footprints appear to be parallel, not in keeping with Simpson's gait. Dennis suggests that a man "so dumb as to leave a knit cap and gloves" at the crime scene couldn't be smart enough to alter his gait. But I'm not suggesting he meant to change his stride. Instead, I believe murdering two people is enough to throw anyone—even O.J. Simpson— off stride, especially for the first few steps after the death struggle. It was, after all, only the first few steps that produced red footprints.

Deedrick also presented evidence that carpet fibers much like those in Simpson's Bronco were found both at the crime scene and on the glove Fuhrman discovered behind Simpson's house. Defense attorney F. Lee Bailey tried to suggest that the fibers could have come from any of the uniformed policemen who walked around the crime scene. But Deedrick said the fibers matching the Bronco's were so unusual that he had never seen any like them. The jury only heard that much of Deedrick's findings, but the public heard even more. The FBI agent reported the fibers found on the glove and the wool cap could only have come from Ford Broncos built in 1993 and 1994. Simpson's car, later returned to the Hertz Corporation, was a '94 model. That piece of information was kept from the jury because Deedrick failed to give defense lawyers a report on the topic. But everyone else now knew that Simpson didn't just leave his blood and hair at the murder scene, but also some polyester strings from his car.

Failure to get all the fiber evidence before the jury was a blunder almost as costly as the demonstration in which Simpson acted convincingly as if the murder gloves didn't fit. "The fibers from the car could have been some of their strongest, absolute killer evidence," said longtime defense lawyer Luke McKissack, who represented Sirhan Bishara Sirhan in his trial for the assassination of Robert Kennedy. "None of us knew how rare those Bronco fibers were, and now the jury never will."

With all that evidence, it is inconceivable to me that Simpson was not at the scene and a participant, at the very least, in the killings. With all the evidence before the jury, it was unbelievable that Simpson could be acquitted—if the verdicts were reached strictly on that evidence. Defense attorneys knew all this as early as a year before the verdicts. They also knew the evidence was all circumstantial: There were no eyewitnesses. So they set about systematically to discredit the collection and handling of the evidence, contending it had been contaminated.

The question they never answered, however, was this: How

does contamination cause someone else's blood and hair to turn into that of O.J. Simpson? For contamination to be the cause of evidence implicating Simpson, this would have had to have occurred. But this plain reality didn't faze defense attorneys. They attacked virtually every police figure, starting with officer Robert Riske, the first cop on the scene. He secured the crime scene immediately. But he made at least one mistake: He picked up the kitchen telephone in Nicole's condo to call for help. Had the murderer left fingerprints on it, they would have been destroyed by Riske's action. Of course, if Simpson's prints had been found on the phone, they could have been explained away easily enough. He visited the condo often.

Neufeld and Scheck then led the assault on Fung and Mazzola, who collected most of the blood evidence. Fung touched the envelope bearing Mrs. Brown's eyeglasses with his bare hand, Scheck claimed. When Fung denied it, Scheck produced a videotape, triumphantly gloating, "How about that, Mr. Fung?!" But he never answered the key question—so what? What if Fung did pick up the envelope without using a rubber glove? Useful fingerprints are almost never found on plain paper, so it was highly unlikely that Fung's alleged carelessness could have caused any harm.

Scheck and Neufeld also tried to establish that Fung and Mazzola collected multiple blood samples without changing gloves. The implication: Blood from one drop might mix with blood from another to render both meaningless. In fact, if such mixing, or "contamination," as Cochran, Scheck and Neufeld insistently called it, had resulted, lab tests would have showed mixed blood types and mixed DNA. But there were no such results. So any mistakes made by Fung and Mazzola made little or no difference to the facts of the case, even if they served to discredit police in the eyes of the jury.

The defense, in fact, brought on one witness almost exclusively to criticize the alleged contamination in the police crime lab. That was John Gerdes, clinical director of the Denver firm Immunological Associates. Gerdes said the LAPD lab "has a substantial contamination problem that is persistent...." The worst he'd ever seen, he said. But even Gerdes stopped short of saying he saw actual proof of contamination in the Simpson case. His most telling point came when he noted that criminalist Colin Yamauchi handled the reference sample test tube of Simpson's blood about the same time that he examined the bloodstained glove found at Simpson's estate. But even if that had resulted in some of Simpson's sample blood dripping onto the glove, it would have produced a mix if some other blood was already on the glove.

Planting in the jury a sense that the blood was contaminated in the LAPD laboratory or even at the crime scene was vital to the defense strategy of discrediting the DNA evidence at the heart of the prosecution case. For defense lawyers failed in all their efforts to show there might have been contamination or mixups in the two outside labs where DNA tests were conducted. So they had to convince jurors that the scientific evidence was suspect, at best, before it left the LAPD and went to the DNA laboratories. There is no doubt they accomplished that task.

They also attacked the statistics that placed the odds at one in more than one billion that anyone besides Simpson was the source of the blood at the scene. This attack was based on the argument that the pool of African Americans from Detroit whose genetic makeup was compared with Simpson's was far too small to supply definite conclusions. It was an argument that raged before the California Supreme Court even as Simpson's case proceeded. At issue was the conviction of Jesse Venegas, the so-called "Supermarket Rapist" imprisoned for raping and robbing a woman in a Bakersfield, California, parking lot.

As in Simpson's case, there were no eyewitnesses to identify Venegas as the suspect. But semen taken from the victim was found to be a DNA match for Venegas. An FBI criminalist testified in his trial that only one person in 65,000 could have the same DNA markers found both in the blood of Venegas and the semen from the victim. Those odds were far lower than the odds on Simpson, but they were enough to satisfy the Venegas jury. His lawyer, Donnalee Huffman, promptly appealed. "It all depends on the accuracy of the statistics," she said. "A DNA match is really a 'non-exclusion.' It just means you can't exclude the person as a possible donor on the basis of the DNA. Without reliable statistics showing how many people will have similar DNA patterns, it's no good."

That was the same argument Scheck made to the Simpson jury, which arrived at a far different conclusion from the Venegas panel. The Simpson defense also could have called on Kerry Mullis, Nobel Prize-winning inventor of the polymerase chain reaction (PCR) method of DNA analysis, who was ready to testify that the PCR testing done in Simpson's case should not have been considered conclusive.

In the end, the arguments about contamination and purity swayed the jury. "I didn't find the scientific evidence very convincing at all," said the former juror number 6, Lionel Cryer. Put that together with the suspicion pushed by Cochran that at least some of the evidence was planted by Fuhrman or other police officers, and it was enough for this jury to acquit.

One persistent question that has dogged prosecutors since the trial ended is this: Could the outcome have been different if they had presented more evidence? For sure, they had more evidence, both physical evidence and evidence of Simpson's behavior at the time of the crimes and earlier. But it's uncertain how useful it could have been.

One set of evidence the jury never saw was the material in Al Cowlings' Ford Bronco during the slow-speed chase on which he and Simpson led police during the afternoon and evening of June 17, 1994. Taken from the car when the two men finally gave themselves up in the driveway of Simpson's mansion were $8,750 in cash, six checks in a sealed envelope, Simpson's passport and a false beard. Defense attorney Robert Shapiro claimed from the moment of Simpson's capture that Simpson and Cowlings had merely planned to visit Nicole Simpson's grave before he turned himself in. But the Bronco was spotted heading toward Mexico on the San Diego Freeway several miles past the appropriate exit for the cemetery. The confiscated items and the location could have been used to argue that Simpson was trying to flee the country before the chase began. The chase also could have been used to counter the melodramatic descriptions given by his family of Simpson's demeanor in the days following the trial.

But it wasn't, partly because of police bungling like the mistakes that began almost as soon as the bodies were discovered. Detectives Tom Lange and Philip Vannatter booked most of the contents of the Cowlings Bronco—including the money and checks—not as evidence, but as the personal property of Cowlings, who wasn't a suspect in the murders or any other crime. One result was that the chase was never mentioned to the jury, several of whose members had watched at least parts of it. William Hodgman, who supervised the prosecution team, later said, "If you knew some of the evidence we were dealing with, you would understand what the cost-benefit analysis was."

But the jury did see several red herrings tossed its way. One was the Ben & Jerry's ice cream Nicole apparently bought for her kids on the night of the murders. A small cup of the ice cream was found on a railing in Nicole's condo after the murders, but police paid little attention to it because they saw no signs that the killer or killers had entered the unit, even though its door was wide open. But defense lawyers made much of the ice cream, trying to show that it was partially melted well after 10 p.m., which would have considerably narrowed the time available to Simpson for the murders. Prosecution and defense both tested the melting rate of the ice cream, eventually proving nothing. All this did was leave before the jury the defense suggestion of a warped timeline.

And some evidence was simply lacking. Where were the killer's presumably bloody clothes? Where was the murder weapon? These were never found, in spite of weeks of ransacking every dumpster and landfill in the West Los Angeles area and every vacant lot near Chicago's O'Hare Airport. It occurred to me early in the trial that if he committed the murders at about 10:15 p.m., as prosecutors argued, Simpson had plenty of time to rush the three miles down to the Santa Monica Pier, drop it all in the drink and still return home shortly before 11 p.m., as limousine driver Allan Park reported he did. As for the clothes, there was that telltale Louis Vuitton garment bag which Simpson carried to and from Chicago the night of the crimes. It was carried— stuffed full—from the Simpson home the next afternoon by faithful pal Robert Kardashian. But the next time it appeared in court fully eight months later, it was empty. Kardashian said he never opened it and didn't know what it contained. But the defense resisted mightily when prosecutors sought to call him as a witness. And there were reports in publications as august as *Time* magazine that at a point when some Simpson lawyers considered a plea bargain to a charge of manslaughter, Kardashian was willing to plead guilty to being an accessory. And there was the mysterious black bag that Kaelin said Simpson didn't want him to touch, the bag that never returned from its presumed trip to Chicago.

The upshot is that there was plenty of evidence that the defense, as it were, never laid a glove on. They never came close to proving that any policeman ever planted so much as a single drop of Simpson's blood along the macabre trail leading from the bodies to his bedroom. The uncontroverted hair and fiber evidence alone would have been more than enough to convict 90 percent of defendants, in spite of Cochran's ridicule. Even though Simpson plainly planned carefully, Goldman's inadvertent presence added some unforeseen physical factors, and this was no longer the perfect crime. But considering the huge mass of hair, fiber and blood evidence, this should instead have been the slam-dunk case police and prosecutors at first thought it was. It didn't quite turn out that way.

DENNIS SCHATZMAN

Since You're So Smart,
Where's the Knife?

Everyone remembers watching the FBI video production of *John DeLorean and the Five Kilos of Cocaine*. It appeared on television screens all over America about 10 years ago. In that epic, DeLorean is captured on videotape sipping Dom Perignon with a few undercover FBI agents who had just sold him some of the world's finest Peruvian flake. Then came the punchline. This was a bust. Out came the handcuffs and the movie would forever be etched on tape.

Fortunately for DeLorean, he had the common sense to hire two brilliant lawyers named Donald Re and Howard Weitzman, who figured out a way to convince a jury that what they saw on the videotape didn't really happen. It's like the old joke about the man who was caught by his wife in bed with another woman. A few moments later, while the wife is screaming her head off and threatening divorce, castration and God knows what else, the man looks up from his evening newspaper and asks: "Who are you going to believe. Me, or your lying eyes?" And so it was with the DeLorean case.

The evidence against DeLorean appeared airtight. But Re and Weitzman persuaded the judge to throw out some of the evidence; the jury was told that DeLorean was entrapped, and the former automaker walked out the courtroom door a free man. Was there any outcry about letting a drug dealer go free? Not that I recall. Was there any clamor for a change in the "criminal justice system" because DeLorean danced through the legal raindrops? Nyet. Was there a call for the heads of the jury? No. Or, as former Los Angeles County District Attorney Robert Philibosian would say, "Were the jurors enthralled by DeLorean's 'celebrity' status and his poster-boy good looks?" I don't think so.

Such, however, was not the case with Orenthal James Simpson. Of course, Simpson, a black man, was accused of killing two white people, one of them his estranged wife. DeLorean, a white boy, was merely caught buying drugs to sell to little black and brown kids in the ghettos of the Land of the Free. America, what a country.

Let's not stop there. What about the first three trials of John Gotti, that celebrated Mafioso America loved to love. The FBI had the goods on Big John. They had informants, snitches, wiretaps, you name it. They had what one might call "the proverbial dick in the pussy." But he, too, walked out the courtroom door. So once again, justice got screwed. Was there an outcry from anyone other than the FBI or the American Civil Liberties Union? Not that I recall. Can you recall? Hell no, you can't recall. Because there wasn't any. Was there a clamor to change the jury system? Nada on that one, too. There was an earthquake of indignation, however, when O.J. Simpson walked out the courtroom door. But, of course, Simpson is black; Gotti is white. I know you white folks hate hearing that, don't you?

Now we come to two of my favorite cases; *The People vs. Soon Ja Du*, better known as the woman who shot and killed Latasha Harlins, and *The People vs. Laurence Powell, Ted Briseno, Stacey Koon and Timothy Wind*, the LAPD officers who tried to kill black motorist Rodney King. One of the similarities is that both brutal scenes were captured on videotape and played on news shows all over the country.

In the *Du* case, the grocer was caught on tape blowing the back of Harlins' head off as the girl was leaving the woman's store. Du had accused the black 15-year-old honor student of attempting to steal a $1.79 bottle of orange juice. Even though the student had been holding the money in her hand, Du violated the cardinal rule of the ghetto: Never put your hands on anyone. She grabbed Harlins by the collar and the girl went upside Du's head and down the other. Du pulls the gun and Harlins turns to leave and "POW"! One dead black girl. The woman didn't even budge to see if Harlins was all right. Not one bit of remorse oozed from Du. Not one milliliter.

A jury found her guilty of manslaughter. But the judge, a

Jewish princess named Joyce Karlin, let Du walk out of the courtroom door with a $500 fine and some community service time. It was the height of insult, not only to the black community—of course, who cares about that?—but also to the "criminal justice system." Karlin said that she wanted to promote healing. Can you believe that? Worse, when she ran for election to the bench the following year, her fellow judges almost unanimously supported her financially. Even a black "handkerchief head" (that means "Uncle Tom") judge named Alban Niles chipped in $200 toward her election. Every time I hear his name, I want to throw up.

Worse still, a truckload of lawyers supported Karlin, this woman who let a murderer go free (oops, did I say that? Now where did I get that phrase from?). Marlene Adler Marks, the managing editor of Los Angeles' *Jewish Journal*, turned Karlin's election into a *cause celebre*. I'm paraphrasing here, but in short, Marks told her readers, in March 1992, that supporting Karlin was a Jewish thing. What she did was within her rights as a judge, so we Jews must support her. Let me pause while you think about that for a minute.

On a talk show, *Which Way, L.A.*, a National Public Radio program hosted by the brilliant Warren Olney of KCRW-FM Los Angeles, discussing the Simpson trial, I brought up the Karlin decision. I lambasted my colleagues for turning tail and running away from the issue. I believed that the media should have sliced Karlin up during the campaign, much like they're doing to Simpson even as we read.

Also appearing on the show was Lou Cannon, Los Angeles Bureau Chief of the *Washington Post*. He used the old white-boy defense against criticisms coming from blacks, which is to take offense to, and feign hurt because of, my comments before a predominantly white audience. Cannon, who was on leave from the *Post* to write a book about the LAPD—that qualified him to be on the show, I suppose—claimed to have written reams of copy on the Du/Harlins/Karlin incident. But to write a couple of six-graph stories that appear on page A-17 is one thing, and to write story after story that pounds and pounds and pounds hard on this travesty of justice is another thing entirely. Lou failed on that score, as did virtually every other white journalist and white-owned medium. Of course, the victim was a poor little black girl named Latasha Harlins, not a white socialite named Nicole Brown Simpson. A bit different, wouldn't you say?

The odyssey of Rodney King: Now that's a story in which we can compare how evidence is viewed differently by blacks and whites. We all know the story *ad nauseum*. King was videotaped being beaten to a pulp by the cops in the middle of a parking lot in front of dozens of witnesses. The cops lied on the police report. They lied to their superior officers. They lied, lied, lied about what they did to King. But as with DeLorean and Du, the videotape tells all. At least that's what I thought.

During the trial, which was moved to Simi Valley, where damn near all the white cops live, the tape was played again and again and again. It showed that King laid down when he was told to lay down; he got up when he was told to get up. But in each instance, while they called him "nigger," the cops beat him unmercifully with their nightsticks—in the end, a total of 57 times. Despite this "airtight evidence" the all-white jury (and one Filipino, but they consider themselves white) let the marauders walk out the door as free men. Several of the jurors who gave interviews claimed that the public wasn't privy to "all" of the evidence. But they were. Of course, they never said what that evidence was. I suspect it was because there was no other evidence. They said that just to get themselves off the hook. The verdicts so disgusted me that I committed to memory the names of the jurors—who were responsible for burning my city down. Here they are: Dorothy Bailey, Alice Debord, Thomas Gorton, Henry King, Retta Kossow, Virginia Loya, Gerald Miller, Christopher Morgan (I almost wanted to say Darden), Amelia Pigeon, Charles Sheehan, Kevin Siminski and Anna Whiting. Loyal Americans, all. Strike that. Loyal white Americans all. They protected and served the LAPD. Daryl Gates must have stuck his chest out with pride.

What I'm saying is this: There is a double standard being played out when it comes to what is considered evidence and what is not. In this country, it's "majority rules." Translation: if the white man says it's so, then it's so.

Which brings us to the issue at hand: the evidence in the Simpson trial. My colleague, Tom Elias, has eloquently laid out the blood evidence and the DNA evidence and the hair follicles and the fibers from the Ford Bronco found at the Bundy murder scene. I'll concede to all of that. The shit was Simpson's, okay? Are you satisfied? But that doesn't tell the whole story in this very complicated double murder. Remember what the jury instructions said: If it's found that a witness has lied on one issue, one can and must assume that the witness may be lying in other areas as well. So the blood found at the scene, and in the Bronco, and on the Simpson walkway, and testified to by detective Philip Vannatter, could be challenged because Vannatter had lied before. He lied about the reasons why he sieged Simpson's estate without a search warrant. He committed perjury. That makes Vannatter a liar, doesn't it? You bet your sweet ass it does. Therefore, the blood and how it got where it was found is fair game for criticism, unless one believes that the LAPD detectives wouldn't lie. Elias would call that splitting hairs. But I don't. Lying is lying, period. A black man who lied on his job application about whether or not he has ever been arrested is fired for lying on his job application. And that's the truth.

Let's talk about the strategy of Simpson's DNA attorneys Barry Scheck and Peter Neufeld, two blood experts from the Big Apple. Tom says that was just a sin and a shame that these two barristers would pick on poor little old criminalists Dennis Fung and Andrea Mazzola just because they fucked up the integrity of the blood evidence they collected. So they have a few faults, Tom would say. But this is a murder case in which blood is at the heart of the prosecution's case. Just as the role of the defense attorney in this case is to pick holes in the prosecution's armor by raising reasonable doubts. That's their job, like it or not.

Elias explains that even though there were tremendous screw-ups in the collection and preservation of the blood evidence, it's still Simpson's blood. Yes, Tom, but to raise the issue of screw-ups is "in play." After all, it's in play whenever whites complain about Affirmative Action. You've heard the comments before. "The workplace has been contaminated because we have these 'inferior' blacks and browns running around not knowing what they're doing." Or, "I would hire blacks, but we can't find any who are *qualified*." Then if incompetence, or the perception thereof, is fair game in race relations and Republican politics, then it's certainly fair game in this case. Scheck and Neufeld were past-masters in exploiting the major *faux pas* of the prosecution's blood evidence. Now everyone is mad at Scheck and Neufeld. Do you think they care? I don't think so. The simple fact is, if your work product is piss-poor, your ass gets called on the carpet. In this case, the carpet was a jury and an international audience.

Juror Brenda Moran, for example, completely dismissed the domestic violence evidence outright. I agree with her. It proved that Simpson was an ogre, or was once an ogre, but it didn't prove that he killed his estranged wife. The government spent an inordinate amount of time advancing this "if-he-slapped-her-around-once-upon-a-time-then-he-must-have-killed-her" argument. It got to the point where it became boring as well as irrelevant.

Then there was the veiled non-evidence covering the whole area of where was Simpson between 9:40 p.m. and 10:45 p.m. on the night of the murders. The prosecution got all bent out of shape just because no one saw him chipping golf balls into the children's sand box, or taking a nap or taking a shower or any of those alibis Simpson gave the police. "Aha," said the big, bad wolf commonly known as the district attorney's office. "This and this alone proves that Simpson killed Brown Simpson and Goldman. No one saw him do any of those things. His alibi is flawed!" Back to reality, however: If it was a fact that Simpson was indeed at the Bundy murder scene during that time frame, why did no one see him there either? Where's the evidence?

What else can we talk about? Oh yes. The "plaintive wail" of the dog. Seems to me that if the dog saw all or part of the murders, and it was Simpson who dunnit, this would have been a traumatic episode in the dog's life. They don't forget things like that. I remember once as a college student, every time I came over to my father's house, his dog would growl at me and bare his very impressive canines. One day, Dad's dog got a little too close with his act and I picked him up and threw his ass over the porch railing. From that day on, that dog would run away from me every time I approached. Even when he was locked up in my father's house for three days because my father had keeled over and died of a heart attack, when I went to check on him, the dog bolted out the door when I opened it. He never forgot that free flight in the air I gave him. Had I been the prosecuting attorney, I would have waltzed little Kato into the courtroom and brought him over to Simpson to let the jury see his reaction. See if he wails plaintively, or some such. Well, anyway, it seemed like a good idea to me.

On the subject of the bloody glove found behind Kato Katlin's guest house. Now this is one for the show *Jeopardy*. Let us recap. Fuhrman checks out Kato's story about hearing and feeling three thumps on his wall by the air conditioner by going outside to investigate and lo and behold, there is a bloody glove lying right there in the bushes—and it looks exactly like the one he saw at the Bundy scene. (Remember, Fuhrman testified that he saw "them" at the murder scene. But who's quibbling over minor details?) The detective testified to all of that.

Further, there's the question of why there are no Bruno Magli-tracked bloody footprints around the area where the glove was found. Nor was there evidence that the spiderwebs that Fuhrman broke to find the glove were broken by a killer who dropped the glove and then re-woven by a lightning-fast eight-legged creature.

We've already been over the fact that O.J.'s bow-legged pigeon-toed walk is inconsistent with the bloody footprints found outside the murder scene. But Tom says that after he killed the victims, Simpson didn't walk that way because he was "off stride." Please. And what about the glove not fitting? After Christopher Darden fucked up that demonstration, the prosecution scurried around to find experts to testify that the gloves shrank nearly one sixth from their original size as a result of the numerous tests they were put through. Try as they might to clean up Darden's mess, a picture was worth a thousand words. *The gloves didn't fit!* And, as Tom Elias reminds us through the words of Johnnie Cochran, "If it doesn't fit, then you must acquit."

In short, evidence is as evidence does. And the evidence just wasn't there to convict Simpson beyond a reasonable doubt. It wasn't there for John DeLorean, and Superior Court Judge Joyce Karlin believed it wasn't there in sufficient quantity to convince her to send Soon Ja Du up the river. If it wasn't there for them, then it's not there for Simpson either. But, of course, Simpson is *black*.

And I didn't even mention the knife.

CHAPTER 10
THE LAWYERS

TOM ELIAS

The Lawyer Who Wasn't There and the One Who Was

An absence of reasonable doubt, William Hodgman told the jury at the end of the state trial of savings and loan swindler Charles H. Keating Jr., does not mean an absence of all doubt. Certainty, he said, is like a glass of water. It can be one-half or one-quarter or three-quarters full or more. But there can still be plenty of water, even if the glass isn't completely filled. Similarly, he told the Keating jury, you can be reasonably certain, certain beyond a reasonable doubt, even if there's still a small amount of room for doubt.

No one will ever know whether an explanation like that or the other Hodgman analogy of the clear liquid running from a kitchen faucet could have changed the outcome of the O.J. Simpson double murder trial. By the time closing arguments began, Hodgman had been on the sidelines of the case for more than nine months, felled by a near heart attack caused by the continual emotional stress of the case. That left the way clear for the rhetoric of chief defense lawyer Johnnie Cochran to convince the jury it could strike a blow against racism by acquitting Simpson—even though the murders of Nicole Brown Simpson and Ronald Goldman had nothing to do with race.

As the case began, the notion that Cochran would be a key man at the finish and Hodgman wouldn't was very unlikely. For Cochran was a late addition to the defense team, while Hodgman was a strong prosecution presence from the very first. But Cochran spent more than a month agonizing about whether he should help defend his old friend Simpson. He considered the same question Howard Weitzman had already answered in the negative: Should a lawyer defend a personal friend? Of all the dozens of lawyers who would be involved in the so-called

"Trial of the Century," no others had similar qualms.

"I didn't hesitate for a moment when I was called," Robert Shapiro told me during the fall of 1994. Shapiro headed Simpson's defense team until it became clear there would be no plea bargain, that the case would go to trial. But Cochran and Weitzman hesitated. An old Simpson pal who had played tennis with O.J. for years and watched most of the football games he played at the University of Southern California, Weitzman was the first lawyer Simpson called. But he bowed out of the case when it was just two days old, bouncing it over to his friend Shapiro. Weitzman, famed for winning an acquittal in the drug trial of onetime automaker John DeLorean despite apparently overwhelming videotape evidence, accompanied Simpson to police headquarters in downtown Los Angeles the day after the murders, but became visibly upset when Simpson insisted on talking alone to homicide detectives Philip Vannatter and Tom Lange. Rumors—never confirmed—circulated for months that Weitzman quit the next day not out of pique over being crossed by his client, but because Simpson confessed the crimes to him. Weitzman has never revealed what Simpson told him in private, but publicly insisted that he couldn't defend Simpson because their friendship was too old and too close.

That didn't stop Cochran. A flashy dresser who lives in the mostly-white Los Feliz district of Los Angeles and drives a Rolls Royce to his Wilshire Boulevard offices every day, he says Simpson began calling him within a couple of days of his arrest. But he didn't accept the assignment until about two weeks after the preliminary hearing because he worried that his friendship with Simpson might make it difficult for him to work effectively. "I thought about that a lot because I've never defended a friend before," Cochran told a reporter on the day of his first court appearance for Simpson. "But I concluded I can represent him objectively. And besides, who best to be on your side but a friend?"

Once he took the case, Cochran appeared to love every minute of it. He even relished the way reporters seeking fresh quotes followed him into the ninth-floor men's room at every break. Forbidden to give interviews in the hallway outside the courtroom, Cochran and other Simpson case lawyers often talked as they and male reporters stood side-by-side in front of the rest room's three urinals. That's where Shapiro first acknowledged to me the role race would have in the case, where Barry Scheck gloated about how he was exposing the failings of the crime lab and where Carl Douglas hinted at the line of questioning he would use against prosecution witness Ron Shipp.

Cochran's addition to the team Shapiro had already assembled assured that race would be a central issue. "Race plays a part in everything in America," he was fond of saying, in private and in public. Afterward, he would deny that his tactics created barriers between blacks and whites, claiming he merely exposed what was already there. "African Americans have a lot of concerns," he said. "All this did was bring it out."

But in spite of that talk and Shapiro's later complaint that Cochran played the race card "from the bottom of the deck," it was Shapiro, not Cochran, who first injected race into the case. Leaked information about detective Mark Fuhrman reached writer Jeffrey Toobin of *The New Yorker* magazine just after the preliminary hearing. He revealed in July 1994 that Fuhrman's background would become a major issue in the case. Toobin's story reported that defense lawyers knew Fuhrman was a frequent user of the word nigger and that he had made racist complaints in a 1981 effort to gain a stress-related disability pension from the Los Angeles Police Department. Everything Toobin reported was borne out later in the trial, making it clear that even if Cochran had never entered the case, race had to become a central issue. So on this one, my colleague Dennis Schatzman is definitely right: Shapiro did "purchase the (race) cards and bring them to the party."

The race issue actually made the presence of Cochran or someone like him a must. "People didn't want to talk about race," said longtime Los Angeles defense lawyer Edi M.O. Faal, who defended one of the youths accused of the videotaped beating of trucker Reginald Denny at the outset of the 1992 Los Angeles riots. "But O.J. is a black man and Los Angeles is very racially sensitive. For him to have an all-white defense team would have alienated some potential black jurors."

When Cochran, then 56 and a veteran of cases involving entertainer Michael Jackson and onetime Black Panther Party leader

Geronimo Pratt, joined Simpson's team, he brought along his younger associates Carl Douglas and Shawn Chapman, who were to become regular courtroom presences. Like everyone else in Cochran's firm, both are African Americans.

From the moment he entered the Simpson courtroom, Cochran acted as if he were the lead defense attorney, even though that role wasn't formally ceded to him until months later. He made all the dramatic speeches. He strode about the courtroom with the cocksure air of a man who felt he owned the place. Even Caucasian Simpson lawyers soon began sporting African-themed neckties like his. Shapiro began to recede a bit.

Meanwhile, on the prosecution side, it was almost always a non-courtroom presence who controlled what transpired before the TV cameras. District Attorney Gil Garcetti realized from the first moments of the trial that this could be the most important case of his first four-year term. His deputies had blown several major cases both before and after he won election in mid-1992—the McMartin Preschool molestation case, the first Rodney King beating trial, the first Menendez murder trial and the trial of the young men who beat Denny. For Garcetti, this was a chance to redeem his office and to establish that things would be different under his regime than they were under predecessor Ira Reiner.

So Garcetti, a conservative Democrat, determined to manage the case from the start. While he never appeared in court, his aide and chief publicist Suzanne Childs, a lawyer and ex-wife of author and screenwriter Michael Crichton, was a frequent attendee from the beginning. And Garcetti was the first prosecutor to speak publicly about the case. "We saw (in the slow-speed chase), perhaps, the falling of an American hero," he pronounced even as the chase proceeded. "To some extent, I viewed Mr. Simpson in the same way. But let's remember. We have two innocent people who have been brutally murdered...."

Two days later, he predicted Simpson might resort to some kind of diminished capacity defense. "It wouldn't surprise me if at some point we go from 'I didn't do it' to 'I did it, but I'm not responsible.'" Garcetti's conduct from those early moments demonstrated that he knew the Simpson case could be central to his political future. He met daily with his line prosecutors and often watched the proceedings on TV, critiquing their performance. "A conviction would be very, very helpful to his re-election chances," Arnold Steinberg, a Republican campaign manager who helped steer Los Angeles Mayor Richard Riordan's winning 1993 campaign, told me early in the trial. "But he made a major mistake when he commented on the case early on. That told everyone he was steering the prosecution, so he would be personally responsible for the outcome." Added Allen Hoffenblum, another Republican consultant, "If they lose on this case, the (white) people will think it's because of either incompetence or racism. (White) people would blame Garcetti for bringing the case downtown."

With his future at stake, Garcetti carefully placed two of the top people in his office in charge of convicting Simpson: Marcia Clark and William Hodgman. Clark had a strong record prosecuting gang members and murder cases, while Hodgman had been promoted to chief of central operations after he convicted Keating. Clark and Hodgman began to oversee the investigation even as police were questioning Simpson the day after the slayings. They appear clearly in videotape shot at Simpson's house by several television stations that morning, even before Vannatter swore out a search warrant.

From the first, Clark demonstrated star quality, while Hodgman exhibited the same stolid, persistent nature that had served him so well in the Keating trial and scores of others. Almost from the moment of Simpson's first court appearance, it was clear that Clark would become a celebrity. She was well aware it was happening. Instead of returning telephone calls and conversing easily with reporters in the courthouse hallway—the usual behavior for deputy district attorneys—Clark adopted a haughty air and refused to answer most questions tossed at her.

When she changed her hairdo to eliminate the Medusa-like curls that had been her trademark for the trial's first few months, she did a small pirouette outside the courtroom door so every reporter could see the change. That new hairdo was the work of Beverly Hills stylist Allen Edwards, well-known for his work on movie stars. Clark's celebrity-like behavior aroused some sarcasm during the trial from other deputy district attorneys. "You can call me 'the other Marcia,'" said fellow deputy Marcia Daniels, who spent six weeks prosecuting another spousal murder in the court-room just west of Ito's during the Simpson trial. Unlike Clark, "the other Marcia" got a conviction. Resentment boiled over, however, when Garcetti awarded $43,000 in bonuses to Clark, Hodgman and Christopher Darden a month after the trial—just days before Clark and Darden signed big-bucks book contracts. "I am beyond upset," said longtime deputy Lea P. D'Agostino. "And so is everyone else to whom I've spoken…If the office wants to do this, fine, but do it for everyone. What are the other deputies in this office, chopped liver?"

Hodgman, however, steadfastly resisted star treatment. Unlike Clark, who always used a private restroom near the judge's chambers instead of the ladies' room off the ninth-floor hallway, he frequented the public men's room as long as he was a central figure in the case. Unlike the publicity-hungry defense lawyers, he never revealed anything of substance there. But stress soon began to tell on Hodgman. He suffered from the flu during jury selection. He missed several days of pretrial hearings due to ill-ness. Finally, in December 1994, he collapsed. He was never a major courtroom presence again, although he nominally coordi-nated prosecution efforts for the rest of the case.

When the prosecution lost Hodgman, it may have lost the case. For in his meticulous, studious way, he would have taken the jury through every piece of evidence during his final arguments, not allowing himself to be rushed by the judge's desire to end matters quickly. He would have offered to jurors his explanations of rea-sonable doubt, just as he did at the close of Keating's state trial. Focus groups staged by defense jury consultants consistently found he inspired more trust than other prosecutors.

But the role Hodgman might have played was left to Darden, a late addition to the prosecution team. Darden's role in the case began when he conducted grand jury hearings into the actions of Simpson pal Al Cowlings during the infamous chase. Garcetti moved him to the big top in the Simpson circus in November 1994. He was inserted into the D.A.'s lineup only after it became obvious that the jury majority was to be African American and that Cochran would take the leading role on the defense side. "We need more people," Garcetti said about shifting Darden into Ito's courtroom. "The defense has nine lawyers—nine lawyers in the courtroom." Actually, there were some days when I counted 12.

Garcetti said his assigning the black, shaven-headed Darden to the case "could very easily backfire. There could be a juror who says, 'Are you bringing him on just because he's black?' The answer is obviously no." Darden's addition led to the most passionate debates of the case, starting with the one where he and Cochran argued the use of the N-word. Another bitter exchange came when Cochran objected as Darden tried to probe defense witness Robert Heidstra, who had told a friend he heard a deep voice, seemingly that of an older black man, coming from the alley near Nicole Simpson's condominium about the time of the murders. Cochran objected to that line of questioning. "I resent that…" he thundered. "You can't tell by somebody's voice whether they sounded black….That's a racist statement." Darden responded that it was Cochran who had made race a major issue in the case. "That's what has created a lot of problems for my family and myself, statements that you make about me and race."

Darden, forced into a role where he had to try to protect Fuhrman from questioning about his racist past, felt awkward from the first. He resented the fact that many whites always looked upon him as the prosecution's token black. "All too often people see me (and) other black professionals and they always want to minimize our accomplishments," he said in one-mid-trial interview. "They never accept the fact that we have sacrificed greatly….I've invested 15 years in this office as a prosecutor. For someone to suggest that I'm on this case because I'm black is to minimize my accomplishments, my efforts, my energy that I have put into this job." But Darden, who usually spoke in monosyllables when I approached him and never gave urinal interviews, didn't shake that "token" label until he delivered his passionate closing argument.

There was high irony, too, whenever Darden and Cochran took up verbal cudgels against each other. Not only had Cochran been a top assistant district attorney under then-D.A. John Van de Kamp at the time Darden was hired, but rumors constantly floated around the courtroom about each of them being a batterer. Those stories held that Cochran had beaten his first wife Barbara and that Darden did the same to one of his girlfriends. The rumors were never substantiated, but they lent an odd air when the pair grappled in the courtroom over the importance of Simpson's known wife-beating.

There was also a link between Cochran and Hodgman. Cochran hired Hodgman into the D.A.'s office, and the pair had nothing but respect for one another before the Simpson case began. "He's simply a thorough, untiring worker who usually gets his man," Cochran told me about Hodgman. Hodgman returned the compliment. "We knew this would really be tough the moment (Cochran) joined the defense team," Hodgman said.

There were no such ties between prosecutors and other defense lawyers. Shapiro, for instance, had rarely tried any cases in court, but made his reputation as a deal-maker. This led to early speculation that Simpson would eventually plead guilty to either manslaughter or second-degree murder. That speculation didn't last long, however, once Cochran entered the case. But it had some basis in fact while it lasted.

Simpson pal Robert Kardashian, a lawyer whose main public roles in the defense were to buck up the defendant's morale and to bring him crisp, freshly-cleaned custom-tailored suits to wear every day, said after the trial that early in the case, Shapiro discussed a possible manslaughter plea, wanting Kardashian to fall on his own sword and plead guilty to being an accessory, presumably for his handling of the mysterious Louis Vuitton garment bag and its missing contents. Kardashian said he wasn't ready to go along with that, "because I didn't do anything." He said the session where all this was discussed was also attended by Simpson's business lawyer Leroy (Skip) Taft and by F. Lee Bailey. "I told him O.J. would never go for it," Kardashian told a reporter. "I told him it's not a subject to be brought up to Simpson." And it apparently never was.

Meanwhile, Garcetti consistently denied the frequent plea-bargain rumors printed in supermarket tabloids. "The evidence is so strong in this case that we can't consider anything other than first-degree murder," he told me. And political consultant Steinberg said "It would be political suicide for him to agree to anything less."

This made it almost certain that Shapiro's role would recede as the case neared opening statements. Shapiro had managed the early phases of the case similarly to the way he handled the defense of actor Marlon Brando's son Christian, who shot his sister Cheyenne's Tahitian lover Dag Drollet in the head at point blank range in 1990. Shapiro got him off with a 10-year prison term when he could have faced a life sentence. He also represented baseball players like Darryl Strawberry, Vince Coleman and Jose Canseco in their brushes with the law and briefly defended parent-killer Erik Menendez. He has helped actress Linda Lovelace, rapper Vanilla Ice and movie producers Ivan Nagy and Robert Evans. Strawberry was an obvious favorite of his. Through most of the summer of '94, Shapiro delighted in regaling reporters with stories about the slugger's attempted comeback from drug and alcohol problems, speaking of Strawberry with obvious affection. Said one prosecutor, "Shapiro is the ultimate dealmaker. He never goes to trial."

The one previous Shapiro case with the most impact on Simpson's was his 1982 defense of fellow lawyer Bailey on a drunk-driving rap in San Francisco. Besides creating a friendship that lasted until the pair began feuding in December 1994, his defense of Bailey provided some portents of what Shapiro would do in the Simpson case.

In the 1982 trial, Shapiro pounded at the credibility of police, calling one witness who said that he, too, as Bailey claimed he had been, was physically attacked by the arresting officer. Then he read a list of others who claimed they had been choked, beaten or assaulted by the same cop. It's a common tactic for defense lawyers to discredit prosecution witnesses when their own cases are weak. But Shapiro's willingness to do it in the Bailey case—with far less at stake—should have alerted Simpson's prosecutors that Shapiro and Bailey would look closely at the background of every policeman in the Simpson investigation. Knowing this, they could have found out enough about Fuhrman to keep him off the witness stand. But once he testified in the preliminary hearing, there was no way to leave him out of later proceedings. And sure enough, the defense made Bailey its specialist on Fuhrman, letting him attack the ex-Marine and portray him as an out-of-control rogue cop.

The Bailey-Shapiro friendship began to break apart when Bailey backed Cochran's bid to become Simpson's lead lawyer. In fact, Bailey sided with a Cochran effort to remove Shapiro from the case entirely, a move thwarted only when Simpson stepped in and insisted Shapiro must stay. Animosity between Cochran and Shapiro became so strong in the winter of 1995 that Shapiro was frequently excluded from defense strategy sessions. Meanwhile, the lawyers said little publicly about their private resentments, staging a "dream team" unity press conference in December 1994 to announce the passing of the lead role to Cochran. Only after the trial did true feelings emerge, when Shapiro announced he would never work with Cochran again and would never again speak to Bailey.

Money was part of the dispute, as fee arrangements made early in the case had to be altered when the roles of Cochran and Bailey expanded. "There is constant tension between the three," a Simpson friend told me in February 1995. "It undoubtedly impedes the kind of coordination this case requires."

Before that ill will broke out, Shapiro also brought in Gerald Uelmen, the retired dean of the Santa Clara University law school who had helped him with the Brando defense. Uelmen successfully argued in that case a motion which prevented prosecutors from using against him statements Brando made to police. Shapiro immediately thought of Uelmen because Simpson also spoke to police without a lawyer present—when he essentially dismissed Weitzman. And Shapiro recruited Harvard Law School Professor Alan Dershowitz to advise his team on strategy and motions. Dershowitz only rarely appeared in court, but filed a constant stream of faxes to defense lawyers. He had worked with Bailey on the defense of publishing heiress Patty Hearst, who eventually was convicted of participating in a robbery after her mid-'70s kidnapping by Symbionese Liberation Army terrorists.

Only Simpson's money permitted such a team, augmented by DNA specialists Scheck and Peter Neufeld. One reliable source estimated the total attorney's fees Simpson paid at $4 million. He spent at least $1 million on professional witnesses like Dr. Henry Lee, Michael Baden and Herbert MacDonell. His fees for jury consultant services ran well above $100,000, while his payments to private investigators probably exceeded that. Because lawyers and others in the case refuse to divulge their fees, those numbers are approximations. Business lawyer Taft doled out the money from Simpson holdings that were placed at $10 million in papers filed during his divorce.

In the end, it was Cochran's arrival that very likely determined the outcome of the case. While Shapiro and Bailey would have used Fuhrman's racism to undermine him, it was Cochran's rhetoric that led the jury to consider all police in the case equally untrustworthy. Neither Bailey nor Shapiro could have argued the race card nearly as effectively as Cochran. Shapiro, for example, had a visceral opposition to Cochran's comparing Fuhrman to Adolf Hitler in his closing argument, a tactic suggested to him by an outside defense lawyer, Charles Lindner, whose family fled the Nazi terror. It was also Cochran with whom most jurors bonded. They made it apparent that they weren't especially fond of Douglas or Darden, the other black attorneys with major roles in the case. But they appeared to hang on Cochran's every word. Beatrice Wilson, the 72-year-old former juror number 12, routinely closed her eyes as she listened to some attorneys cross-examine witnesses. But whenever Cochran spoke, she was completely alert and attentive.

It seemed to me that the eight black female jurors viewed the three African American lawyers as potential sons, and the one they most liked, the one they most admired, was Cochran. This may have been helped along by the encomiums dealt out to him during the fall of 1994 by various black community activists. He was grand marshal of one parade and received copious coverage in the *Los Angeles Sentinel* for another award citing him as an "outstanding role model."

None of that was what Shapiro would later resentfully label "playing the race card from the bottom of the deck." But it was calculated to fix an image in the minds of the black jury majority long before they were sequestered. And because Hodgman wasn't there at the finish to remind jurors about what reasonable doubt actually is, they were easily swayed by the emotionalism of Cochran's appeal. I felt during those closing arguments that Hodgman's absence was probably as important as Cochran's presence. For with the often-bumbling Darden and Clark giving the prosecution's final arguments—the same pair who regularly misused evidence and failed to make adequate use of whole areas like domestic violence—there was no one to offset the smooth racial appeals with which Cochran sent the jury off to its so-called deliberations.

DENNIS SCHATZMAN

"First, Let's Kill All the Lawyers"

Whoever came up with the phrase, "First, let's kill all the lawyers," was probably talking about defense lawyers like Johnnie Cochran, Barry Scheck, Peter Neufeld and F. Lee Bailey. After all, who else could they have been talking about? I personally would have nominated Robert Shapiro and District Attorney Gil Garcetti as candidates for the gallows as well. Shapiro for being a liar, a turncoat and a crybaby. Garcetti for sticking his nose into the day-to-day nuts and bolts of the case where it didn't belong and ultimately gumming up the works. But who's listening to me these days? In this chapter, I want to discuss the role of the lawyers in this case, their tactics and how from my vantage point I believed they were perceived by both the mass media and the general public.

First, let's look at the attorneys for the defense; its leader, of course, was Cochran. This Loyola University-trained attorney was brilliant in court. No one can honestly deny it. Instead of being praised, as Leslie Abramson was for her textbook defense of parent-killer Lyle Menendez, Cochran was skewered and even lampooned—as by my colleague, Tom Elias—for his "flashy dress" and because he "drives a Rolls Royce to work every day." That's funny, since Elias considers wearing a pair of khaki trousers and a camel-hair blazer as the apex of high fashion. He even insulted me in front of our book publisher and two film producers about my penchant for wearing African clothing. When he first saw me in that garb, he told those men he thought I looked "silly." It was only later, he said, that he realized I had a great work ethic and a good mind. Thanks, Tom.

Cochran is accused of hitting below the belt in both his opening and closing arguments and all throughout the trial. His opening argument was blamed for sending William Hodgman to the hospital. And in the closing argument, he ignited a firestorm by invoking the name of Adolf Hitler to compare to Mark Fuhrman, and imploring the jury to "send a message" to the cops that *Thou Shalt Not Bear False Witness Against Thy Defendant*. He crushed the prosecution when he reminded the jury, "If it doesn't fit, you must acquit." That's why he was hated, not because he was a dirty player, but because he was accurate and effective almost to a fault. And all of this was seen by millions of television viewers. Critics also didn't like him because he was proficient at being able to take, as journalist Terry Melia writes, "seemingly trivial bits of information and stretching them into long, drawn-out dissertations, thus making the jurors think twice as hard about any given issue."

Fred Goldman, father of Ronald Lyle Goldman, really despised Cochran. Following Johnnie's closing statement, Goldman called a press conference and tearfully called Cochran "the worst kind of racist." Goldman, like virtually all other whites, doesn't know the difference between a "racist" and a "tropistic." As I explained earlier in this book, blacks in America are not racists *per se*. Blacks are tropistic. This means that they are responding to the racism that is heaped upon them day after day, and thus often react by showing hatred toward whites. Whites, on the other hand, despise blacks largely because of the color of their skin and how inferior and/or dangerous whites perceive them to be.

In the face of all that, Cochran's team managed to win anyway. But bias against the defense attorneys also took other forms. Even the voice tones of a Simpson lawyer became unfair game for criticism. Peter Neufeld, the Brooklyn-reared DNA expert, was often criticized for his accent. While cross-examining one of the LAPD criminalists, Neufeld repeatedly called Andrea Mazzola "Mazzoler." Judge Ito even took one occasion to tell Neufeld that his "Brooklyn accent" and the speed of his verbal delivery was giving the court stenographer a hard time, and that slap went nationwide. The *New York Post* poked fun at the incident with this front-page headline: "Bronx Cheer for Brooklyn."

Neufeld's partner Barry Scheck was detested, by and large, because of his take-no-prisoners approach to cross-examination. For nine days straight, Scheck pounded criminalist Dennis Fung into the sand with all the subtlety of a Tasmanian Devil. He would raise a question and then lance the criminalist with, "Now isn't that *right*, Mr. Fung?" When Ito didn't like Scheck's attitude, the New York lawyer would either challenge or simply ignore the jurist. There were times when both appeared to want to settle their differences out in the parking lot. One of the good points about Scheck was that his courtroom activity in attacking the DNA evidence kept all of us awake.

Many of the men and women in the journalist pool, particularly *New York Daily News'* Michelle Caruso and the Associated Press' Michael Fleeman, would poke fun at Robert Blasier's high-pitched voice. Blasier, a Sacramento-based DNA lawyer, proved, however, that he was no shrinking violet when conducting himself in the courtroom. A generally deferential man to both the judge and the prosecution, Blasier wouldn't back down when attacked. On a few occasions when Ito said something Blasier didn't like, the bald, diminutive lawyer would whip off his reading glasses and glare at the judge, as if to say, "You are not dealing with Pee-wee Herman here." And Ito wasn't.

F. Lee Bailey drew a lot of criticism in the media largely because many journalists and pundits felt that he didn't live up to his advance billing. They also didn't like him because he wouldn't talk to them. When the West Palm Beach-based lawyer cross-examined Mark Fuhrman, many critics unfairly felt that Bailey, in Perry Mason style, should have left the detective a jellyfish sobbing uncontrollably on the witness stand. "Bailey created such expectations, and did not deliver," opined Laurie Levenson, a professor of criminal law at Cochran's alma mater, Loyola University of Los Angeles. "Maybe he didn't have the right ammunition." Bailey would later have the last laugh. But he also got into a little sexist tiff with Marcia Clark when they pretty much called each other a boatload of liars.

Shapiro started off as the darling of the news media. While he was "handling things," the Beverly Hills attorney never met a reporter he didn't like. It was Shapiro who introduced the world to the seamier side of Mark Fuhrman. Shapiro would arrive each day in his chauffeur-driven automobile and descend the steps in front of the courthouse in full view of the cameras like he was freaking Loretta Young or something. Billed as a fixer and a plea bargainer, Shapiro's handling of witnesses was surprisingly very good. One of his greatest contributions to the case came during the first three days after the murders when Shapiro inked the deals on most of Simpson's expert witnesses. He is also responsible for bringing in virtually all the lawyers except Cochran. But Shapiro lost me after the verdict when he turned 180 degrees and criticized his colleagues for, as he says, injecting race into the trial. It was a pitiful way to ride off into the sunset.

Harvard's Alan Dershowitz became known as the long-range missile. He monitored the trial from his office in Cambridge and would fax comments and legal opinions to his colleagues while court was in session. Dershowitz drew venomous attacks from legal pundits and police groups nationwide when he accused the law enforcement community of teaching the practice of "testilying," the art of lying in court. Never mind that his accusations were partly borne out by detectives Fuhrman and Vannatter, many jealous legal critics, such as former Pennsylvania governor and U.S. Attorney General Richard Thornburgh, never forgave him, apparently, I suspect, for talking out of school.

Early in the proceedings, Dean Gerald Uelmen sent shock waves throughout the land when he told the court that his client would be heard using the word "fuck" on the 911 tapes. When I sidled up next to him at a urinal during the morning break—I believe I'm the one who started shadowing male lawyers into the men's room—I said to him, "Pretty interesting comments you made this morning." While shaking things off, Uelmen responded, "You do what you have to do." He then looked at my press credentials and instantly clammed up. A constitutional law scholar and former dean of the Santa Clara School of Law, Uelmen became the architect of many of the motions the defense submitted to the court. Generally, he was treated with deference and respect.

Carl Douglas, a partner in Cochran's firm, performed many functions. He was notorious for engaging in spin doctoring, giving as he gave the media cogent and precise comments on various aspects of the trial as he walked either into or out of the courthouse parking lot. He was the most effective lawyer in this case to engage in this practice. He always appeared to be busy and in a hurry to get to the side of his client while conducting these interviews. Douglas, I believe, earned the respect of the judge because Ito would often call upon the Northwestern Law School-trained attorney to inform the court about certain legal minutiae. Douglas' cross examination of Simpson's so-called friend Ron Shipp didn't set well with many reporters and probably the general public. Many thought he was too heavy-handed. Pointing over to Simpson, Douglas would lash out at Shipp and say, "You are really not this man's friend, *are you?*"

A few lawyers, like the University of California at Irvine's William Thompson, a population expert, and James Ferguson, the Greensboro, North Carolina attorney who represented Simpson on the Fuhrman tapes in his state, made cameo appearances. But the more interesting appearances came from two female attorneys, Shawn Chapman, an associate in Cochran's firm and Sara Caplan, who held a similar position in Shapiro's office. My comments about them are strictly sexist in nature and I make no apologies for them.

Although Chapman was a bust as a litigant asking questions of potential jurors during *voir dire*, she damn sure looked good doing it, waving her hair in the air. After that, Cochran relegated her to doing research in the case. Caplan, the University of Michigan-trained blonde, looked, as my late father would say, "good enough to drink." Although she spoke very little during the trial, and was rarely seen after Shapiro was demoted, she was definitely the belle of the ball. I don't think there was a male reporter anywhere in the courthouse who didn't express an interest in taking a couple of laps around the judge's sofa with her.

Moving on to the prosecution team, I'll lead off with District Attorney Gil Garcetti. His behavior throughout the trial should have proved that prosecutors are politicians first and attorneys *second*. Garcetti let it be known that he was going to be in charge of the strategy, often calling two meetings a day with the lawyers working on the case. There's no doubt in my mind that he was a hindrance to the process and not a help. Early on, Garcetti made his first mistake by publicly calling Simpson a "murderer" while the bodies were still warm. Jumping the gun this way is considered a no-no in the legal world. It hurts the defendant's right to a fair trial by trying to influence potential jury members.

Garcetti's decision to have the case tried in downtown Los Angeles was criticized universally, largely because the venue of original jurisdiction would have been predominantly-white Santa Monica. The reasoning Garcetti gave to the press was that (1) since his office opted to initially take the case before the Grand Jury, the case should then stay at 210 West Temple Avenue, and (2) He wanted the case tried downtown because a conviction coming from a multi-racial jury would have had more meaning. I thought both explanations were bogus. I think it was just a stupid move on his part.

The district attorney also drew criticism for not opting to seek the death penalty. But this was probably the smartest decision he made in this case. Under what I believe was largely bluff pressure from Los Angeles' black leadership, Garcetti told the leaders that he wouldn't do it. His real reasoning was that he believed—correctly, I might add—that no jury would convict Simpson if there was a possibility that he would go to the gas chamber. Ironically, the meeting, held at the offices of the Los Angeles Urban League, was also attended by Cochran, who had not yet been added to the defense team.

William Hodgman had few, if any, critics. A gentleman and a consummate professional, Hodgman was the head man on the case and was doing an admirable job as far as I could see. The public has been told that he was relegated to serving in an advisory role after his hospital stay. That's bullshit. In reality, Hodgman got sick and tired of Garcetti getting in the way. So he took the advisory role way out. I may be reaching here, but I think he's our next elected District Attorney after Gil Garcetti hangs up his shingle and runs for mayor of Los Angeles or state attorney general.

Marcia Clark lived up to her billing as a no-nonsense, "tough-as-nails" prosecutor. From the very beginning, she was the HWIC—head woman in charge—for the prosecution. She was a master at getting her way in court. Whenever Judge Ito was on the verge of issuing a ruling favorable to the defense, Clark would cock her head slightly, bat her eyelashes at the jurist and that was that. Compounding her already tough job of trying to make lemonade evidence out of lemons, Clark had to battle her estranged husband Gordon (what a scumbag) Clark over the custody of their two young boys.

Clark was also smitten by the Hollywood media bug. As the trial went on, she first changed her hair style and then she spruced up her wardrobe, all of which prompted a local pilot to fly around the courthouse dragging a sky banner asking her for a date. She frequently had lunches delivered to her office from the Normandie Club, a legal gambling joint in southern Los Angeles County. As mentioned earlier, Clark engaged in several verbal skirmishes with Bailey, but she also stood toe-to-toe and slugged it out with Cochran in a couple of legal bouts. Although she was representing the prosecution, Clark was generally respected in the black community. People would come up to her and give her their two-cents worth about how she was railroading the football Hall of Famer. But in the same sentence, they would often ask, "By the way, will you sign my T-shirt?"

Christopher Darden. Oh Chris, how do I fault thee? Let me count the ways. At first, I felt sorry for him because of his "damned-if-you-do-damned-if-you-don't" situation. But it didn't take long for him to start crying after he joined the prosecution's team in mid-November 1994. First he cried about the use of the "N-word." Then he cried because he felt the black community didn't like him because he was trying to pack Simpson away on ice. And he cried and cried and cried to anyone who would listen about how he felt that Johnnie Cochran was picking on him. When things didn't go his way, Darden cried the blues and threatened to leave the legal profession, as if anyone was going to miss him.

I first began defending Darden by telling television and radio talk show audiences that he wasn't disliked because he was a prosecutor. I explained that over 60 percent of all African American lawyers work for the government, many of them prosecutors. Blacks understood that. What they didn't like about Darden was how he peacocked around the courtroom scowling at Bailey and Cochran for no apparent reason. They didn't like how he would bait Cochran by telling a press conference audience that his adversary should "put up or shut up." When Cochran later put up, and chumped Darden off all at the same time, the Bald One, you guessed it, started bitching and moaning. After the jury rang in the new month of October with the acquittals, Darden couldn't control his emotions at a Garcetti-led press conference and sobbed his way into the waiting hands of the Goldmans and of white America.

For all Darden's trouble, Garcetti blessed him, Clark and Hodgman with whopping bonuses and a publisher inked him to a million-dollar book deal. I found that book situation extremely nauseating. Here is a man who screwed up often in court, who embarrassed the profession and, above all, was on the losing end of the case. But he gets a book deal. It reminds me of the financial rewarding of Peter McNeely, the boxer who lasted all of 87 seconds with slugger Mike Tyson. Even light-in-the-ass Tom Elias could have lasted two minutes with Tyson. McNeely's ineptitude nonetheless landed him a lucrative advertising deal to promote a brand-name pizza. Tyson got bupkis. I don't get it. But then again, whites always take care of their own.

Even though I exposed his secret life as a woman abuser, there's no question that the trial was good for Darden's social life. He rollerbladed along the Pacific coast with University of Oklahoma law professor Anita Hill and made the major gossip columns. After the trial, he was rumored to be romantically linked with Marcia Clark. I couldn't help but chuckle at the thought of Chris and Marcia hooking up. If he would so much as raise his hand toward her, she would have literally kicked his ass.

Hank Goldberg, the 32-year-old prosecutor, was the epitome of the nice guy if ever there was one. His problem was that his monotone was so pervasive that he made watching grass grow a must-see attraction. A knowledgeable lawyer, he just couldn't keep from putting everyone to sleep. The same thing with Lisa Kahn, the prosecution's in-court point woman on the domestic violence and other non-germane issues. She definitely knew what she was talking about, and she wrote some mighty fine legal briefs. She was just boring as hell.

Rockne Harmon and George "Woody" Clarke were two DNA experts brought up to the major leagues from the Alameda County and San Diego County farm clubs respectively. Clarke was called in to examine the government's FBI and state Department of Justice DNA experts. Other than that, Clarke neither hurt nor harmed the government's case. Harmon, a native New Yorker and Annapolis graduate, was an Alameda County prosecutor who came to the party with a reputation as an ass-kicking litigator. He did his best to shake up Dr. Henry Lee both inside and outside the courtroom. Harmon harassed Lee's colleagues at a medical conference held in Seattle in 1994 by stalking and then grilling them after the researchers had finished holding hallway conversations with the eminent forensic pathologist. Despite his Rasputinesque reputation, however, Harmon was a very affable guy. He always took the time to talk to me or any other reporter, especially about matters unrelated to the trial. One of Harmon's hobbies was growing things in his backyard, and one day he brought me a bag of dried red peppers he had grown. I really appreciated that.

Brian Kelberg's job was to try to make everyone forget the preliminary hearing testimony of the error-prone Irwin Golden, the deputy coroner who performed the autopsies on Brown Simpson and Goldman. He had the coroner use a ruler to show how Simpson supposedly grabbed each victim from behind and hacked them up. His problem, however, was that outside of the theatrics, Kelberg was annoying. He talked too much and he talked too long.

I remember getting on the elevator with him and several other district attorneys and employees during one morning break. I complimented him on his thespianesque approach to criminal litigation. "It's a good thing I didn't have holes in my shoes," Kelberg deadpanned as the elevator crowd chuckled." That's right," I responded good-naturedly. "Because I would have written about that in the *Sentinel*." To which he responded, "I'm sure you would have."

I want to say something about the lawyers who doubled as media analysts, or "pundits," if you will. In my opinion, most of them were pro-prosecution shills who took their post-verdict sour grapes to the airwaves almost immediately after the acquittals were announced. Heading this list was Geraldo Rivera, CNBC's host of "Rivera Live." The host, who formerly went by the name of Jerry Rivers, never tried to hide the fact that he thought all along that Simpson was guilty. And most of his guests reflected those same sentiments. On occasion, he would bring on someone like me. But after I left too many bodies intellectually sprawling on his studio floor, a CNBC insider told me that I was—pardon the pun—blackballed from his show. Rivera also put his money where his mouth and heart were by donating nearly $35,000 to Denise Brown's charity.

Among the more objective analysts were USC's Erwin Chemerinsky, Georgetown's Greta Van Susteren, KNBC's Manuel Medrano, Loyola University's Laurie Levenson and Charles Rosenberg and Professor Norman Garland of "E." I appeared on several shows with Chemerinsky and I found him to be very knowledgeable, balanced and fair. Van Susteren parlayed her numerous quality appearances into landing her own show, CNN's *Burden of Proof*, co-hosted by onetime Los Angeles attorney Roger Cossack. Levenson often sat next to me in the courtroom in the CBS seat. She often shared some of her notes with me, so you know I like her. She received reams of free publicity from the *Los Angeles Times* as a daily contributor to the paper's quick-analysis column.

The pro-defense-oriented pundits were led by two African Americans, Beverly Hills' Leo Terrell and Oakland's John Burris. Burris was a criminal defense attorney with a more measured approach to the spin-doctor field. Terrell, however, was a more lively and combative television warrior who often rubbed people the wrong way.

UCLA's Peter Arenella, who shared the *Times* daily analyst column with Levenson, was pretty much pro-prosecution. Add to that list Dick Thornburgh, Loyola's Stan Goldman, former L.A. County district attorney Robert Philibosian, KTLA's Al Deblanc, Los Angeles Southwestern Law School's Robert Pugsley and a host of others.

I was really curious to see Thornburgh in this group. I've known the former U.S. Attorney General professionally for nearly 20 years. He was one of the few Republicans that had any credibility in Pittsburgh's black community. As the city editor for the *New Pittsburgh Courier* in the late 1970s, I was one of a select group of black leaders, known as "the truth squad," who helped Thornburgh win the Pennsylvania governorship over Pittsburgh's Democratic mayor Pete Flaherty.

Thornburgh had an image of being a squeaky-clean non-politician politician. In reality, however, he was just as morally suspect and borderline criminal-minded as any Democratic ward politician in the Commonwealth. Readers may remember the infamous Computer Technologies Associated scandal that hit Pennylvania in the early 1980s. A Newport Beach-based computer whiz named John Torquato, the son of a corrupt Pennsylvania Democratic Party county chairman of the same name, masterminded a scheme to fleece the Commonwealth's 600 public school systems out of some $40 million in FICA recovery money. Thanks to a federal court ruling, governments and some private businesses were obligated to refund FICA tax payments extracted from sick pay between the years 1979 and 1981. A bill was drafted, passed by both the state senate and state legislature and signed by Thornburgh, all within 30 days, authorizing then-state treasurer R. Budd Dwyer to hire a firm to do the collection work. Dwyer chose CTA, Torquato's firm, who coincidentally drafted the bill. Imagine that.

My point is this: Thornburgh signed the bill, which makes me believe that somewhere in the mix, he knew what was going on. So I find it strange that Thornburgh would lead the charge to change the jury system to allow convictions with the vote of only 10 jurors "in the spirit of justice." In my opinion, I believe that the former U.S. attorney general came close to serving time himself.

One of the good things about having had this case televised was that it allowed the world to see how the criminal law system and its lawyers actually operate. What we saw more often than not, as retired New York Supreme Court Justice Bruce Wright most eloquently told Linn Washington, author of *Black Judges on Justice*: "Law and not justice is what is emphasized in America."

CHAPTER 11
A FACE-TO-FACE DEBATE

The Lessons and the Legacy
of the Simpson Trial

Schatzman: New York State Supreme Court Justice Bruce Wright has said that racism in the American criminal justice system is camouflaged by politeness, but everybody knows that African Americans are considered the inferior group in that system just as they are in American society, and they are treated accordingly. The system treats them differently than others, whether you're rich or poor. The O.J. Simpson trial hasn't changed either that reality or that perception, and that's the obvious lesson we should learn from this case—that we haven't learned anything. The criminal law system as it is practiced in the United States is unchanged. One of the glaring phenomena is how white America has taken it personally that a black man managed to win justice and proved that not just white people can win in this system. They're past-masters at rationalizing how it happened by saying the jurors were stupid. They say the jurors were mesmerized by Mr. Simpson's celebrity status. They blame the lawyers for doing their job. So, in a nutshell, we have learned that things have not changed at all.

Elias: I would say that one of the lessons we've learned from this case is that racism goes two ways. We've learned that blacks can be racist, too. We saw a jury that was selected by the defense on the basis of race, with the presumption that they wouldn't want to convict a black hero. In fact, that was one of the points Johnnie Cochran made during the jury selection process: that O.J. Simpson was a black hero and that the prosecutors were trying to keep blacks off the jury. This was absurd, as proved by the final results. We also learned that police can be corrupt and still catch the right man. And I think we learned that we need to change the jury selection system. I don't think we need to change the system of unanimous verdict—the system that exists in 48 of the 50 states. But the selection of this jury was an absolute joke. People who were knowledgeable about the case were simply excluded— that is, the people who admitted they had any knowledge about the case were simply dismissed. This meant that you were stuck with this jury of people who claimed they hardly read anything, because it was impossible not to be somewhat knowledgeable about this case if you so much as read a newspaper in the months leading up to the trial. As to what whites resent about this case, my feeling is that whites don't resent a black winning because he's black. Whites resent a guilty man walking because of a jury that voted on the basis of race.

Schatzman: A couple of things you've said need to be corrected: First and foremost, a black cannot be considered a racist in a system where he has no power. Rather, if I may quote former Maryland Congressman Parrin Mitchell, blacks are "tropistic," a biological term that means they are responding to negative stimuli. Blacks are more tropistic than they are racist. Number two: Whites object to black people beating them in areas other than sports, entertainment and some forms of food preparation. They always have. And when they're beaten, they get you back. But when whites "beat the system," there is never any outcry about how bad the criminal law system is. When John DeLorean went out and bought drugs and got away with it—drugs that wound up being sold to little kids in the ghettos—nobody raised more than a minimum outcry. John Gotti, who was head of the New York Mafia, beat the rap and walked out of the courtroom three different times, and there was no cry from the press or anyone else about changing the jury system. It only happens when black people win. That's a fact.

Another thing is that whites have become past-masters at speculating what really happened in the Simpson case. They say O.J. did it—but they can't really prove it. And neither did the prosecution. The evidence just wasn't there. They claim the jury was mesmerized by his fame—but there's no proof of that either. They say the jury was unintelligent, that they couldn't think for themselves—but that's just another slap at black people. I dare say, based upon the instructions they received about reasonable doubt, it would have been impossible for any jury to convict Mr. Simpson—unless you're trying him in Simi Valley, where often-times they seem to feel an obligation to do the wrong thing for "the right reasons."

Elias: I disagree that blacks can't be considered racists because they're only responding to white racism. Blacks can very definitely be racist in America. Take Louis Farrakhan as an example. He refers to the Jewish religion as a "gutter" religion. He refers to Jews as "bloodsuckers." If any white man referred to the First A.M.E. Church in that way, if any white man referred to any particular black group as a bunch of bloodsuckers, he would be instantly labeled a racist fanatic. So why can't we label Farrakhan the same way? Yeah, some people object to blacks beating them at certain activities. But I think those people would object to anyone beating them, whether they're black or not. There are plenty of whites in this country who work for black bosses, black managers, black company owners. And they're perfectly happy with their jobs. That has even spread to athletics, where you have black coaches; people like Dennis Green and Ray Rhodes who are perfectly well accepted and do a great job.

Dennis, you just said that there was no outcry in some of these other cases where the verdicts were absolutely absurd. That's not true. There was a huge outcry about the hung jury in the first Menendez trial. I mean, these are two guys who went in and shotgunned their parents. There was also a huge outcry when the cops who beat Rodney King were acquitted in the Simi Valley trial. It was a white President, a Republican President, who demanded they be retried. It was George Bush's Justice Department that put Stacey Koon and Laurence Powell on trial the second time for violating King's civil rights. Bush didn't have to do that. He did it because it was the right thing to do. So all whites are not racists.

Now, you say the prosecution didn't prove that O.J. Simpson was guilty. Well, let's look at that for a minute. His blood is at the scene. You don't deny that. His pattern of behavior with the domestic violence, you don't deny that. You put the two things together, as Jimmy Breslin wrote in a magazine not long ago, you'd have to be a cabbage not to know the guy's guilty. As far as saying black people can't think for themselves, when I talk about this jury and the way it was selected, I'm not just talking about white jurors getting thrown off because they were informed. There were plenty of potential black jurors who were thrown off because they were informed about this trial. What you ended up with was a jury that by definition had to be almost illiterate. And because they're people who don't read newspapers and magazines, the chances of them understanding the blood evidence, as complex as it was in this case, are pretty slim. What we saw is the final result. They just didn't understand it.

You find jurors like juror number 6, Lionel Cryer, saying the scientific evidence was "garbage." He was buying what Barry Scheck was trying to sell, which was the concept that if you let blood deteriorate for a while, somehow it deteriorates into O.J. Simpson's blood. That's simply not the case. Why couldn't those jurors understand that? If you could find O.J. Simpson's DNA in that blood, it hadn't deteriorated to the point where it was useless. More than any other single piece of evidence, the blood establishes that the man is guilty

Schatzman: Okay, let's recap here. You say Louis Farrakhan is racist because he doesn't like Jews. Farrakhan says Jews who own businesses in the black communities—and also Koreans and others—rarely give anything back to the community. That's a fact. That's not speculation. I don't recall anywhere that Farrakhan or any of his minions killed Alan Berg, that Jewish talk show host in Colorado. I don't know of any members of the Nation of Islam who have bombed Jewish synagogues. I don't know any who have in any way done anything to Jews. So I don't want to hear anything else about Farrakhan. If you people have nothing else to say, you go after Farrakhan. So there are black basketball coaches who have made it. Isn't that nice? But Johnnie Cochran made it on his own in a much tougher arena. He's been skewered, allowed to twist slowly on a stick because he did his job. As opposed to Leslie Abramson, who represented one of the Menendez brothers, who admitted they killed their parents. She was praised for the job she did in defending him. She even got a shot at her own talk show. The double standards go on and on and on. You can talk till you're blue in the face, but that's a fact of life.

As for the jurors not being intelligent enough to understand what was going on, people say that because they can't think of any other rationalization for losing the case. Given the rules laid down by the judge for evaluating circumstantial evidence, "not guilty" was the only possible verdict, and it had nothing to do with whether they or the defendant was black or white.

Elias: Technically the jury did follow the rules. They elected a foreperson, and they reached a verdict. But in the amount of time they took to make up their minds, they obviously didn't look over any of the evidence very closely, if they looked it over at all. After a trial that lasted eight and a half months, I wouldn't call a three and a half hour deliberation any kind of deliberation at all.

You also say you don't know of Farrakhan and his minions defacing any synagogues or doing anything to Jews. Neither do I, but after the Rodney King verdict in Los Angeles, do we know that none of his followers participated in the riot that ensued, burning down structures that belonged to Koreans, who are on his list of bloodsuckers alongside Jewish shopkeepers with stores in the ghetto? In this day and age, in the city of Los Angeles, Koreans live and work in much closer quarters with black people than Jews do. So the Koreans are a much handier target. Vandals would have to go a little farther to find a synagogue to deface. As for defacing synagogues, plenty of synagogues around this country have been defaced. We don't usually find out who does it. But words are powerful. So when Farrakhan calls Judaism a "gutter" religion, calls a whole ethnic group a bunch of bloodsuckers, he's doing damage, whether you care to admit it or not.

You also mentioned that the Nation of Islam has never been involved in bombing a synagogue, but you might be interested to know that when the First AME Church in Los Angeles was threatened to be blown up by a right-wing fringe organization, it was the Anti-Defamation League of B'nai B'rith that first exposed that group, reporting them to the police before it could happen. So you might say that they saved Reverend Chip Murray's church.

Why was Johnnie Cochran skewered? Cochran wasn't skewered because he did a good job. He was skewered because from the very first day he was on this case, he said that race was going to have to be a major element in the defense. He and Bob Shapiro chose the jury on the basis of race, he played that card throughout the trial, and then when he made his final appeal to the jury, he did that on the basis of race too. "Send a message to the police," he said. "You can police the police," he told the jury. Well, this trial wasn't about the police. This trial was about O.J. Simpson, or at least it should've been. That's where it went off track. It became a trial about Mark Fuhrman and the cops. And thanks to Johnnie Cochran, the jury allowed themselves to be misdirected. That's really the nub of why he's criticized.

Schatzman: What he did was win. Isn't that his job? Johnnie Cochran is a lawyer, a litigator. Lawyers battle for their clients. Sometimes they stay inside the white line, and oftentimes they don't. If you're on defense while a football player on the opposing team is runnin' for a touchdown, you do whatever you have to do to stop him. Even if you lose fifteen yards for grabbing his face mask, it's better than letting him score.

You also said Cochran and Shapiro chose the jury. Might I remind you that the prosecution was equally involved in that decision? If they let eight or nine blacks on the jury, whose fault was that? And it wasn't the defense that chose to come downtown rather than try the case in Santa Monica; it was District Attorney Gil Garcetti. You know who else kicked a lot of people off the jury? Lance Ito. For innocuous things like watching cartoons. Next you'll blame the jury for that too. The fact of the matter is the rules apply to everyone. You can't get mad and cry about it if the case doesn't come out your way.

Elias: We're going to agree on something. As far as jury selection goes, you're right about Judge Ito. He eliminated a lot of jurors for absurd, trivial reasons. But I think he has to be held even more accountable for what he didn't do. He had a responsibility to stop Cochran at least a dozen times during his closing arguments. Because he wasn't arguing evidence anymore. He was arguing something completely extraneous. But Ito gave him free rein, in keeping with his habit of letting lawyers blather on about almost anything they wanted. He didn't have to allow it. He could've just banged his gavel and said, "Enough of that, Mr. Cochran. Get back to the point."

I think that Lance Ito is at fault in a major way for the composition of the jury. Because the pool from which the jurors were drawn was an absurd pool. If you're trying to match the demographic composition of Los Angeles County, there should have been some Asians on the panel, some Latinos, some Caucasians—

not just African Americans. And there was virtually nobody in that pool who read much of anything. The questionnaires weeded those people out. And that applies to the whites in the pool, the blacks in the pool, everybody in the pool.

Schatzman: Well, the way you tell it, all black people are illiterate. You don't like the way we talk. You don't like the way we dress.

Elias: That's baloney.

Schatzman: You're already on record about whether it's baloney or not. All you're saying is, you believe they're illiterate because they voted to exonerate O.J. Simpson. If you want to blame anybody for how the case turned out, don't blame the jury. Don't blame Johnnie Cochran. Blame Lance Ito. Blame Garcetti. Blame Marcia Clark and Chris Darden. They're the ones who fucked up. So quit rationalizing with this sour grapes behavior that you're exhibiting here. They blew it. Too bad.

Elias: There were certain presumptions that went into the jury selection on both sides. And some of those presumptions were wrong, in particular on the prosecution's side. One reason the prosecutors didn't make more peremptory challenges was because they presumed that most women would be responsive to the domestic violence evidence, regardless of their race. What we saw in the final result was that the black women who composed the majority of the jury weren't very responsive at all to the domestic violence evidence. They said it was completely irrelevant.

I think it's because of what was going on around them. I think a lot of violence goes on in the black community that doesn't get punished. That's in large part because the police don't care. They don't do much in the black community. And so what seems like a big deal elsewhere may not seem like such a big deal in the black community. And Dennis, even in your chapter about domestic violence, when you talk about the cases you adjudicated in Pittsburgh, you don't talk about a pattern. You never say any of those people had a pattern of behavior. Simpson did, and this pattern of behavior led down a path that ended with these murders. You can't ignore that pattern of behavior. If he had excoriated and humiliated Nicole in public once, that wouldn't have been a pattern. You could disregard it. You could say that it didn't have much to do with their relationship. But we have a pattern that went on for seventeen years. That's a long time.

And then you come to his blood at the scene. Then you come to the victims' blood in his car. Then you come to rare fibers from cars that are particularly like his car at the scene of the murders. Then you come to his hair on the shirt of one of the victims. Then you come to blood on Simpson's driveway. Sure, the case is circumstantial because there was nobody actually there to watch the crime. But when you leave blood behind all over the place, and when you're dripping blood onto your car and somehow you smear some blood from one of the victims into your car, you have left a pretty darn good clue as to who the murderer is. It's tough to get around all that.

Schatzman: Well, there's something else that's tough to get around: the history of race relations in America. Only a fool would think that this case was not in part about the racial issue, simply because a black man is accused of killing two white people, one of whom was a white woman who happened to be Simpson's ex-wife. We don't have to go too far back in the history books to see how it drives white people crazy when some black man takes one of their women. So it took me all of what—three hours?—to figure out that race was going to play an important role in the case, despite all the arguments to the contrary. That's a fact. That's not speculation.

With respect to domestic violence, no one ignored it. The jury just felt that it wasn't all that relevant. There was no indication that he did anything physical to her after 1989. That's five years before the murder. Yellin' and screamin' doesn't constitute serious domestic violence. It shows that Mr. Simpson is an asshole. As are most athletes, myself included. We do things in loud, boisterous ways. We're physical. We do stupid shit sometimes. That doesn't make it okay. But once you say motive, you'll spend three months talking about domestic fucking violence. Okay. You only do that when you got nothin' else to talk about.

Now with regard to Simpson, yes, his blood was at the scene. His hairs were found on Goldman's shirt. Blah, blah, blah, blah. Okay. But there's also evidence that the police played fast and loose with much of the evidence. The police lied under oath.

We're just supposed to forget that. You say, "Oh, yeah, well they lied. But so what." Well, it's not so what. You ain't supposed to lie. If you think you got the guy, you're supposed to lie? Make up shit? That stuff happens all the time. 'Cause, see, white folks don't mind that when you're talkin' about niggers. Niggers are throw-away people, you see. So nobody cares except us. And that's what this whole thing is all about.

Elias: No, that's not what it's about.

Schatzman: I'm not finished. It's all about how people perceive them. You'll notice that my colleagues, along with all these commentators, don't have any evidence, and they're saying, "I feel that O.J.'s guilty. I feel that he did this and that. And I feel that Cochran wasn't 'responsible.'" You know how many people are dead and are in jail because somebody felt they were guilty? Emmitt Till is dead and buried because some white boys felt he insulted one of their white women. See, when you're black, you just can't feel and deal in the white world. You better have it down, because white people are vindictive. They'll get you back. Okay? So if you're gonna go out on the skinny branch, you better have the shit down pat. 'Cause you're gonna catch hell. They're gonna lose their jobs, they're gonna lose their homes. Because I understand how white people are.

Elias: You claim that I said, "I feel, I feel, I feel," about a lot of things. I don't think I ever said that, not in this conversation, no. I said I watched the jury being chosen and people who read newspapers and magazines systematically excluded. That's what I saw. People who said they got most of their news from magazines and newspapers were eliminated. Now, the problem with the domestic violence evidence wasn't that it was emphasized too much. The problem was that it wasn't emphasized enough in the case. The problem was that the prosecution never showed the importance of this pattern of behavior. They tried to do it in the closing argument when they talked about the "long fuse." But they never produced any evidence proving that people who commit other acts of domestic violence are also prone to murder at a certain point in their life. They could've done that, but they didn't. Their excuse was that they didn't have enough time. My God, they took five, six months with their case. They spent two months on blood evidence alone. It's ridiculous to say they didn't have enough time. They could've taken a little more time if they weren't so afraid of losing the jury. But if they'd lost this jury, so what? They'd have had a mistrial and had to do it over again. But at least you wouldn't have a guilty man walking the streets.

Forgetting all the shortcomings in the prosecution's case, let's talk about the evidence they did present. I don't believe the jury had grounds for reasonable doubt that the evidence, the physical evidence, was convincing of his guilt. I'll tell you why. They may have had grounds to think it was possible someone could've tampered with the blood evidence. The tampering that Barry Scheck and Peter Neufeld suggested went on was that somebody took one milliliter of blood, a very tiny amount of blood, and spread it all over the place. They spread it on the gate, they spread it on the floor, they spread it on the blood swatches, they spread it in the car. You have to understand what a tiny amount of blood one milliliter is—and you have to remember that the man who drew Simpson's blood testified later that there wasn't any blood missing.

But even if we accept the initial assertion that there was one milliliter missing, they would have had to carefully take a tiny eyedropper and just smear a tiny bit. Now, let's say they take O.J. Simpson's blood and they put it on a swatch of blood that's been picked up at the crime scene, and the blood at the crime scene is not O.J. Simpson's. If you take a teeny bit of O.J. Simpson's blood and put it on that same swatch, then you go test it for DNA, you don't get purely O.J. Simpson's blood. You get a mix. They didn't get a mix anywhere except in the car, where they found a mix of Simpson's blood with the victims'! Now, I haven't emphasized that aspect a great deal because I do know the car was tampered with. And I do know that prior to the car being tampered with, the detectives had access to the reference samples of blood from the victims. So, if you make the assumption that people are going to go out and risk their lives and careers and prison terms for doing that kind of thing, if you assume that they're gonna make that kind of a move just to cement their case against Simpson, then you have to disregard the evidence of the victims' blood in his car.

But you can't disregard the evidence of Simpson's blood at the crime scene. It simply can't be ignored. It means that O.J.

Simpson was there. He might have had company. He might have had help. But he was there and a participant in these murders. Of course, the prosecution hung their hat entirely on the single-assailant theory. And that's only a theory. We don't know that Simpson was alone in committing these crimes. He could've had a lot of help. There were other theories that were bantered about during the preliminary hearing. We heard a lot about the Jason Simpson theory. We heard that Al Cowlings might've been helping him, and so on. That was all disregarded. I don't know who helped him, if anybody helped him. But from the evidence, I do know he was there. And there is no reasonable doubt of that.

Now, about the evidence that the police lied. You're right, it's not a so-what. Mark Fuhrman should be put on trial for perjury. And Phil Vannatter should be disciplined for lying in the process of getting a search warrant. No question about it. But those are the only police lies we know about in this case. And those lies don't change the evidence I was just talking about. The evidence is there. This trial was not the trial of Mark Fuhrman and Phil Vannatter. This was the trial of O.J. Simpson. It was his blood at the scene. It was his record of beating this woman for years previous. That's what eliminates reasonable doubt. And to say the sweep of black history somehow justifies this verdict is absolutely absurd.

Schatzman: As usual, Tom, you have bored me with your blather about all the evidence. Let's go back to the jury. What constitutes an informed juror? I'm sure you've read the 1960 book by Jacques Ellul, who talked about how the most intelligent people, the most well-read people, are the people most likely to be influenced. They're not always as smart as their reading materials would suggest. So to suggest that the people who read the most are the smartest, and can make the best decisions, is just pure horsepuckey. And that's been proven down through the years. Josef Goebbels made a pretty nice living indoctrinating very smart people to the point where they felt that they were better than everyone else, including the Jewish people. So, you know, you don't have to have a Ph.D. to understand what's going on. These jurors spent nine months on the case.

With respect to all the blood evidence you've been talking

about, you conveniently vacillate between what's real and what's speculation, depending upon what kind of argument you want to make. You know his blood was at the scene and all that. But we still don't know how it got there. No one saw O.J. Simpson doing anything. I do agree that he was probably at the scene, but not necessarily to kill anybody. We know for a fact that the prosecution does intimidate and threaten witnesses. They did that with Thano Peratis, who drew O.J.'s blood. I mean, after all, who does he work for? The police. He says one thing one time, and all of a sudden he changes his story. The prosecution was real good at threatening the woman who worked with their Torrance, California, office, who they claim knew Marguerite, Simpson's first wife. I mean, they threatened her. They threatened her livelihood, her job. You know they threatened Bea Williams, who used to live with Chris Darden and can testify about his penchant for domestic violence and abuse. They threatened her. They threaten people. They beat people up. They put people in jail to keep 'em from testifying. So, contrary to what you say, these people are not pure as the driven snow. They're not nice guys. They are out to get you. And they're out to win at any cost.

But so is Cochran. So don't blame Cochran when the prosecution is doing the same stuff and has more fire power. We're talkin' about the State. The State has unlimited resources. Unlimited. They can call upon the Department of Justice, the FBI, the fucking CIA, everybody else you can think of. Probably Interpol, if they want to. They sent a guy all the way to Italy to find some shoes in this case. They spent eight thousand dollars on this guy, he ate the finest pasta, and what does he testify to? That O.J. Simpson wears a size twelve. I mean, Carl Douglas wears a size twelve. You know what I'm sayin'? We spent eight thousand dollars on some guy and what he finds out, he could have done with one phone call.

Elias: Dennis, I think it's marvelous that you agree at last that O.J. Simpson was at the scene.

Schatzman: Probably.

Elias: Probably at the scene. Why don't you tell me how his blood got there if he was at the scene and he wasn't a participant?

Schatzman: I don't know.

Elias: Then what was he doing there? Standing around and watching while somebody else murdered them? That would make him an accessory.

Schatzman: Not necessarily. He might have simply happened onto the scene while the murder was in progress. Have you ever seen anybody die? You ever seen anybody get killed? You ever see people walk out in front of a car and can't move because they're mesmerized, they're so shocked they can't move? So we don't know what happened.

Elias: If he was too mesmerized to get involved, even to try and stop the crime or grapple with the killer, then why did he suffer a cut on his finger?

Schatzman: O.J. says he cut his finger on a drinking glass in Chicago. You can't prove he didn't.

Elias: However he got the cut, the fact remains that you just admitted for the first time that he was there.

Schatzman: Probably. Probably. But even if he was there, we don't know who committed the crime. How come he couldn't have come across four people who were killing them over a drug deal? Mary Ann Gerchas said she saw four men leaving the scene.

Elias: Well, if you believe her at all—and there's good reason not to—Gerchas says she was about a block away from the scene, you'll recall. And it was the dark of night; there was only a quarter moon. She said she saw four men, two Hispanics and two whites, running to a car from the scene. Right? Well, I'll take you there at night with the moon in the same condition, and I'll defy you to tell a Hispanic apart from a white. Under those conditions, that's absolutely absurd. But let's say O.J. was there and found the murder in progress by parties unknown. If he tried to stop them and tried to fight off the assailants and got cut, wouldn't he be likely to admit that or even proclaim it afterwards? Or would he assume that people would think he did it himself?

Schatzman: Well, it depends on who these killers were. If they're drug dealers, they might well kill his kids. And everybody else on the block.

Elias: So now you're suggesting that O.J. Simpson was a good Samaritan that night when he just happened to be lurking outside her home. Well, in one of your chapters you already made an outlandish comment about hitmen parked in the black Mercedes outside the Mezzaluna that night. You can't prove that either.

Schatzman: Just 'cause you don't have the story doesn't mean that I haven't. Just 'cause you believe what you want to believe, don't make it true. That's one thing about white folks. Basically the best argument they have is just to completely dismiss what somebody black says. And that's the end of it.

Elias: That's not the case here at all. But if you're willing to concede that O.J. was probably at the crime scene that night, what was he doing there when he had a plane to catch?

Schatzman: Maybe he was going to stop off and look through the windows, as he liked to do, at a time when she would believe he couldn't be there, just when he was about to leave town on a trip to Chicago.

Elias: If he was really at Nicole's condo that night—for whatever reason—why did Cochran tell us he was home playing golf in his backyard? And why did Simpson himself claim later that he was upstairs taking a nap? What the hell was he doing?

Schatzman: I chip balls in my backyard. I also take naps.

Elias: You know, there was a small army of people out there in Brentwood walking their dogs that night, as you well know, and nobody saw him playing golf. And some of them walked right past his house.

Schatzman: Nobody saw him at Bundy either.

Elias: We're going around in circles. Can I ask you for a personal opinion? The jury found legal reasons to believe that he was not guilty on the basis of reasonable doubt. And you've made a strong argument why that was a rational and understandable decision for them to reach, given the flaws of the prosecution's case. But given the fact that you feel O.J. was probably at the crime scene, do you still believe that he didn't do it?

Schatzman: Yes. I do for a couple of reasons. One, when the man threw Nicole out of the house, he was loud. When he kicked her ass, he was loud. Loud. Loud. Loud. But nobody heard a sound while the crime was taking place. Number two, let's talk about the footprints at the scene. You may scoff at this, but it's true. Mr. Simpson is bow-legged and pigeon-toed. When he's comin' out of the jail, when he comes to the court, he's pigeon-toed.

That's just how he walks. But the footprints at the scene weren't pigeon-toed. It seemed like the prosecution would have pointed that out, but they didn't. We've also got the glove. This bloody glove found behind Kato's room. It's just sittin' there, no blood drops around it. No broken spiderwebs. We've got these blood drops all over town. Except where we should have blood drops. How can that be? Then we got cops in Simpson's house six to seven hours before they get a legal search warrant. Stuff like that. God knows what might have been happening. 'Cause after all, Mark Fuhrman has a history of destroying evidence.

That's the evidence, and it's badly flawed. According to the definition of reasonable doubt, Cochran more than made that case. Black people didn't make up any of these rules and regulations. White people did that. They say it's the stupid jurors, that they can't pay attention. But they paid attention to reasonable doubt. All they did was pay attention for nine months, so don't be shocked if it only took four hours to acquit him afterward. You wouldn't have objected if the verdict had been conviction.

Elias: I'm gonna have to ask again: If you don't believe he did it, why do you think he was at the scene? Now, you say that it's highly unlikely that a guy who's so tired from having run around all day can kill two people, and do it in a way that no one can hear. But that ignores the fact that he had just been training within the previous two months before the murders for the planned television series "Frogmen," training in exactly this skill—how to knife somebody in the neck, slit their throat without anybody hearing it. He had had training from experts in this. And this is a guy who, when it comes to physical skills, is one of the most coachable people in the world. And he's got physical strength.

Then we come to the footprints. I would suggest, yes, O.J. Simpson is a little bit pigeon-toed. Not to the degree that you say, but he's a little bit pigeon-toed. He walks slightly toward the middle, not as much as he used to when he was a world-class athlete. But I would also suggest that even O.J. Simpson, after he's murdered two people, the first few steps he takes might be a little bit off stride. I would say that after you've killed two people, just about anybody might be a little bit off stride, might even be staggering. And remember, the red footprints are only just a few steps. There're not very many of them because the blood wears off as the killer walked away, and you can't see it anymore.

Then you come to the glove at the estate. Look, I'm gonna concede that Mark Fuhrman could conceivably have planted that. But I have another theory for how it might've gotten there without a cop planting it: O.J. Simpson arrives at his house. He knows there's a limousine waiting to take him to the airport. This limo service is always early. So he knows they're there, even though he parks on the other side of the house. And to get his bag into the house without anyone observing him, he first walks up across his neighbor's lawn and tosses the bag over the fence—that's what thumped against Kato's air conditioner. A glove falls out of the bag when it hits the ground. Then, in those few minutes that he's home after he goes in the front door, he goes out again and retrieves the bag. That may be the black bag that later disappears. The one he wouldn't allow Kato to pick up and the one that never showed up again after his return from Chicago.

But even if you forget about the glove, if you eliminate Fuhrman from the case entirely, if you eliminate all the evidence they got at Simpson's estate, you'd still have enough to convict the guy because his blood is at the scene, and his pattern of behavior is what it is, and there's blood on his car. There's no challenge to the blood on the outside of his car, either. That was fresh O.J. Simpson blood. Right above the door handle of his car. Nobody questions that. It couldn't have been from the reference sample. The reference sample wasn't drawn until nine hours later. So if you eliminate everything Fuhrman found, you still have enough to convict him.

Schatzman: Let's talk about the knife. Where is it?

Elias: Well, I have a theory about that too.

Schatzman: Don't give me no theories. We don't even know that he had a knife.

Elias: We know he had a collection of knives.

Schatzman: Were there any missing?

Elias: I don't know. The cops would have had to have a catalog of every knife the guy owned to know that.

Schatzman: Well, they went and found out he bought a knife on May 3rd, 1994—but that wasn't the murder weapon. So where is it?

Elias: I'll tell you where it is, in my opinion. I think it's in the ocean.

Schatzman: It could be anywhere in the damn world. The point is, you don't know, and neither does anybody else. How about the missing shoes? Are they in the ocean too?

Elias: They're wherever that black bag is. Or possibly they're with the contents of the Louis Vuitton bag that Mr. Kardashian took back to his house full, and somehow brought to court empty. First you see a picture of the case full, then you see it empty.

Schatzman: Prove there was anything incriminating in it.

Elias: I can't prove it. That's just my theory. God and O.J. Simpson are the only ones who know for sure. And maybe Bob Kardashian. Look, Dennis you make a good case for the defense, but you also admit that O.J. was probably at the crime scene that night. Yet you still claim he's innocent. Which is it?

Schatzman: It's not as simple as that. You agree with me that the prosecution made a poor case for conviction, and I agree with you that O.J. was probably at the murder scene. We just don't know what happened there, because there were no witnesses to the crime. The rest of the case is entirely circumstantial. In my opinion—and the opinion of the jury—that wasn't enough to convict the man. And that should be that. End of case. End of subject. I'm sick and tired of seeing every black person in America put on trial about the verdict. It's like there's a litmus test of whether you're a good nigger or "one of them."

Elias: Not as far as I'm concerned. In my mind, O.J. Simpson is a murderer. It's that simple. I didn't say anybody else was. And I don't blame the rest of the black race for feeling the way they do about it. But black history does not justify what he did.

Schatzman: Were you as indignant about the first Rodney King verdict?

Elias: Yes, I was, and I said so in writing at the time. So did hundreds of other journalists. There was such an outcry that President Bush called for the federal government to retry the police officers involved for violating King's civil rights.

Schatzman: Why didn't that happen in the case of Latasha Harlins?

Elias: That was a rank injustice. There's no question.

Schatzman: I suppose that's reflected in your writings of that time.

Elias: Yes, that's reflected in my writing.

Schatzman: But not in the *Los Angeles Times*.

Elias: I can't answer for them. I can only answer for myself.

Schatzman: You're part of the media.

Elias: Just as you are. I don't have to answer for the media either. Just as I don't answer for the Jewish people, though I'm a Jew. I am accountable only for myself.

Schatzman: So are the jurors in the O.J. Simpson trial. They don't answer for all black people.

Elias: I didn't say they did.

Schatzman: Yes, you did. You called them stupid, you said they were illiterate.

Elias: That's because of how they were selected, not because they're black. Dennis, you've implied that I'm a racist for believing that the jury was wrong to find O.J. not guilty. Do you think it's possible for a white person to believe O.J. is guilty without being a racist?

Schatzman: Yeah, it's possible to think that he's guilty without being a racist. But to believe that he's guilty based upon the evidence that was presented in the case, that raises a great deal of speculation about one's underlying beliefs. There have been some polls suggesting that black people were more in tune with the evidence than white people were. That white people came to their conclusion that Simpson was guilty based upon a feeling as opposed to what the evidence says. Big difference.

So when you ask me if it's possible to think he's guilty without being a racist, the answer is yes—but racism plays a role in predisposing whites to feel a certain way, simply because of the past history of what goes on with respect to black people. So you can believe he's guilty without being a racist—but I don't think you can feel that way without ignoring the rules of evidence. For the public to believe the arguments of commentators who have tried this case not in the courtroom but on the air, and in the press, just goes to the stupidity of white people. But let me turn your question around: Wasn't it possible for the jury to find reasonable doubt without themselves being racist?

Elias: I suppose it's theoretically possible to believe he was innocent without being a racist—but not without being ignorant. those of us who followed the trial in great detail know more than the jury, actually. We know more about the fiber evidence than the jury did, for instance, because the jury wasn't permitted to hear all of it. We know much more about the domestic violence evidence, because the prosecutors chose not to present it all. So I don't think it's possible for someone who's reasonable and has observed this trial in detail to believe that Mr. Simpson was not present at the scene. Even you concede he was present at the scene. And if he was there, he's at the very least an accessory.

Schatzman: So each of us has accused the other one of being, at the very least, ignorant for not agreeing with him. That's the larger issue that lies behind this trial, and so much else of what goes on between black and white here in America. Whatever progress you may say there's been in the past 30 or 40 years, only a fool or a blind man would deny that this is still a racist country. White people still grow up thinking of black people as inferior to them. They've been taught that from what they see on TV, what they see in their neighborhood and what their parents tell them. So I think that while most whites may not be guilty of being racists, they are likely to be guilty of perpetuating racism in their belief system, in their thought process, in their subconscious. They're perpetuating racism even if they simply accept it as a fact of life in America and do nothing to condemn it in others or combat it in themselves.

Where I live in Ontario, California, if I'm walking across the street on Foothill Boulevard, going up to get the paper at the big newsstand and I'm walkin' across the street with the light, I hear all these little clickity-clicks. Everyone's locking their doors because they're scared of me. They think I'm gonna hijack 'em. It's subtle little things like that that you experience every day if you're black. Things you can't begin to understand even as the most well-intentioned white person. Take a guy like Tommy Lasorda, manager of the Los Angeles Dodgers. I'm sure he'd be deeply hurt if anybody called him a racist, but at a game one after-noon, I saw him run over and rub the head of one of the black infielders for good luck. One of the things I heard growing up was that if you want good luck, you rub a nigger's head. It's a white world.

Elias: I've seen Lasorda do that myself. But I never thought about it until you pointed it out, Dennis

Schatzman: That's precisely my point. White folks don't notice, or they even think some of these things are cute.

Elias: It's something each of us has to look at in his own heart. When I meet a person like you for the first time, it's certainly obvious that you're black. Fiercely so. But to many whites that can be intimidating. I was a bit intimidated myself the first time I met you. If that makes me a racist, so be it. But if you try to accept black people and give them the same chance that you give whites to prove themselves to you as people, then I think it's pos-sible for a white not to be racist. I don't think I'm entirely free of racism, but I have a long record of trying to get past it. I was arrested desegregating a restaurant in Atlanta in the early Sixties, when I was in college down there. I've had guns pulled on me when I've been doing conciliations for the Westside Fair Housing Council in Los Angeles after someone's been denied an apart-ment on the grounds of race. Dennis, do you think you're untouched by the same brush that you use to paint white people? Do you feel you are ever susceptible to racist assumptions about white people?

Schatzman: Well, I think I'm very "tropistic" with respect to my feelings toward the white race, based on how I've been treated and how I've seen other black people treated all my life. Quite frankly, I really feel on a daily basis I never know what white people are going to do. I have a good understanding about what black people are going to do. From the young punks to the profes-sionals, because that's the experience I come from. But with whites, I'm of the same opinion as Arthur Ashe. He talked about growing up in Richmond, Virginia, being trained to always look over your shoulder for trouble from the white man. I'm the same way.

Now, I daresay I would not be sitting here with the superior intellectual preparation that I have without the help of white people. With the exception of three black teachers, every teacher I had from kindergarten to 12th grade was white, and each and every one of them was top notch. Some were rotten racists. There was one in particular, but you know, when she was teaching white folks, she was teaching me too. So I had some great teachers. There was one Wayne Sadowski, my 11th grade chemistry teacher, and as soon as this book comes out I'm gonna go back to Pittsburgh and give him an autographed copy. He said something I think about every day of my life. He said to me, "It's not how smart you are, it's how well you know how to get the answers." And I had top teachers at the University of Pittsburgh. And I think of my Little League coach. I remember my old mail carrier. He always had something nice to say to me. Asked to see my report card. He delivered mail every day from kindergarten to 12th grade, and he was one of the nicest guys I ever met. I don't forget these things.

Elias: I don't think that I come from that different of a place than you do. I come from a refugee family. My parents escaped from Hitler. They weren't in the concentration camps. They escaped. They went from country to country to country, ended up in America. So I too was raised with a kind of an attitude, an atmosphere where you're always looking over your shoulder. My parents were the first Jews to move into Deerfield, Illinois, outside Chicago. And I will never forget how the area that we moved into was quite raw. I was about seven years old when we moved in there, and the other kids in the neighborhood came and attacked my brother and me with rocks. We were behind a pile of dirt, and we were throwing dirt clods back at them, because this was war with these little kids. All because we were Jews. They're yelling "dirty kikes" and all this kind of stuff at us. I have a scar on my lip, you can't see it because I have a moustache over it. But I have a scar from that. I ended up in the emergency room that night, with three stitches in my upper lip because of racism, or anti-Semitism, call it whatever you want. So I know where you're coming from. I don't claim to be free of racism myself, but all of us in some way have been victimized by it in this country. You gotta remember, America is a country of refugees, one way or another. The only people who aren't here by choice are the blacks. But everybody else was running away from something. All except the Indians and the blacks.

Speaking for myself, as far as this case is concerned, I care only if O.J. Simpson was guilty or innocent. I don't care if he's black, white or purple. His blood was there, and as far as I'm concerned he did the crime. And it has nothing to do with his race. That I can say with utter confidence. I would like us to get to the point where we can see everything and everyone like that. Where we look at Joe, Sam and Henry as individuals, and we get past their skin color or their ethnic heritage. I've gotten past it with you, Dennis. I know you're black. I'm aware of it when I'm with you. But I think society presses that on me. And you press it on me, too, in a way, because you shout it at me and everybody else. But that's all right, because despite all our differences, I've gotten to know you, and respect you, and care for you as a fellow human being.

Schatzman: Most eloquent. Where I think we have to go from here is to simply acknowledge that we live in a society that is still racist. I blame white people for the problems with police. There are good cops, but there are bad ones, too, and the good ones don't rat on the bad ones. White people don't walk away when somebody tells a racist joke; I don't care if it's about a Jew, an African American, an Arab or a Pole. We don't marshal the full weight of society to deal with issues of race. We just kind of forget about it. When the issue of Fuhrman came up, about his history, eight or nine months went by before anybody outside of the system did anything about it. Now, that's just racism by default. We can't keep blaming the problem on black people. White people have to share it, the large burden of responsibility, because they're runnin' things. They control virtually all the institutions of our society. You know, Lyndon Johnson made the bold step of signing The Civil Rights Act in the 1960s. He met with all kinds of resistance, but he did it because it was the right thing to do. If he hadn't been tough, I wouldn't be sittin' where I am today.

Elias: I think you'd be doing fine. But there's no denying the truth of what you've said. Even if we disagree about everything else, we agree about that. In my opinion, race should never have become an issue in the Simpson trial, but since it did—perhaps inevitably—what can we learn from it? What is the legacy we'll be left with? Will it push us even farther apart, or can it help to bring us together? I can't speak for all white liberals. I can speak for one white liberal, which is me. And I don't think this case either discouraged me or gave me hope. But honest dialogues like this book give me hope. Because you and I can disagree as diametrically as we have all through the trial and as strenuously as we do in this book, and we still come out of it talking to each other. And that is the ultimate message. We don't have to agree and we don't have to be the same to learn how to live with one another. Rodney King asked, "Can't we all get along?" I think we can. We just have to try.

Schatzman: I couldn't agree more.

INDEX

Christopher, Warren, 165
Christopher Commission, 165
churches, African-American, 24, 34
First A.M.E. Church, 24, 257, 259
circumstantial evidence, 108-109, 213
civil court, 34
Clark, Libby, 197
Clark, Marcia, 75, 79, 94, 108
  Bailey and, 243
  behavior, 233-234, 246-248
  bonus paid to, 234, 248
  on hair samples needed, 81
  Ito and, 150, 167, 246
  jurors and, 97
  on jury selection, 94, 95
  on police search, 68
  at preliminary hearing, 81, 85
  Schatzman on, 246-247
  Shively questioned by, 75
Clark, Tom, 126
Clarke, George "Woody," 248-249
CNN, 36
Cochran, Johnnie, 108, 131, 149, 225, 258
  behavior, 230-231, 241
  closing argument, 18-19, 27, 33, 38, 99, 166-167, 179, 212
  Darden and, 235-236, 247-248
  and double-standards issue, 38-39
  Elias on, 230-232
  female jurors and, 239-240
  Fuhrman compared to Hitler by, 38, 166-167, 239, 242
  Fuhrman's use of N-word and, 157-159
  Goldman on, 18-19, 38, 166-167
  Hodgman and, 236
  and introduction of racism into trial, 158, 159, 259-260
  Ito and, 151, 260

jurors and, 25, 99, 101
  on jury's job, 167, 259-260
  presence on defense team, 230, 231-232
  qualms at beginning of case, 229-230
  reaction to verdicts, 30
  Schatzman on, 241-242
  Shapiro and, 238
  on unanimous jury requirement, 146
  on Vannatter's credibility, 164
  white media and, 37, 38-39
Cohen, Richard, 173
Conn, Billy, 30
Conyers, John, 37-38
Cotton, Dr. Robin, 183
Couric, Katie, 37
courthouse, downtown Los Angeles
  choice of, 70-72, 80, 91, 246, 260
  press room, 74
courthouse, Santa Monica, 71, 246, 260
courtroom seating
  awarding of seats to reporters, 9-11
  decisions about dividing shared time, 11-13
  press seating chart, 9, 10
  public, Phillips and, 32
Cowlings, Allen C., 49-50, 58-59, 193, 216, 265
Cox, Bobby, 120
Cravin, Willie "Bobo," 97-101, 107-108, 165
criminal justice system, racism in, 51-52, 255
Cryer, Lionel, 98, 123, 183, 216, 258
Current Affair, A (television show), 36
cuts on Simpson's hand, 56, 197, 267

D

Daily Breeze, 78
Daniels, John, Jr., 59-60
Daniels, Marcia, 234
Darden, Christopher, 117,

122, 123, 131, 150, 157, 225, 248, 266
  bonus paid to, 234, 248
  Cochran and, 235-236, 247
  on Fuhrman's use of N-word, 157-158, 165, 167, 171, 247
  and glove demonstration, 180, 202
  Ito and, 151
  role in case, 234-235
  Schatzman on, 247-248
  on Simpson's record of domestic violence, 23
Darrow, Charles, 57-58
Davis, Eric, 84
Davis, Reverend Jordan, 24
Deblanc, Al, 250
DecisionQuest, 94
Deedrick, Douglas, 185, 212, 213
defense team. *See also* names of attorneys
  assault on DNA analysis, 215-216
  bias against, 241-242
  black jurors as advantageous to, 72-73
  cost to Simpson, 238-239
  discrediting of evidence by, 208-209, 213-218
  and domestic violence incidents, 118-119, 120-121
  drug-dealer theory, 100, 191, 267-268
  on Gerchas, 193
  Ito and, 138, 149-150, 151
  and jury selection, 93, 96, 97
  and racism as issue, 159, 160
  Schatzman on, 241-245
DeLorean, John, 219-220, 225, 230, 256
Denny, Reginald, 76, 147, 231
Dershowitz, Alan, 179, 238, 244
Deukmejian, George, 138, 144, 150

celebrity treatment of
Simpson, 135-136
Clark and, 150, 246
Cochran and, 166-167,
260
defense team and, 138,
149-150, 151
Elias on, 135-146,
138-139
goal of, 137, 138
gun carried by, 150-151
on high-profile cases, 147
interviews, 135-136,
144-145
jury pool rules and, 99,
104-105
jury selection and, 91, 92,
93, 94, 145, 260-261
and Keating trial,
136-137, 139, 140
lack of control in
courtroom, 151
need to control, 143-146,
147-149
Nicole's diary not
admitted by, 115, 116
on press quarters, 74
press seating chart of,
9, 10
private sessions, 141
prosecution team and,
138, 149-150
and public's right to
know, 140-141
on relevance of
Fuhrman's racism,
152-153, 157, 160, 162
retentive memory of, 149
Schatzman on, 126,
147-156
television and, 137
treatment of defense
team, 138-
treatment of press,
140-145, 146, 147-149
wife (see York, Margaret
"Peggy")
wit of, 149
I Want to Tell You (Simpson
and Schiller), 182

J

Jackson, Michael (radio
show host), 36, 38, 39
James, Rick, 171-172

Jeanette-Meyers, Kristin,
140
Jewish Journal, 221
Johnson, Jack, 170
Johnson, Lyndon B., 38,
276
Johnson, Rabbi Gary, 24-25
Joyner, Al, 53
"J.R.," 201
jurors, 107-109, 257-259.
See also verdict
artists' portraits, Ito on,
141
behavior of, 97-101,
107-109
and carpet fiber
evidence, 213
Cochran and, 99, 101,
167
and DNA evidence, 97,
145, 216, 258
on domestic violence,
115, 116, 117, 224
female, 239
few domestic violence
episodes heard by,
115-119
hidden agendas, 98-99
ice cream evidence
and, 217
and life after trial, 100
lying by, 95, 96-97,
98-99, 100-101, 107
message sent by, 167
and N-word, 157, 162,
165
Park's testimony
reviewed by, 31-32
payments to, 92
and police officer
credibility, 163-164
race issue and, 165-166,
272
racial backgrounds, 31,
91, 103-104
and racism as issue in
trial, 23, 165-166, 272
retirees, 92
Schatzman on, 265 on
scientific evidence,
97-98, 217
sequestration of,
99-100, 116, 117
suspicions of blood
contamination and, 216
time to select

forewoman, 31
white media on, 37
jury pool
downtown Los Angeles,
71-72, 80, 91-92,
260-261
Elias on, 260-261
initial size, 104
racial distribution, 71,
91-93
jury selection, 255-256, 272
consultants, 93-94
defense team and, 93,
94, 96, 97, 259, 260
Elias on, 91-97, 263
factors skewing, 92-93
failures of, Elias on, 93
final agreement on,
96-97
first number drawn,
91, 94
hardship questionnaire,
92
honesty of potential
jurors and, 95
Ito and, 91, 92, 93, 94,
145, 260-261
juror questionnaire and,
104-107, 261
police record in, 106-107
prosecution team and,
93, 94, 96
questioning process,
92-93, 94
reading and viewing
habits in, 105-106
Schatzman on, 102,
103-108, 260, 261
Shapiro on, 93
weaknesses in,
145-146

K

KABC, 36
Kaelin, Brian "Kato," 84,
85-86, 169, 175, 211-212,
218
grand jury testimony, 79
at preliminary hearing,
73, 85-86
at trial, 188-190
Kahn, Lisa, 248
Kalb, Marvin, 58
Kammer, Jerry, 143